A PATH TO WHOLENESS

TASHENE WOLFE

*To Dea!
May you find peace & joy
on your Path to Wholeness!
Love
Tashene!*

A PATH TO WHOLENESS

TASHENE WOLFE

NEW AUTHOR PUBLISHING

A PATH TO WHOLENESS

TASHENE WOLFE

Copyright ©, Tashene Wolfe 2014

All rights reserved

Second Edition

New Author Publishing

Brockville, Ontario, Canada

www.newauthorpublishing.com

Library and Archives Canada

Cataloguing in Publication

Tashene Wolfe

ISBN 978-1-928045-09-0

TABLE OF CONTENTS

DEDICATION 1

ACKNOWLEDGMENTS 2

FOREWORD 3

PROLOGUE BY TASHENE 5

GROUND ZERO 13

    The Total-Self 17
    Your Spiritual-Body 18
    Your Emotional-Body 19
    Your Mental-Body 19
    Your Physical-Body 20
    A Healthy Total-Self 21
    How Your Clouds Were Formed 23
    How Clouds Distort Your Emotional Perceptions 27
    Clouds Contain Your Defensive-Mechanisms 29
    Scripts 31
    The Original Cause of Addictions 34
    What is an Addict? 45
    How Your Clouds are "Triggered" 47

A CLOSER LOOK AT YOUR CLOUDS 55

    Victim 59
        Victim Scripts 60
        Victim Control Tactics 60
        Victim Rules of Conduct 60
    Persecutor 61
        Persecutor Scripts 61
        Persecutor Control Tactics 61
        Persecutor Rules of Conduct 62
    Rescuer 62
        Rescuer Scripts 62
        Rescuer Control Tactics 63
        Rescuer Rules of Conduct 63
    The Victim State of Mind 66

Transition Time from Victim to Persecutor 69
The Persecutor State of Mind 70
Transition Time from Persecutor to Rescuer 76
The Rescuer State of Mind 78
Other Dangerous Habits that Support the VPR Cloud 83
Making Excuses 83
Mistakes 85
The Need for Secrecy 90
The Scapegoat 91
The VPR Cloud in Daily Life 93
Possible Repercussions When You Step Out of the VPR Triangle/Cloud . 102

EMOTIONAL ELEMENTS IN THE VPR CLOUD 109

Fear 117
How to Reduce Fear in Your Life 119
Anxiety and Worry 120
How to Reduce Anxiety and Worry in Your Life 123
The Blame, Shame, & Guilt Triangle 124
Blame 127
Shame 129
Guilt 131
How to Reduce Blame, Shame, and Guilt in Your Life 133
Anger 134
How to Reduce Anger in Your Life 144
Frustration 147
   Victims *148*
   Persecutors *148*
   Rescuers *148*
How to Reduce Frustration in Your Life 149
The Belief in Lack & That You are Unworthy 149
   Victims *152*
   Persecutors *152*
   Rescuers *153*
How to Release Lack and Unworthiness in Your Life 156
Loneliness 161
   Victims *162*
   Persecutors *162*
   Rescuers *163*
How to Reduce Loneliness in Your Life 164
Resentment 165
   Victims *167*
   Persecutors *167*
   Rescuers *168*
How to Reduce Resentment in Your Life 168
The Belief That You Need to Control Others 169

- *Victims* 170
- *Persecutors* 171
- *Rescuers* 172
- How to Reduce the Need to Control in Your Life 172
- Unfounded Hope 174
- How to Reduce Unfounded Hope in Your Life 175
- Insecurity 176
- How to Reduce Insecurity in Your Life 178
- Emotions Specific to Each Position 183
- Emotions Specific to the Victim State of Mind 184
- Self-Pity, Helplessness, Hopelessness, Inadequacy, Powerlessness 184
- Disappointment and Despair 186
- Depression 189
- Emotions Specific to the Persecutor State of Mind 191
- Rebelliousness 191
- Defensiveness 193
- Competitiveness 194
- Emotions Specific to the Rescuer State of Mind 195
- Superiority, Arrogance, and Disrespect 195
- Self-Righteousness 197
- Fatalism 199
- Overly Sensitive to Others 200

RETHINKING THE BELIEFS IN YOUR CLOUDS 207

- The Belief that You Have to Struggle to Survive 213
- The Belief that You are Powerless 214
- The Belief that You Need to Escape 216
- The Belief that You are Too Stupid to Choose Well 217
- "Shoulding" on Yourself or Others 220
- The Belief that You Have to Be "Nice" to Get What You Want 227
- The Belief that You Have to be "Clever" to Have Your Needs Met 230
- Other Self-Limiting Beliefs and Scripts 231
- About Me: 233
- About Living on This Planet: 234
- About Relationships: 235
- About the God Force: 238
- About Mother Earth: 239
- How to Release Your Dysfunctional Beliefs and Scripts 242

INTRODUCING HEALTHY HABITS 249

- Preparing For Take Off 249
- Acceptance 249
- Acceptance 250
- Embracing Your Ego 253

    Making Healthier Choices 262
    Risks 265
    Remorse as a Healing Force 269
    Letting Go of the Need for Approval 274
    The Way You Look 275
    What You Think 277
    What You Say and How You Say It 278
    What You Believe 280
    Letting Go Of Control Dramas 283

REINVENTING YOUR LIFE 293

    Reconnecting With Your Body 293
    The "White Devils" 297
    "The Black Devils" 297
    Rethinking Selfishness 308
    Healthy Selfishness 310
    Real Lasting Pleasure 314
    Instant Replay 318
        Step 1 – Connection 319
        Step 2 – Commitment 320
        Step 3 – Replay 320
        Step 4 – Assessment 322
        Step 5 – Self-Acknowledgement 325
        Step 6 – Your New Plan 325
        Step 7 – Letting Go and Letting God 327
    Reconnecting With Your Parents & Siblings 328
    Building Healthy Relationships 338
    Learning to Love Unconditionally 349

NEW BEGINNINGS 353

    Defining Your Sacred Circle 353
    Creating A Personal Sacred Space 357
    Reconnecting with the Source of Your Being 362
    Reconnecting With Your Authentic-Voice 367
    The Right Use of Your Will 371
    Expressing Your Balanced Total-Self 386
    Testimonials 394

Dedication

To my mother Lily Wurster, who taught me independence and the courage to fight for my life, even when I made choices of which she disapproved. To my grandchildren, students, clients, and friends who carry the promise of the future on their shoulders.

Acknowledgments

This book could not have been written without the help of both my teachers and students. I am deeply grateful to you all. There are many people who have been instrumental in making this book a reality. A special debt of gratitude to my soul family who helped "birth" the first edition-Carol Alaimo, Valery Catton, Amanda Smith, Bobbie Kalman, Andrea McCabe, and Hanneke van Overveld. New people have pitched in with the revisions and improvements of this edition. Many thanks to Helene Darisse, Elaine Murray, Susan Clyde, Jenny Davey, and Fran Walsh for their encouragement, support, and many hours of editing. Special thanks go out to Salvadore SeBasco for his book critique and review and his many suggestions that have been utilized to improve this edition. A special tribute goes to my soul brother, Chris Todd, whose unwavering support and guidance have sustained me through the last months of revising this edition.

Foreword

A Path to Wholeness changed my life! I was in the VPR Triangle and did not even know it! I purchased my first copy of this book from Tashene sometime in 2006. It was a time when I was in a very unhealthy relationship and feeling completely out of balance. I quite honestly did not know up from down anymore and was in a constant state of instability and confusion. I kept asking for insight, what was I was not getting?

I read this very insightful book for the first time shortly thereafter in a plane many thousand feet in the air (I was on my way home from another miserable holiday with my partner). As I read, I began to excitedly and feverishly highlight the most relevant text for me; and on that flight, I found my great AHA moment. You know that moment when all the pieces of a puzzle you have been working on finally come together? I suddenly realized that I was in a VPR Triangle with my partner! It was a pivotal moment in my life and in that relationship.

The most interesting thing that happened was, as soon as I became aware of the VPR Triangle, I was immediately able to step out of it! All of a sudden, I found myself looking at my partner from a completely different and detached perspective. I marvelled at how and why this person (sitting next to me and fussing and complaining about the long flight) had so much control and power over me. He suddenly seemed so powerless, absurd, like a fish out of water. I realized that he was not stronger or smarter than me. He was not better than me in any way. His only power over me was that he was completely adept in the Triangle. Then, I realized that I must be also, otherwise we could not have danced so skilfully together within the workings of that Triangle. A Path to Wholeness clearly showed me my part within the VPR Triangle; and in seeing it, I could step out of it into my Personal Power. The information in this book set me free!

Each relationship we have has the potential to be within the VPR Triangle. I do get caught up at times and dragged back into the Triangle, when I am not paying attention; but now I know how to identify what I feel when I am in there, identify which role I am playing; then face my part of it and get the heck out of there again as quickly as possible. This book has enabled me to empower myself to have more authentic relationships with those around me – to no longer be a victim. Thank you Tashene for the insights I was seeking!

Debbie Boehlen, Founder and owner of the Canadian Centre of Indian Head Massage www.indianheadmassage-canada.com

Prologue by Tashene

My personal journey toward wholeness began in 1971, during a Near Death Experience. After extensive testing, the doctors told me that I had only a few months to live. I went through all the stages of dying – denial, anger, bargaining, depression, and finally a place of acceptance and peace. During the actual death experience, however, I became aware of the hope that I could heal my body. I remember saying, "I'm ready to go, but if there's anything that I need to do in this world, show me how to get well." With that as my commitment, I was thrust back into my body. Over the next few months, I was shown how to eat and drink very specific things that gradually healed my body.

Soon, I went back to school to learn about human psychology and healing. My plan was to become a social worker; but before I could even graduate, I was recruited to train as a Reality Therapist with the Addiction Research Foundation. My background in psychology and the fact that I was a "clean and sober role model" had qualified me for the job. Everyone in the groups that I led was "a serious addict," who had been referred by, either their doctor or a judge, due to their dangerous behaviour. I soon realized that I had found my life work, because I could see that I was actually helping people get their lives back on track.

Even though I was the one who was supposed to be the teacher, the "addicts" were amazing teachers for me. As I began to more fully understand the concept of addiction, I began to realize that I wasn't so "clean and sober" after all. I realized that I was physically addicted to several socially accepted substances, as well as many non-physical patterns of relating to my environment. In the beginning, I was too self-righteous to consider that *my* seemingly *innocent* addictions were anywhere near as *bad* as drugs, alcohol, or gambling – the habits that had so adversely affected the "addicts." Gradually, I began to see that this wasn't true. I couldn't go anywhere without my *stash* of soda and chocolate. My belief that those substances were essential for my wellbeing was the same kind of belief that I repeatedly heard from people who were labelled "addicts." I became painfully aware of the similarities between us, rather than the differences. I also, gradually became aware of the *emotional* component of addiction – whether it was to a substance, person, or thing.

I began the self-discipline of keeping a constant vigil to catch myself, whenever I experienced that *desperate, addictive sensation*. Each time that I was honest enough to identify that specific emotional sensation, I would consciously strive to prevent myself from acting upon it; honestly look into the source of what I was experiencing;

and *wakefully wait*, until I could find a healthier way of relating to the situation.

My outlook on life again changed dramatically after another time of spiritual awakening in the 1980s. I left my old way of life and set out on a spiritual journey. I spent 10 months studying Bio-kinesiology, which is the use of kinesiology to connect with the soul vibration. I began to see auras and became very intuitively connected with people. I had been trained as an iridologist and herbalist and as I worked with people, I realized that I was seeing things that were not scientific – I had become a medical intuitive. I could explain to a person where their health challenges were simply by looking at their aura. I began to notice dark spots in my clients' auras. These spots usually corresponded with a physical disorder, which the client already knew about or one that I knew would soon manifest.

I began to call these dark areas "clouds," because I realized that these clouds were made up of dense particles of dysfunctional thoughts and emotions – like dirty water droplets. As I clairvoyantly assessed and defined the cause of those dark particles – the mental or emotional blockages – I found that many of them could be dissipated very easily, when I revealed the situations that had caused those thoughts and emotions to become "stuck."

I was shown that much of our daily stress and emotional pain is the direct result of clouds of confusion in our lives. I could see that the clouds were dysfunctional energy packages that were stuck between the Mental and Emotional Bodies. This led me to believe that our bad habits are simply the products of unhealthy notions that we have become emotionally attached to – dysfunctional beliefs. Due to my background in addiction counselling, I soon concluded that we become emotionally attached, or addicted, to our bad habits, because we are under the false impression that they will *make us feel better* – the way addicts think about their addiction of choice. As I poured over every available book on the subject of addictions, I realized that much of the existing literature was limited to the addiction to certain substances, such as drugs and alcohol; the dysfunctional behaviour of gambling; or the enabling behaviour of partners or family members (co-dependency). This just didn't seem to be a complete picture.

Over the years, as I counselled clients, I observed that, even though there *are* people who use self-abusive substances to avoid looking at the pain and confusion in their clouds, there are even more people who live in misery by focusing their time and attention on seemingly "normal," but dysfunctional habits. For example: I noticed how some people spend most of their time and attention on competing with others to become *"a somebody"*, because they feel so inadequate. They make most of their choices based on whether or not others will approve. Or, there are people who spend all of their time and attention on destructively stressful activities – such as controlling everyone and everything in their environment, so they will feel safe. Or, there are people who run away from their problems by spending most of their time taking care of others, working, or playing sports, or watching TV, or playing video games. I began to help people sort out their bad habits and understand the beliefs that fuelled their bad habits. I began to see that the habits fell into three distinct categories – that of Victim, Persecutor, and Rescuer. I realized that the Victim, Persecutor, Rescuer Triangle is a huge cloud that envelops most of our present society and that very few people actually live free of its influence.

It was many years later when I learned that Samuel Hahnemann, the founder of Homeopathy, had written about clouds (which he called miasms) in a work that was published in 1828. He claimed that miasms are the cause of every disease. This corresponded so closely with what I had seen intuitively, I began to study his theories and I have concluded that we are probably talking about the very same phenomena.

I began to realize that most of us have clouds and we use addictions to avoid looking at them. Our addictions don't have to be physically harmful, like alcoholism or drug abuse; they can be as simple as wasting our precious time by watching too much TV, or playing video games, or arguing with people over trivial matters, or, in my case, spending too much time reading books to avoid my real issues.

I eventually came to see that by making conscious choices about what we focus our attention on, and by changing the inefficient patterns of our dysfunctional thoughts, feelings, words, and actions, we actually change our world.

When we look carefully at the history of human society, it shows that dysfunctional beliefs, traditions, and behaviours have consistently prevented harmony in human relations. We can see how dysfunctional beliefs and behaviours create conflicts between people, groups, religions, and countries, all over the world. I am now convinced that, if enough of us penetrate our clouds and see the truth of whom we really are, we will gradually change our individual patterns of relating to our environments; in so doing, we *are* changing the world.

As I began to see the individual conflicts as indicators of a global problem – a microcosm that reflects the macrocosm – I began to understand that our darkest personal clouds are those that separate us from our soul connection. In essence, we have become disconnected from our truth, so we follow along in our learned patterns of relating that continue to confuse us and cloud our judgment. That clouded thinking is reflected in the choices that we make in our daily lives.

I began sharing the ideas in this book in the early 90s and they have been used to support, encourage, and heal the lives of many people in my private practice as a minister, counsellor, teacher, and healer.

Since the first edition was self-published in 2005, it has found its way across North America. In fact, it won an Honourable Mention Award in the Body, Mind, Spirit Category at the Independent Book Publisher (IPPY) Awards in 2006. What a thrill it was to go to Washington, D.C. to receive this prestigious award! It has been an even greater thrill to hear how this book has changed people's lives. I have received many emails and letters thanking me for writing it. One man said, "The first time I read your book, it was because I like you. I read it the second time, because I figured that I had missed something. I have just finished reading it for the third time and I now realize how much your book has changed my life for the better."

This type of comment has convinced me that this book may also help you bring your life into greater balance. Please don't think, however, that you can change your life just by reading it. You can only change your life *IF* you are willing to conscientiously review and revise your old beliefs and the habits that have clouded your thoughts, feelings, words, and behaviour, until a new way becomes natural. Anything that you have *learned* in the past can be *unlearned* and new habits and behaviours can be established.

Everyone's path is unique; but the one thing that we all want is to be happy, to feel whole. If this is your mission, this book will encourage and support you on your path. It will assist you in understanding how you were influenced or conditioned in the past; what conclusions you formed during certain stressful situations; how to rethink those conclusions; and how to shed the light of truth into any area that holds a cloud. By penetrating your clouds with the light of truth from your soul/Spiritual Body, you will be able to restructure your beliefs, allowing you to make healthy choices that support you along your personal *Path to Wholeness* – to find and fully express your Total-Self and create the life that you were meant to have.

Chapter One

Ground Zero

Long ago and far away, there was a happy royal family who were loving and kind to each other and their subjects. However, there were some people in the land who were greedy and power hungry who tried to dethrone the king to gain power. Even though the king was just and fair, his opponents created trouble throughout the land. This struggle lasted many years during which time the queen gave birth to several daughters. Each time a daughter was born, the troublemakers would rejoice, because they didn't see girl children as a threat to their plans.

Finally the queen gave birth to a son. She was afraid for his life; so she made the ultimate sacrifice and he was taken from the palace secretly to be raised by distant relatives in a tiny village in the country. Because his adoptive parents were poor peasants, he grew up believing that he too was a poor peasant. When he became a young man, however, a royal emissary arrived in the village to tell him the truth and asked him to assume his position as the royal prince of the kingdom. He couldn't accept the truth, so he ran away and denied his birthright.

This story is a metaphor for your life. You are a divine-spark – a part of the Creative Force of the Universe – the God Force. You are a divine spirit having a human experience. You are a prince or princess of the royal family – the God Force; however, you have been conditioned to believe that you are "just a human being" and you are, therefore, "less than" and "disconnected from," the God Force. This is not true; but a story that you have learned to accept as truth. Just like the prince in the above story, you can run away and deny your birthright, or you can accept it. You have free will to choose which perception you will believe to be true.

Many teachers and religious leaders throughout the history of humanity on this planet have taught us to believe that we are separate from the God Force. Unfortunately, some people continue to believe these stories, until many generations later, our light has become dimmed by the lack of truth about whom we really are. It may have seemed easier to deny that we are in charge of what is happening in our lives; because we realized that, if we accept the truth, we will have to face the fact that we *are* responsible for our kingdom – our reality.

Many of us are now in a position to accept the truth, because we know that we can't run away from ourselves any longer. We now understand that everything that is presently in our world *was created by us*, through our thoughts, beliefs, words, and actions – the things that we learned to believe about ourselves, and our patterns of relating to our environments – including the lies that we have told ourselves and our dysfunctional habits. Therefore, if your world isn't exactly how you wish it to be and you want to create a happy and healthy life, you must rethink any untruths that were internalized during your earlier experiences – those that have clouded your thinking and kept you in unhealthy patterns of relating to your environment.

The process of spiritual awakening is the peeling away of the lies or untruths that you have held in the past – the lies that have clouded your thinking and have kept you feeling separate from the God Force. As you penetrate those clouds with the light of truth, your world will automatically reflect the changes that you have made.

Consider for a moment the idea that, before you came into this world, you were consciously aware that you were a part of the God Force. You were whole and connected with every aspect of your being. You had a natural connection with Mother Earth and the God Force – you were directly linked. You were supported, nourished, and sustained by that connection. Somewhere, deep in your consciousness, you remember this connection. That's the reason that you are dissatisfied with anything less. That's the journey you are on – to find the fullness of that connection again. This book is designed to help you remember whom you truly are behind the lies that you have learned to believe about yourself – your clouds.

If you want to let your light truly shine, instead of just barely surviving on this planet, you will need to understand, rethink, and release some of your old habits and beliefs. By rethinking and adjusting the way that you make your choices, you will begin to activate your creativity and engage your will to consciously make changes in your life by awakening spiritually and creating a new way of being in your world.

You are a complex being, so the following illustrations and definitions are designed to help you understand the different parts of your Total-Self in a clear and precise way. By dissecting your Total-Self into these four parts, you can become consciously aware of how each part of you interacts with your Total-Self; whether you have clouds of unhealthy habits and beliefs that dim your potential; and how to release your clouds to reveal your authentic self.

The Total-Self

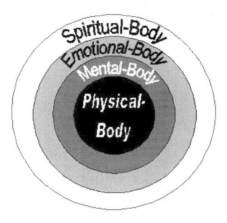

This is the way your Total-Self would look if you were a perfectly balanced person living in total harmony with every aspect of your being.

The term "Total-Self" represents your total consciousness – the totality of all your parts – your Spiritual-Body, your Emotional-Body, your Mental-Body, and your Physical-Body. Your Total-Self is balanced when all your parts are functioning in harmony and integrity with each other.

If you were totally balanced, your decisions would be made from a place of consensus between all your parts. If you think that something is missing in your life, it is because you are not making your decisions from a place of harmony with your Total-Self – there is something out of balance – there is a cloud in a specific area of your consciousness.

Your Spiritual-Body

The outermost circle of the above illustration represents your Spiritual-Body. It is shown as clear in the above illustration because it is invisible to your physical eyes and has the least dense energy. Your spirit is whom you were before you came into this world and what will be left when you no longer have a physical form. It is your natural connection with the rest of the Universe. Ideally, it penetrates or overlaps every part of your being.

If you were, at all times, consciously connected with your Spiritual-Body, you would always know how to cope with every situation in a healthy, stable manner. Your choices would be based upon what is *right* or *good* for you; and you would know how your decisions would affect your future and your future relationships.

Some people call your connection with your Spiritual-Body "activating your fullest potential" or "self-actualization." Sometimes, your Spiritual-Body is called your soul, your higher-self, your superconscious mind, your "authentic-self" or your "authentic-voice." (Your "authentic-voice" is actually your soul-voice from your Spiritual-Body and will be more thoroughly discussed in Chapter 7.) Whatever you call it, a strong connection with your Spiritual-Body is the goal of most spiritual seekers.

Your Emotional-Body

The next layer, in the above illustration, is your Emotional-Body. It is a slightly denser energy than your Spiritual-Body, because it contains the desire to be part of the physical reality of this planet. It contains sensors that are designed to perceive and evaluate the non-physical reality around you. Your emotions are designed to give you information about the energetic atmosphere or "climate" in your environment, both internally as well as externally. When you become fully conscious of your Emotional-Body, you are fully aware of what you are sensing at all times. By using your natural senses, you can perceive the energy in each new environment to decide whether it is beneficial to you, or whether it would be better for you to remove yourself from that space. When you are able to accurately sense the energy around you with your intuition, then you can use your Mental-Body to define and label what you are experiencing and choose the role that you want or need to play in each environment.

Your Mental-Body

The layer that is closest to the Physical-Body in the above illustration is your Mental-Body. It is darker in colour, because it has the capacity to hold onto mental energy, until it is manifested into a physical form. Your Mental-Body is like a computer database that stores factual information about your life experiences and your physical environment. It holds your conscious and unconscious memories – all the information and concepts (packages of information) that you have learned from your previous experiences in your environment. It holds all your memories and logical conclusions about your previously experienced reactions and responses. It holds the information that you have learned about your connections with other people, your environment, Mother Earth, and the God Force.

You "tune into" your Mental-Body whenever you consciously observe and label things in your environment and come to conclusions about what is happening. You make decisions about each situation and decide what is in your best interest according to what is stored in your memories. Your Mental-Body processes information by defining how external stimuli and information will affect your life and your relationship to the world. You then file the necessary information into your memory banks to be used at a later time. Some people call your Mental-Body your "mind" (both conscious and unconscious). When you are consciously aware of your mental processes, your mind is clear and precise. When you are unconscious of the way your mind is working, your thoughts are clouded and unable to process your options in a clear way.

Your Physical-Body

The dark shape in the centre of the above illustration represents your Physical-Body. Its shape is the darkest in colour because it is the densest manifestation of your Total-

Self. Your Physical-Body is everything that is visible to the human eye in your personal world and outwardly expresses who you are into your environment. It, of course, includes the physical body in which your spirit lives; but it also includes all things that you have created in your physical environment, your home, and your possessions.

A healthy Physical-Body represents your uniqueness and expresses what makes you different from others as well as the qualities and values that you share with other people. Your Physical-Body is often referred to as how you express your ego into the world. It is the physical manifestation of everything that you have created with every aspect of your Total-Self.

A Healthy Total-Self

Your Total-Self is what we often call your "personality." A healthy Total-Self contains a healthy body, mind, emotions, and a close alignment with your soul/Spiritual-Body. This balance is called your personal integrity. Ideally, each part of your Total-Self is seen as equally important, respected for its value, and given the appropriate support and encouragement to grow and evolve. A healthy Total-Self also creates a layer of protection for your identity – healthy boundaries.

Healthy boundaries create a safety net around your Total-Self to prevent harmful external stimuli from affecting your identity. For example: If you are an honest person and someone were to call you a liar, a healthy Total-Self would automatically reject that false accusation, because you know that isn't who you are. Therefore, your whole being would prevent you from being affected by that person's opinion, because a firm knowledge of your high level of honesty is in place. You would simply deflect that opinion away from you and say, "That isn't who I am." That allegation would just bounce off your being and you would not be affected by it, making it possible for you to respond with such a clear message that your attacker will easily understand.

The reverse is also true. If someone were to call you a liar, and, if the boundary around your Total-Self were less than strong and healthy, you would allow that accusation to penetrate your being and you would be affected by it. This would reveal that you had previously formed an unhealthy (and perhaps unconscious) belief about your ability to be honest – a belief that clouds your perception of yourself. This awareness is an opportunity of healing – an opportunity to review a self-limiting belief and release it.

Every belief is simply a package of energy that holds facts, ideas, memories, and concepts to which you have attached an emotional value. Every belief was formed because you have come to conclusions based on your previous experiences. In other words, beliefs are created when you mix facts and feelings together. Each belief is your creation. It is like a baby that was birthed in the energetic field between your Mental and Emotional Bodies.

If the belief is in alignment with the truth in your Spiritual-Body, it will naturally float to the perimeter of your Total-Self and create a safeguard from external doubts, fears, or false projections from others – a healthy boundary. If, however, it is a false belief that is based on misinterpretations or misrepresentations of your truth, it will stay stuck between your Mental and Emotional Bodies; and it will diminish or even stop the light of truth from your Spiritual-Body from enhancing your life.

How Your Clouds Were Formed

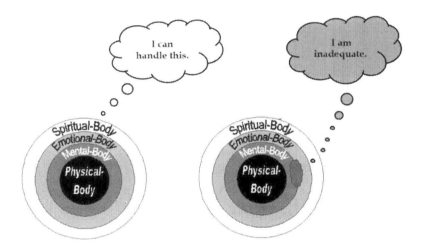

The above illustration shows that a good belief will be a clear energy package, like the one on the left and it will serve as a safety net around your being. It is in harmony with the light of truth from your Spiritual-Body so it will enhance your life. If, however, the bubble is filled with self-limiting beliefs, it becomes a dense cloud like the one shown on the right and it will remain stuck between your Mental and Emotional Levels.

Every cloud is made of a variety of distorted or unclean ideas – almost like droplets of dirty water – that have gathered together due to similarities in their vibrations. As we go through life, we collect these soiled energy packages for a number of reasons: They may be based on memories of our experiences in previous lifetimes; we may have absorbed them from the attitudes and beliefs that were demonstrated in our early childhood; or they may have been assumptions that we came to during our experiences in past or current environments.

In other words, we have gathered those polluted ideas together into a solid cloud that defines and limits our perception of ourselves and our environments. Then, we have built a story to define our clouded thinking. Our stories say that what we believe is true: however, a belief may, or may not, have any value or basis in reality.

Let's also examine how facts, concepts, and ideas/theories/stories/scripts influence our clouds. The word "fact" represents a certainty – something that most people will agree to be true. It is a fact that you are reading this book. If you are sitting in a chair, while you are reading, it makes the statement, "You are sitting in a chair," also a fact. Now, we have brought the word "chair" into this narrative. Most of us would agree that the word "chair" represents a "concept" that includes the presumption that a chair is simply something that one sits upon; but it's not something to eat, or a vehicle to drive to the market. Therefore, a concept is a grouping of ideas that we use to refer to a specific subject or object. A specific word (such as the word "chair") is used to embrace the parameters of that concept.

The concept, which comes to mind when you hear the word "chair," is totally unique to you. It contains information about what your imaginary chair looks like and is made of. For example: The word "chair" may activate thoughts and pictures about one that is made of wood, or metal, or it may be upholstered. While you are still thinking unemotionally about "facts" regarding your chair, it is still in the realm of concepts.

As soon as you begin to add an emotional charge or attach a value to your mental image of your chair, it moves into the realm of beliefs. For example: You may have an emotional attachment to a specific chair, because it has sentimental value; or it is very comfortable; or you think it has more value because it cost a lot of money. Each of these emotional components adds dimension or value to your perception of the images that you created in your mind as you explored the word "chair."

You begin to create a theory or story to substantiate your reason for valuing that particular chair. Some of your theories regarding the value of your imaginary chair may be very practical and logical. You might say, "I like this chair because it supports my back while I'm reading." That belief is a conclusion that you have come to through experience: You value the chair because of its comfort level. If, however, I were to offer to exchange your chair with another that you found more comfortable, very likely you would accept it willingly.

However, when you add a stronger emotional attachment to a specific chair, you would begin to add more energy to the value of your chair. For example: You may have a favourite chair that was given to you by someone you loved and you want to continue to feel their love as you sit in their chair. These are good feelings that you enjoy; so you don't want to part with the chair, because you don't want to let go of those loving feelings.

Conversely, if you were to add fearful thoughts to your belief package regarding your chair, it begins to create a whole new perception. Let's say that you begin to build a theory/story about it that suggests, "The only time that I will feel the presence of my loved one is when I sit in their chair." Or, "They won't love me, unless I keep their chair forever." You start creating a story that makes you feel controlled by them because of those conditions. You may even believe that they will be angry with you and stop loving you, if you were to sell or give away their chair.

Your theory has devolved into a cloud that contains beliefs that are so distorted that they have no resemblance to the truth. It is simply a mental construct that you have begun to believe in. The resulting story that you have created has become a cloud – an illusion or delusion – that has the power to cripple you and prevent you from using your free will to make healthy decisions in the future.

How Clouds Distort Your Emotional Perceptions

Scientists have now proven that you have receptors in your brain (that were already functioning before you were born) that are designed to intuit information about your environment, allowing you to assess the energy around you. Your intuition is a natural function of your Emotional-Body that allows you to accurately perceive every element in your environment. This perception then allows you to respond appropriately to each new situation and keep you safe.

If your early environment was confusing or unsafe, your intuition may have become overloaded with sensations and you concluded that you had to turn down its volume to survive. For example: If everyone in your environment was bigger and stronger and more powerful than you, or, if you were consistently diminished by the thoughts, feelings, words, and actions of those around you, you may have concluded that the best way to survive in that environment was to pretend that they had all the power and you had none.

If you were consistently conditioned to mistrust your observations as a child, your ability to read the signals and sensations in your Emotional-Body gradually became less accurate. By shutting down your conscious awareness of the nonphysical reality around you, this disconnection confused or even disabled your Emotional-Body. You became less able to make healthy choices, because you were not receiving accurate information from your Mental-Body. In other words, a cloud was created between your emotional sensors, and your thinking processes. Consequently, you became less and less capable of using your natural capacity to react appropriately to challenging or dangerous situations.

For example: As a small child, you may have had experiences where you were criticized or even punished because you didn't know something. You may have felt emotionally hurt by the energy coming from the people who were upset with you. They may have also said that "you should know better" and you interpreted this to mean that you were "stupid." This may have affected your perception of your mental abilities. You may have then combined the two components – the words that they told you, plus your hurt feelings – to create a clouded belief that you were inadequate – just because you didn't know that particular thing.

Now, whenever you experience a new or different type of situation, where you are inexperienced, you automatically criticize yourself (tell yourself the same story, in the same way) by calling yourself "stupid." Each time a situation arises where you are either told by an outside source, or come to that conclusion by yourself, it reinforces the cloud, making it denser. Once that cloud is in place, you continue to act in a way that is in agreement with the energy of the cloud. In this case, you would act "stupidly;" making the cloud more and more dense through reinforcement.

Clouds Contain Your Defensive-Mechanisms

As has been mentioned earlier, it is the function of a healthy Total-Self to define your personality, your identity, and to protect you from the external influences that could adversely affect your life. Therefore, when you were a child, it was natural for you to develop ways to automatically react to your environment. These reactions were supposed to make life simpler and easier, but also to protect you from harmful external influences. You probably unconsciously internalized some of these habits by observing the older people in your environment.

Some of those habits are functional coping-strategies, because they are aligned with your Total-Self, and allow you to respond appropriately to situations. Others are dysfunctional defensive-mechanisms that have become stuck between your Mental and Emotional Bodies, and continue to cause you to react inappropriately to the threats that come toward you.

A healthy coping-strategy naturally brings about a healthy, harmonious result. A defensive mechanism is an unnatural process that you have invented to protect yourself, because you are in a state of fear. If you keep in mind that every "mechanism" is a man-made, mechanical invention that is not natural, you will see that it is outside the realm of healthy or harmonious results or effective solutions to the challenges in your life. It is merely an artificial weapon that you have invented to protect yourself. All defensive-mechanisms are abnormal ploys that we use to protect ourselves and to pretend to be in control, even though we feel powerless. In reality, they are lies that we have invented to defend us whenever we feel vulnerable.

If your environment was consistently unsafe, you most likely developed defensive-mechanisms that were not in your best interest then, and are definitely not in your best interest, now. Keep in mind that children who are raised in confusing environments quickly learn to focus all their curiosity and creativity on ways to protect themselves. This is how defensive-mechanisms become habitual. Now, as an adult, some of those habits may automatically control you, especially when you are in uncomfortable situations. They automatically click into place, whenever a specific energy approaches you.

Some of your defensive-mechanisms may be: believing that *every* environment is unsafe, so you have to protect yourself against *all* people, especially people of different races, religions, or nationalities; believing that it's a "dog-eat-dog world," so you have to make yourself *important* or be aggressive to feel good about yourself; or believing that no one is going to like you, if you tell them who you really are, so you have to create a false persona or mask to be accepted or to prevent others from knowing how vulnerable you feel.

You eventually gathered those beliefs together, until they created dense clouds that have their own "voice" – words or scripts, which you continue to use as a mask or false face to protect you, whenever a specific type of threat approaches your being. Sometimes, this "voice" is what you automatically project toward others, through your vocal chords; but often, this "voice" is just words in your head that diminish your truth, create confusing emotional sensations, and, consequently, muddy your perception of yourself. So, I call the voice of your false-self your "phony-voice" – false perceptions about yourself and your world; as opposed to your "authentic-voice" that expresses the truth about whom you truly are – an awareness of your divinity – the truth from your Spiritual-Body.

Scripts

"Scripts" are internal dialogue or self-talk that are the products of unhealthy beliefs – stories that you have told yourself. Scripts are simply a grouping of lies that you have gathered together to protect yourself – a defensive-mechanism. Each script is spoken from a false persona or "character" that you have created to project a false image of yourself. Your "character" automatically "reads" from your script, according to the role that you have chosen to play in the drama of life.

Have you ever noticed how your tone of voice changes when you are insecure or threatened? This is because your phony-voice is reading from a script that was created to protect you from further confusion, rejection, or abuse. You believe that, if you play your role *correctly*, using the *right* words with the *right* tone of voice, you will be safe. So, your scripts are *tools* that you have invented – defensive-mechanisms that click into place to make you *believe* that you are in control. They are also designed to fool your audience into believing something about you that is not true.

You created your scripts to prevent people from knowing that you feel vulnerable (insecure or afraid). They were designed to throw other people off track, so they won't continue to abuse you for being you. That phony-voice tells you lies about yourself and your abilities, as well as gives incorrect messages to the other people in your environment. Over the years, that voice may have become louder than the truth of whom you are. For example: If you were really intelligent as a child, it may have caused trouble with people who wanted to dominate you. They may have told you that you were inadequate and eventually, you began to agree with their perception. You began to tell yourself that you had to pretend to be inadequate, so you wouldn't get into trouble again. Unfortunately, you repeated that lie to yourself so often that you began to believe it. It became automatic – an unconscious script that you began to believe was true.

Another example: When someone tries to intimidate you, you might automatically "read" from a script that says, "Don't tell me what to do! I'm in control." This script is designed to fool the other person into believing that you actually know what you are doing; when in reality, you may not, you aren't sure, or you are afraid that you have just made a mistake. This is your attempt to control others by using your phony-voice to puff-up (fill with hot air) your clouded beliefs and prevent others from knowing that you are actually feeling insecure.

You may also have a cloud that is filled with stories or scripts that you have internalized, because you have become convinced that you *deserve* abuse. Every subsequent situation that causes similar scripts to be triggered exposes memories that are recalled with amazing clarity and accuracy – often with the same, or very similar, levels of distress. Also, some of your unconscious scripts are lies, which you have absorbed directly from your early childhood environment. They may have become totally subconscious and hidden behind stories that have no basis in your present reality.

As you become more conscious of your scripts, you can more easily deal with them. You will then be able to release your unhealthy patterns of relating and the subsequent false personas and scripts that you have built around them. You then have a clean slate to invite in new information from your Spiritual-Body, make decisions based on the truth of whom you are and fully express your Total-Self into the world around you.

The Original Cause of Addictions

Whenever unhealthy beliefs or behaviour are prevalent (disempowering or confusing behaviour, beliefs, ideas, or reactions), a cloud of confusion is formed. This cloud contains all the different particles of thoughts, beliefs, and emotional reactions that were ever expressed by the people in that environment. If you lived in such an unhealthy environment, it was natural for you to become confused.

As a child, if you were subjected to confusion on a daily basis, eventually, you began to consider it as the normal way to be and you became conditioned to it. You were told that you "should" be able to cope with it. You began to focus all your attention on dissecting the confusion to regain some semblance of order and control. If you couldn't sort out those confusing elements, you may have begun to search for ways to temporarily hide your areas of vulnerability. However, if you were being denied the elements that you actually needed to feel safe and secure, you probably used your imagination to find another method that could give you a temporary respite – an artificial substitution for the real thing – an addiction.

Those substitutions may have been the only solutions that you could think of or the only ones available to you at that time. Even though you realized that they were not what you *actually* wanted, you were desperate – you wanted to *feel better* – so you accepted *second best*. Second best left something to be desired; so you began to use your imagination to tell yourself a story about how you "needed" your addiction of choice to make you feel complete. Your story became a belief or illusion. However, your stories could never make your addictions truly satisfying – because no matter what story you told yourself, the substitutions/addictions were not the *real* thing. Your stories were simply scripts, which your phony-voice was telling you, to divert your attention away from your reality, so you could *pretend* that you were *feeling better.*

All external confusion (big or small) affects your Total-Self if you don't have healthy boundaries. When you were a child, if confusing messages were consistently repeated by your peers' or elders' words, reactions, or behaviours, unnatural conclusions or patterns were established in your Total-Self. That confusion may have turned down the volume of your authentic-voice (from your Spiritual-Body); diminished your connection with your intuition (from your Emotional-Body) that influenced what you perceived as the right or wrong things to do; imprinted more lies and confusion in the clouds that were lodged between your Emotional and Mental-Bodies; confused your logical mental processes (in your Mental-Body); and eventually, affected your Physical-Body. Your self-image and your perception of the world around you had become totally confused. This confusion prevented you from developing naturally into the self-sufficient being that you were intended to be.

Considering that it is much easier to control a person who is confused, we might then ask, if the act of confusing another person is actually a form of abuse. We know that, if you were to hurt your body repeatedly, the physical wounds would become deeper and more difficult to heal. Then, consider that this is also true with wounds that are the product of emotional and mental confusion. Unfortunately, non-physical wounds may not be considered as harmful, because they are not obvious to the naked eye; however, they are very real, as they create dense clouds in your energy body.

During your childhood, some emotionally or mentally abusive patterns may have been diminished, underestimated, or ignored, because they were the result of a parent's or caregiver's unhealthy habits. They became *familiar* to you. It is common for familiar abusive attitudes to be considered "normal" by family members and they are eventually accepted by the entire family. Consequently, you were *conditioned* to accept that specific type of abuse. At times, you may have even denied that it *was* abuse, simply because the story that you told yourself about it was stronger than the truth.

It is important, at this time, to understand a simple formula to define abuse. If you perceived yourself physically wounded in a situation, it was abusive in some way. If you were mentally or emotionally confused, it created a cloud in your consciousness. If you were told confusing ideas about the God Force, your connection with your Spiritual-Body was diminished, disrespected, dishonoured, or disempowered. The people who were doing these hurtful things may not have *intended* to wound or confuse you, but it doesn't matter. If you *felt* harmed, it added density to your clouds. It is important, however, to keep reminding yourself that, in most cases, the people who had previously confused or hurt you would not have acted that way had they known any better. It is also important to keep reminding yourself that all wounds can be healed in time with adequate love and attention, so there *is* hope!

Every addiction is an attempt to distract our attention away from our pain. During a time when we felt vulnerable or helpless, we developed a plan that was designed to make us *feel better.* However, whenever we act on that plan, even though we may temporarily find relief, very soon we feel worse, so we believe that we need *more*. This repetition strengthens our scripts about how helpless we are; and our addictions are anchored into our clouds.

Every addiction is a learned behaviour. Whether people are addicted to *substances* (such as alcohol, drugs, food, chocolate, cigarettes); *ideas* (such as self-limiting beliefs); or *behaviours* (such as shame, self-abuse, continuing in unhealthy relationships, or living a stressful lifestyle); a pattern emerges pointing to one root cause for the addicts' misery. They are using addictions to *attempt* to avoid pain in their lives – to numb the pain in their brains.

Every addiction is a substitution – not the real thing! For example: When you were small, a situation may have arisen where you felt wounded or confused, so you wanted a hug and some reassurance from your parents; but they offered you a candy instead. You were left with two options. You could complain and say, "I don't want a candy, I want a hug." In this case, however, you would then run the risk of being rejected or hurt again, as well as possibly losing out on the candy, which you probably had enjoyed in the past. So, you say, "Well … this is better than nothing," and you *settled* for the candy – *second best.*

Eventually, this "settling" created a pattern in your mental and emotional processes that clicked into place whenever you wanted a hug or reassurance; so now, you automatically reach for candy, whenever you experience that desperate feeling of neediness. However, the candy doesn't truly satisfy you, so your mind has to build an illusion around it to make it seem satisfying. You may have invented a story that says, "Wow! This candy is so good! It's even better than a hug!" Your phony-voice continued to repeat this script, until you almost believed it; so you continue to use it to protect you from experiencing the pain of not receiving the love, support, and encouragement that you *actually* need.

Your addiction to food may have been established at a very early age, when you were given a "treat" instead of the hug or reassurance that you actually needed. Or, it may have been demonstrated by your parents or caregivers as you watched them use food to hide the pain in *their* lives. This behaviour may have been internalized into your consciousness, and it became a habit – a "normal solution" to that empty sensation – and you developed a script that your phony-voice told you would make you feel better.

If you are addicted to food, you focus all your attention on eating, because your attention is focused on the belief that you will *feel better IF* you have something to eat. Or, you may be obsessed by something more specific, such as the belief that you *need* a particular type of food – a pizza, a hotdog, ice cream, potato chips, etc. This could have started when your parents or caregivers were absent or unsupportive, making you aware of "that empty sensation." However, when they fed you certain foods, you accepted the *illusion* of being loved. Perhaps, your parents felt guilty for neglecting you; so they brought home a pizza or ice cream. You didn't realize that it was an artificial form of love, so you created a script about the need to attain that specific type of food. This developed into an obsession or addiction to a specific type of food.

As you grew older, you saw people displaying ways that they said made them *feel better* – other types of "fixes." One of your friends may have suggested a "better candy" – drugs or alcohol – and said, "Here, try this. It will make you *feel better*." That empty sensation was so prominent in your life that you were willing to try *anything* to *feel better*.

Every addictive substance, idea, or behaviour is always "less than whole." We are never addicted to something whole and abundant. For example: We can't become addicted to a whole apple or orange, unless we pervert that natural substance with either an emotional attachment, such as the belief that it will make us *feel better,* or we add something to it, denaturing it in some way.

An example of this is the old adage, "An apple a day keeps the doctor away." The story that you will be healthy, as long as you "eat an apple a day," created an emotional attachment – in this case, a delusion. Even though apples are nutritious – filled with vitamins and antioxidants – they are not an insurance policy to prevent all diseases.

Also, if you were to add something unhealthy, such as white sugar and white flour pastry and bake it into an apple pie, it is much easier to become addicted to the final product; because you have added something that is not complete in itself. Then, if you were to add a memory of a beautiful, happy day, when your mother or grandmother baked an apple pie for you, an emotional element is added to the mix. Therefore, if you were to substitute apple pie for a healthy lunch to try to cover up or distract your attention away from feeling lonely or unsupported, you would automatically feel cheated. On some level, you would realize that it doesn't actually satisfy your need. This makes you desire *more,* to look for something else to fill that missing element.

Often, our addictions are so unconscious that they seem *normal,* as is illustrated by the following story. Years ago, while lecturing on the subject of addictions, I would often say, "You can't be addicted to something as healthy as orange juice." Then, I met someone who was. While visiting a friend, I noticed there were several gallon jugs of orange juice in her fridge. My curiosity got the better of me and I asked her about the juice. Initially, she brushed me off by saying that it had been on sale, so she had stocked up. Each time I visited, however, I noticed there was always what I perceived to be an excessive supply of orange juice on hand. Then, I found out that there was also a second fridge in her garage containing more jugs of juice.

As I continued to listen carefully, the root cause of her addiction to orange juice began to reveal itself. My friend was the youngest daughter of a very affluent family. They owned a very successful cold storage facility and were accustomed to having access to lots of food. Every Christmas, her father brought in a large shipment of oranges from Florida. If there were any leftover oranges, they were made into juice on Christmas morning. This became a wonderful, family tradition.

Then suddenly, when my friend was a young teenager, the depression of the '30s hit the area – very hard. People didn't have the money to buy the fruits that her father had brought from the south. Soon, fruit was rotting in the bins and the cold storage business was lost. Their beautiful home was lost to the bank and the family had to move into an old farmhouse in the country where they struggled to survive.

In my friend's vulnerable, young mind, the family's financial struggles created a belief in *lack* and unworthiness. Even though she struggled to become a highly paid professional, she still carried feelings of insecurities. At some point, she began the habit of stocking up on large jugs of orange juice. She had no idea that her need to have several gallon jugs of orange juice in her fridge at all times was an attempt to cover up her sensations of insecurity. It had become *normal* behaviour.

She felt *safer* when she had all that juice on hand – it was her security blanket. She could never get enough orange juice, however, because the solace she was seeking could never be satisfied by orange juice. Her cloud of insecurities had not been healed, so it manifested in abnormal behaviour. Even though she had a very good income, she became a "penny pincher." She was proud of only buying fruit that had been marked down in price. She would spend hours scanning sales flyers and then drive many miles to purchase sale items. She would brag about the fact that her clothes were purchased from second-hand stores. Her insecurities were ruling her life. There were so many activities devoted to "penny pinching" that she had no time to live her life.

> *Every addiction is a cry for help!*

Even though every addiction is a cry for help, our cries may not be heard unless someone is brave enough to draw our attention to them. We may be wasting our time and energy blindly plodding along the same unproductive path that we have previously followed. In the above story, my friend had no idea that her obsessive behaviour was controlling her life, until I drew her attention to it. Then, she had the opportunity to rethink her clouded beliefs.

Every addiction distracts our attention away from our creative ability to find a healthy, natural substance or action that would satisfy our needs. Whenever we engage in addictive behaviour, it wastes time and energy and prevents us from expressing ourselves in more productive and satisfying ways.

There are a great many substances and habits that are accepted as *normal* in our society that may have been introduced into our daily lives due to someone's addictions. Coffee, tea, sugary sweets, soda pop, and alcoholic beverages have become *normal* fare. People simply go along with the crowd, fitting in with their family patterns, their peers, or others in their environments. The self-limiting habits of others have become their "normal" behaviour.

When you *hope* that your addiction of choice – food, alcohol, TV, etc. will make you *feel better* – this is always *unfounded* hope. However, it may be the only hope you have. You may have desperately needed some form of hope to combat the painful sense of *lack* that you were experiencing, so you inserted an illusion or addiction. Or, you may have concluded that you couldn't have the *real* thing and given up hope entirely, so you settled for second best. In either case, you became an addict.

What is an Addict?

The word "addict" is used to describe an individual who has harmful habits that create unhealthy stress in his or her life, and, usually, in the lives of others. Addicts have lost their ability to make healthy choices and have begun to use self-limiting substances, habits, activities, or relationships as a way of life, because they have come to the conclusion that there is no other way to live. They have developed scripts (lies and illusions) that are a set of excuses and justifications designed to support their unhealthy beliefs. Their addictions have begun to rule their life, adversely affecting the personality that they project outwardly to the world. Everyone, except them, sees the clouds that are hanging around in their lives, because their scripts, the messages that they hear from their phony-voice, constantly affirm the *value* of their addictions. Their scripts often become louder than any feedback that they might receive from others.

The degree to which we try to control our environment with our addictions reveals our level of discomfort, frustration, fear, and lack of creativity. For example: People who are terrified of being poor may risk gambling everything they have; someone who is terrified of being alone may stay in a relationship in which they risk abuse;

people who are afraid of starving may overeat or eat unhealthy substances and risk future health problems – all because they are unable to face the truth about what is *actually* going on inside.

When you are addicted to doing something the same way every time, it is as though you are stuck in a *robotic trance*, where you automatically reach for the same solution without any conscious thought. This compulsive behaviour is based on the lie or script that you must do a specific thing, in a specific way, to *feel better* – to relax, to be satisfied, or even to survive.

You may ask, if one is lacking the creativity to find healthy solutions, how can they possibly break their patterns. The first and most important step is to become conscious of how your automatic reactions perpetuate themselves – how your clouds have taken on personalities of their own and have their own scripts. By becoming fully conscious of your scripts, you can ask yourself whether the stories that you tell yourself are in your highest good. This process takes a deep level of honesty and concentration. Secondly, you must become conscious of what triggers you, and how your triggers control your thinking processes. Then, you will be able to take back your Personal Power – your will to live – to choose something different – something that is in harmony with the truth of whom you are.

How Your Clouds are "Triggered"

Whenever you are confused or "upset" for more than a few minutes and you can't clear your mind, one of your clouds has very probably been triggered. This is because your clouds contain a whole range of particles of energy, beliefs, scripts, and memories that you have collected throughout your life. Each cloud contains so many different elements that your attempts to sort them out can seem insurmountable. Whenever a cloud is "triggered," all that residual energy is exposed to your conscious awareness at the same time. It feels like a swirling energy vortex, because you are rapidly changing from your emotional sensations to your old scripts and self-limiting beliefs and back again. You may feel stuck in a rut or even paralyzed. You may become a scared, helpless child, and you don't understand why. One client said that, when she was triggered, it "stops me in my tracks." She can't think of anything except her old scripts and emotional reactions.

Your clouds may be triggered by obvious input from others; but they may also be triggered by a variety of subtle elements – a sound, a smell, a colour, a tone of voice, or even the unspoken, projected emotions of others. Or, you may be carrying a painful memory in one of your clouds and you may automatically *expect* a specific reaction from the people in your environment. For example: You may *expect* that you will automatically be rejected, whenever someone tells you that they are upset with something you have said or done, because that is what has previously happened. Or, you may assume that a specific result will *always* take place, whenever you have a difference of opinion.

These automatic reactions are usually habits or patterns of relating that you have developed over the years, to deflect your pain or distract you from what you are feeling. However, when you insert one of your excuses, justifications, scripts or lies into your thinking process, you automatically "stuff your pain under the rug" again. If you continue to abdicate your Personal Power, you give away more and more of your life to unhealthy habits.

Recognizing the fact that you are stuck in a cloud is the first step out of dysfunctional thinking and into your Personal Power. When you can objectively observe your process, you have already activated your Personal Power to create a different reality. So, practice just observing what is going on. Put labels on your most obvious thoughts and emotional reactions. Then, dig deeper into your emotional sensations and label what other emotions are being triggered.

You may need to explore the subtle messages that are implied in your scripts. What are they telling you? You may need to ask yourself why a specific slight or criticism affected you, and realize that it *hurt* only because you had a dysfunctional belief about yourself that resonated with that specific type of cloud. Own your reactions. Own the fact that you have carried those reactions for some time. Own the fact that you have created them to protect yourself. And then, own your right to change your reactions into appropriate responses.

It is very important to differentiate between abuse and the pain that you feel when a cloud has been triggered. Original abuse was the first time that you experienced that type of pain; while a trigger is the activation of an unconscious memory of that original pain. Keep in mind that you may assume that someone is being hurtful, when they are, in actuality, refusing to support your self-abusive patterns of relating. Or, you may assume that you are being attacked, when someone is actually calling your attention to beliefs or scripts that are disempowering to you.

It may be your defensive-mechanisms or addictions that are actually being attacked – not you. If you come to the conclusion that a trigger is abusive, you will waste time wallowing in self-pity and miss the gift that it is to you – the opportunity to understand an original wound, or perhaps rewrite an old script, or expose a cloud to the light of truth.

As you become better at discerning the difference between your phony-voice and your authentic-voice, you are on your way to a more balanced life. This requires, however, that you accept responsibility for the care and maintenance of your Total-Self. You can no longer blame others for "pushing your buttons," because you are taking responsibility for healing your life. You are taking responsibility for removing your defensive-mechanisms and rewriting your scripts, so you can heal any clouds that are lodged in your Total-Self. In so doing, you have become accountable for your thoughts, feelings, words, and actions.

When you rethink your beliefs, rewrite your scripts, and create a new life, everyone in your circle of influence will be affected. You've probably heard the quip, "Who are you? And what have you done with my wife/husband/child etc.?" When you change, everyone in your environment has to adjust how they relate to you. This may be welcomed by some people in your circle, but, more often, it is resisted, and conflict may ensue.

Humans are creatures of habit and bad habits are hard to break. The good news is that good habits are just as hard to break. We can all learn new ways of being – we can all change! We don't have to be trapped in unhealthy beliefs! This is especially true when you see the beneficial effects of your journey reflected in the lives of those you love, as is demonstrated in the following story.

Sandra was a client who came to me for counselling. However, for several sessions, she kept telling me how "perfect" her life was. My next question was always, "Then, how can I help you?" Gradually, her story began to unfold. She was married to a "nice man;" but they "never talked about anything important anymore." They talked about their children, their home, their responsibilities, but they never shared any mental, emotional, or spiritual intimacy. She felt "guilty for expecting him to change." She said she loved him, but she didn't like him anymore. She realized that something was missing from her life and she wanted more.

She actively began to search for answers. She soon realized that she had married her husband because he was just like her father in many ways – neither man talked about his emotions; neither man was interested in anything except making money; neither man was warm and affectionate to his partner or his children, and both men buried their troubles in alcohol.

Sandra finally concluded that the main focus of her early life had been to beg for her father's approval, which never came. She realized that when she married her husband, she had been looking for what had been missing in her early childhood; but she didn't get it. Next, she realized that she had done the same thing with her husband, as her mother had; she had excused his drinking to "keep peace in the family." Then, she realized that she resented him, because, even though she excused his unhealthy behaviours, she got nothing of value in return.

She began attending a variety of classes and workshops to become more consciously aware of what she wanted out of life. She began to gain strength and build a solid connection with her Personal Power. Gradually, after many struggles and attempts at reconciliation, she finally moved out of their family home. Her adult children were horrified and told her she must be "crazy" to leave a "nice guy" like their father. She bore the brunt of many accusations, until it came to an impasse with her son – they no longer spoke. This hurt her deeply, but she knew in her heart that she had done the *right* thing for her.

She began to let the light of truth penetrate her clouds and understand that the conclusions that she had previously come to were not in her best interest. She began to demonstrate to her children that she was happier in her new way of life. After three years of exploring her old habits and connecting with her authentic-self, Sandra found a soul-mate with whom she could share her life.

Her children gradually began to shift their attitudes and eventually, she began to develop a different style of relating with them. She was able to model self-sufficiency for them and they began to follow her lead by taking responsibility for their thoughts, feelings, words, and actions. She began to appreciate that she had influenced something truly worthwhile in their lives when her son began to share his thoughts and emotions with her. They developed a more honest relationship and she had the chance to model a different parenting style for him.

He slowly began to break the "silent guy thing" that he had learned in his early life. He began to change his scripts about what a "man should be" and change his patterns of relating to his children. He began to spend more quality time with them and became more encouraging to them, instead of putting them down the way his father had put him down. He began to share his true thoughts and experiences with his loved ones and heal his relationships.

It wasn't easy for Sandra to make those huge changes in her life; but now she sees how her decision to release her old patterns has positively affected the people in her world. An unhealthy family pattern was broken and she is creating a new, healthier environment for her family. Her grandchildren are also getting the kind of support from their father that will change their futures. She said, "I didn't do it for them – consciously – I did it for me; but now I see that I also did it for them. My journey was to learn how to listen to my authentic-voice and to be brave enough to walk in my integrity. This gave me the incentive to make healthier choices; but also, it showed the members of my family that they have the right to make better choices for themselves."

Your life changes because you make the effort to change *you*. Becoming totally honest with yourself by exposing your clouds and healing your dysfunctional patterns isn't easy, but it is a very worthwhile journey. Begin by asking yourself, which voice are you listening to? Are you running your old scripts – listening to your phony-voice? Or, are you listening to your authentic-voice? Which voice do you want to follow?

To find true happiness, you must bring your life into alignment with every part of your Total-Self. Once you have a clear picture of whom you truly are and what you want in life, you aren't easily distracted from your integrity or your goals. You *can* find this place in your life. When you love yourself enough to make a commitment to live in your integrity, you are on your *Path to Wholeness* and amazing things will begin to happen.

Chapter Two

A Closer Look at Your Clouds

There are many different types of clouds. There are personal clouds that apply only to your specific personality; there are clouds that are specific to your family grouping; and there are clouds that are more universal, which affect greater numbers of people in our society. As was mentioned in Chapter One, your personal clouds gathered gradually as you came to certain conclusions about the best way to survive in your world. You may have collected ideas from your family and culture that serve you well, but you may also have gathered energy that no longer serves you, because you are now ready to move into your Personal Power.

Each situation that arises in your daily life creates a challenge to which you need to find an appropriate response. Because curiosity and creativity are the areas of a child's development that are most likely to be distorted and diminished in confusing environments, it is much more likely that, instead of developing your own unique way of coping with life's challenges, you blindly followed the energy that was exhibited in the clouds of previous generations.

It is natural for children to unconsciously absorb the "solutions" that others in their family environment have used to cope with situations in their lives, because that is the natural way for them to learn how to handle their own experiences. Therefore, you may have followed the lead of the people in your environment and learned that there were specific ways to cope with specific challenges. These so-called "solutions" may have become your earliest patterns of relating or habits. Or, even though you may have created your own solutions, which were your attempts to explore your world in different ways, those "solutions" were probably very similar in energy to the ones that you observed in your early environment.

You may have chosen to model your behaviour after the people that you thought were the most successful in your environment – the people who seemed to get the most attention or the ones who seemed to have the most influence over others. You may have blindly followed the patterns of relating that were exhibited by your parents or peers. If those patterns didn't bring them great joy, it may be time to look at the possibility that those patterns didn't work well for them and they may not be working well for you. It may be time to consider another way to be.

In my practice as a spiritual counsellor, I have observed over the years that there is one specific pattern of relating that creates more misery in human interactions than any other. It has become solidified into a very dangerous cloud that hangs heavily over our society.

The Victim, Persecutor, & Rescuer Triangle Cloud

The Victim, Persecutor, and Rescuer Triangle Cloud (VPR Cloud) is the most unhealthy, dysfunctional, self-limiting, and pervasive cloud in our society today. This cloud has been floating around our planet for centuries. It has diminished our connection with Mother Earth and the God Force, caused a great deal of misery, and limited the potential of every human who has succumbed to its far reaching tentacles.

Many aspects of our society are adversely affected by the beliefs that are contained within the VPR Cloud. It penetrates to the very foundations of our religions and governments. We are surrounded by its energy, so we believe that it is the natural human condition; therefore, we have absorbed it from the energy in our surroundings. In so doing, we gather ineffective and dysfunctional solutions/addictions/habits from it. Because we have become accustomed to it and desensitized to the misery it creates, we become duped by the ideas that are preached by rescuers, those who suggest that, if we followed its rules, we will find happiness. Unfortunately, it does not lead to happiness. The very nature of the VPR Cloud limits human potential and creates misery.

It is important to understand that the VPR Cloud holds all the confusing memories and the subsequent unhealthy emotional sensations that have been experienced by *every person* who has ever lived in that clouded thinking. The VPR Cloud is like a giant archetype that was created by unhealthy humans and contains all the scripts that keep it in place – all the "shoulds, shouldn'ts, rights, wrongs, goods, and bads" – the automatic value judgments that become our scripts and phony-voices and consequently, our unhealthy patterns of relating to our environments.

People who live in the VPR Cloud, seldom, if ever, realize the misery that it causes in their own lives or the effect that their unhealthy attitudes and behaviours have on the people around them. They don't take any responsibility for the chaos they create, because they believe that it is the only way to be. It seems impossible to comprehend, but this chaotic way of living has become the "new normal."

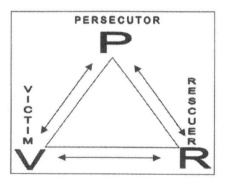

This illustration shows the three positions in the VPR Cloud. These labels represent the state of mind that individuals possess while they are in each position. The arrows represent how easy it is to switch states of mind.

The VPR Triangle always consists of three distinctive roles, and, consequently, three distinctive sets of scripts that are automatically read from. Each role is expressed into the outer world through specific characteristics that create a way of being – similar to the script from which a character would read to portray a role in a theatrical production. The VPR Triangle is the classic drama sequence: damsel in distress, villain, and knight in shining armour. You have probably seen it in many forms – in movies and in real life. The drama is played out, either with three individuals (or a group of people) participating, or within the mind of the person who is living in the VPR Cloud.

> *Every position in the VPR Cloud is a method of control, designed to get attention and power.*

Victim

When you are playing the victim role, you pretend to be a powerless, innocent child, at the mercy of others. You see others (whom you believe to be your persecutors) as *at fault* or the *cause* of your emotional, mental, or physical pain, as well as your spiritual disconnection. You are constantly looking for someone to make your decisions for you and rescue you from yourself or your circumstances. The payoff you receive, when you are playing the victim role, is the *illusion* that you aren't responsible for your thoughts, feelings, words, or actions. You feel shame that you aren't in control of your life, so you project blame toward others, believing that others are the cause of every problem and that they possess the only ways to solve those problems.

Victim Scripts – "I can't do it!" "It wasn't my fault! I just did what I was told to do." "I just said/acted that way, because s/he said/did ….. " "I can't help it!" "Why are you treating me that way/trying to hurt me?" "I'm playing nicely, so why aren't you helping/saving me?" "Please help me/take care of me." "I do what I'm told to do, so I deserve to be looked after."

Victim Control Tactics – They are often passively-aggressive and do or say things behind the backs of the people who don't want to play their game. When others don't look after them, they believe that those people are being cruel. They are very clever at manipulating others by whining and complaining.

Victim Rules of Conduct – Victims believe that they must always comply with others in their environment. They are allowed to whine and complain, but they must not engage their will or step out of their helpless role into their Personal Power. They pretend to be helpless to manipulate other people into looking after them.

Persecutor

When you are playing the persecutor role, you have rebelled from the victim role to gain power, and, in turn, use that pretence to control others. Whenever others try to make you feel powerless or helpless, you react in a way that will intimidate them, trying to make them play the victim role. You strut about pretending to be the *top dog*. This is done, because you believe that it makes you important or stronger, so others won't try to victimize *you*. This is the typical bullying energy. When you are playing the persecutor role, the payoff you receive is the *illusion* that you are *more powerful* than others – based on the belief that that's the only way to survive.

Persecutor Scripts – "Who are you to question my authority? I know better!" "Just do what you are told." "Don't be so stupid/inadequate/lazy!" "This is the right way to do it. You are wrong. I am right." "You have to do it this way."

Persecutor Control Tactics – Persecutors gain control more openly and directly than victims. They are the intimidators and believe that it's okay to "take hostages." They yell and tower over their potential victims to show their superior strength and dexterity. They get a power-high from their control tactics; they despise the victims who use whining and manipulating tactics, seeing them as weak. They will do anything, even violent acts to retain the illusion of control.

Persecutor Rules of Conduct – Persecutors believe that they must dominate others in their environment, so others can't dominate them. They believe that it is "okay" to use whatever force is necessary to bully other people into doing what they want them to do. They use their aggressiveness to control others and to puff up their dominant position.

Rescuer

When you are playing the rescuer role, you pretend that you have more power and control than others. You have learned *all the tools* to cope with life, due to your previous education or experiences. This is reinforced by the helplessness of victims, because they believe that they *need* you to help them cope with the challenges in their lives. You manipulate them by sharing advice and solutions, believing that your advice is superior, and that they can't live without you. When you are playing the rescuer role, the payoff you receive is the *illusion* that you are more *important* than others. Unfortunately, our society holds this illusion in place by honouring rescuers and by praising people who sacrifice themselves for others. Those who are in rescuing professions are frequently rewarded with prestige and higher salaries, anchoring this energy into a more universal problem.

Rescuer Scripts – "You poor thing! Here, let me help you." "I'll tell you how to behave, so you'll survive in this world." "Just stay with me and you won't be afraid." "I'll fix everything. You don't have to worry about a thing." If someone suggests a different solution, the rescuer is quick to say, "That's the way it is. There is no hope for change." "I don't want you to have to worry; I'll take care of everything." "Don't rock the boat. You'll just cause waves and it won't do any good."

Rescuer Control Tactics – Rescuers use much more subtle control tactics than persecutors. Rescuers accept their superior position, so they believe that it is their job to control others. They use a gentle tone of voice, so their victims don't suspect that they are being manipulated. They believe that they are *helping* everyone. They seldom say what they are actually thinking, because they don't want their victims to know how much they disrespect them. Intuitively, they know that their victims won't trust them any longer if they suspect that they are being used.

Rescuer Rules of Conduct – Rescuers are the dominant energy in the VPR Cloud, so they must maintain the upper hand at all costs. They can't display any signs of confusion or weakness, or they would lose their position of authority. They confuse others by preaching the belief that *they* are the only ones who can manage the elements of every experience. Rescuers expect victims to completely accept their suggestions and turn over all their power.

Rescuers actively seek out those who are in distress, so they can look important by rescuing people. They think that they should control them by whatever means are necessary as long as they pretend to be doing it for the benefit of others. They keep the illusion of power over others in place through subtle manipulations. However, their main motivation is to look important and keep the VPR Cloud in place. They have the most to lose, because their entire identity is bound up in their role as a superior being. Consequently, it is the rescuers who have the greatest amount of energy invested in keeping the VPR Cloud in place.

The VPR Cloud is solidified because no one takes responsibility for his or her thoughts, feelings, words, or actions or holds others accountable for theirs. Victims blame everyone, including themselves. Persecutors blame everyone who doesn't comply with their demands. Rescuers blame anyone who doesn't see how superior they are, tries to undermine them, or doesn't comply with the rules of the VPR Triangle.

People may unconsciously fall into old clouds of confusion in the VPR Triangle and feel frustrated, because they believe that there are no alternative solutions to their problems. To cover their frustration and pain, they then resort to unnatural substances or unhealthy behaviours/addictions.

For example: Sue had a crush on Tom, who said that he would call her on Friday night. When this didn't happen, she ate a bag of potato chips while watching a movie, in an attempt to cover up her feelings of isolation. All through the movie, however, she was alert (anxious, on edge) for the phone to ring. She started by hoping that Tom would *rescue* her from her loneliness. As the night progressed, however, she began to mentally berate him for not calling to fulfill his role as her potential rescuer. She had switched to thinking of him as the *mean, old ogre* who ruined her evening. He had gradually become her persecutor. It all happened within Sue's mind, but, in reality, it was her clouded thinking (the VPR Cloud) that ruined her evening – not Tom.

Most people who live in the VPR Cloud prefer one position over the other two because they have played that role so often they believe that it is their lot in life. They become very skilled in their ability to operate within the rules of a particular position. That role becomes *comfortable* to them. However, that so-called "comfortable state of mind" – their control tactics and the scripts they *read* from – also limit them and separate them from their greater potential.

It is very similar to the story of the frog in the pot of water. In this analogy, because the water is heating so slowly, the frog doesn't realize that it is being slowly boiled to death. This is the same type of prison that happens when we gradually give away our Personal Power and allow others to control us. Those prison walls become tighter and tighter, until there is no room to move in any direction. This is the essence of the clouded thinking within the VPR Triangle. Therefore, when we internalize a specific role within the VPR Cloud, it becomes so habitual that we get locked into a specific state of mind.

The Victim State of Mind

People who perceive their reality through the victim state of mind always believe the lie that they are *lacking* in some way – inadequate. They have internalized the belief that they will never be smart enough, good enough, adequate enough, or competent enough to live successfully on their own, without people to look after them, to do their thinking, and to make their decisions for them. They act as if no one has any Personal Power naturally – it has to be earned by manipulating others. They act wounded when others treat them badly; however, because of their belief in their powerlessness, they seldom stop the abuse that is projected toward them.

People who have the victim perspective spend huge amounts of time, energy, and money looking for others who might fill their needs; for example: the *perfect* mate, Mr. or Ms. Right; the *perfect* career; the *right* religion; the *best* way of life; or a *knight in shining armour* who will rescue them and *fix* all their problems. Those in the victim state are usually dissatisfied with everything in their present situation and are constantly looking for the elements that they believe are missing from their lives. However, their sensation of lack seldom guides them to any satisfying solutions. So, they try to cover their pain with addictions.

People who are in the victim state of mind believe that other people *should* provide the solutions, which they think they need to cope with their challenges in life. They have learned that "good children obey," and "should be seen and not heard." They believe that they are simply puppets of the whims of others. Their inner voice, which contains their curiosity and creativity, was stifled during their childhood. This was because family members seldom listened to what they had to say; or, they were not allowed or encouraged to follow their inner guidance. They eventually internalized a belief in the victim role (they "settled" – became emotionally attached to that victim state of mind) and soon believed that it was the only way to cope, get their needs met, or survive. Other people who participate in the VPR Triangle dynamic continue to reaffirm this erroneous belief.

Even though victims resent it when others control them, they may vent their anger in subtle (perhaps passively aggressive) ways instead of clearly saying no to controllers. They may have been taught to suppress their anger and turn the other cheek to be loved, but they soon realize that it isn't working and they are left running their scripts about being at the mercy of an unfair Universe. They may whine, "I have always been good, so why does this always happen to me?" Or, "I've been good to you, so why are you treating me this way?" The erratic and often opposing messages and value systems demonstrated in their early environment have created sufficient internal chaos to suppress appropriate reactions and stifle the creativity that could lead to healthier solutions.

People who are in the victim state often experience resentment or envy whenever they see others with a better career/car/house/husband/wife or life than they have. They are convinced that the God Force has left them "out of the loop." Because they believe that they are helpless, they also believe that they cannot change their destiny.

People who have adopted the victim role live by the credo: "Any attention is better than no attention." They continue to draw attention/energy to themselves by whining and complaining about their life without realizing that they are actually continuing to create this dynamic with their thoughts, feelings, words, and actions. They become attached to this role in life – addicted to misery – to the point where they may even joke about their circumstances, and have a type of pride in how well they deal with their *unfair* and *difficult* experiences.

All victims have ample opportunity to see the errors in their thinking processes; unfortunately, if others don't agree with their perception of reality, victims automatically reject their opinions and put them into the category of persecutor. They usually reject any feedback that is contrary to their clouded worldview.

People who are stuck in the victim state of mind usually stay there, until something significant happens to jar them awake. If they become aware of how they have been abused, demoralized, or disempowered by others, they *may* start fighting back. When they realize there is a different way to think and behave, they go through a quantum leap in awareness. This awareness alters their worldview and shifts the way that they perceive everything and everyone in their environment. They may then begin to rebel against their position in the VPR Triangle and become creative in their attempts to change their lives. Unfortunately, when they move out of the victim position, they usually go directly into the persecutor position, because their whole life has been clouded by the worldview of the VPR Triangle and their role models have all been victims, persecutors, or rescuers.

Transition Time from Victim to Persecutor

People who have previously seen themselves as victims usually believe the progression from victim to persecutor is a good thing, because they are no longer helpless, hopeless, and at the mercy of others. This transition time is a time of great stress, however, due to the major adjustments that they are experiencing. The high level of stress occurs whenever former victims change their usual position in the VPR Triangle and discard their old ways of being – their automatic, victim scripts and their patterns of relating to their environments. They have rejected the obedient, powerless, and compliant *nice guy/girl* image, but they usually replace it with aggression and angry rebelliousness.

Whenever a person who has previously played the victim role moves into the persecutor role, everyone in their environment is confused by their change in behaviour. Victims are confused, because the newly fledged persecutors have become aggressive toward them and they say, "What happened to my old friend?" The other persecutors become angry, because the new persecutors no longer accept domination. The rescuers become frustrated, because they are now unable to manipulate the new persecutors.

There is a risk, at this point in the lives of newly fledged persecutors, that their previous persecutors may become more aggressive in an attempt to put them back into the victim position. The new persecutors become further stressed, because they begin to experience new emotional sensations – those specific to the persecutor role. In some cases, this may be too overwhelming and cause them to fall back into the victim role. However, if they are sufficiently impressed by their new-found illusion of power, they won't be as likely to fall back into the victim perspective.

The Persecutor State of Mind

New persecutors often become angry with themselves when they realize how they have allowed others to treat them previously, so they turn their anger around and project it toward anyone who they perceive as a potential threat. They then have become full-fledged persecutors.

To adapt to the role of persecutor, they have put on a new mask. They no longer accept the domination or abuse of others in their old, passive way; however, because their role models have confused them and clouded their thinking, they fail to see that there is a healthier way to live. They simply use the same methods that their previous persecutors have used on them – to control, intimidate, and dominate others in their environment.

People who live in the persecutor state of mind express the philosophy, "It's a dog-eat-dog world; so, I have to get them before they get me!" Many people who take on the persecutor role are children, or younger siblings of persecutors. Someone has always had the upper hand and they have come to the conclusion that it is better to be the *top dog* than the *underdog*. Persecutors begin trying out their skills of being the *top dog* by rebelling against the established patterns of their families.

This often leads to the idea that it is okay to throw their weight around and soon they become bullies. The issue of bullying is a commonly discussed topic in school and work environments at the present time. However, when we realize that bullying is the product of abuse, it is easier to understand and redirect bullying behaviour.

Aggressive individuals are always seen as a threat to the status quo; therefore, those who have previously held the reins of control will automatically see the new persecutors as a threat to their position of power. This is because the new persecutors may actually come up with unheard of power ploys or disruptive control tactics. Those in the previous position of power don't know how to deal with this new form of manipulation, so they will probably reject the new persecutors.

Newly fledged persecutors are often banished from their family unit or group, as soon as the established persecutors realize that they can no longer force them into compliance. They may be seen as "black sheep" and ostracized. People who tenaciously hang onto the control mechanisms of the past usually view anyone who threatens the established order as *bad* or *rebellious.*

Individuals who become truly rebellious have consciously, or unconsciously, recognized that their parents' or society's structure hasn't worked for them; hasn't provided them with a secure environment in which they can grow; hasn't given them a sense of security or self-realization; or, hasn't created happiness or success. Therefore, these developing persecutors set about to create another reality that they hope will be more secure and happy. Unfortunately, because they have, by this time, become so disconnected from their authentic-voices and their connection with their Spiritual-Bodies, their new way of life is often just as unsatisfying as it was previously.

Persecutors may become part of a counter culture – anything from practicing a different set of values and finding people who agree with their perception of reality, to participating in a radical religious cult. Unfortunately, these rebels often find that they don't have the necessary skills to make healthier alternative decisions, so they revert back to conforming to the rules of conduct within the VPR Cloud.

Throughout history, true rebels, such as Mahatma Gandhi and Martin Luther King have been the forerunners of change, because they were clever enough to think of radically new ways of doing things. Rebels only become enmeshed in the persecutor role *IF* they close their minds to true self-expression and create self-righteous attitudes about their beliefs. When this happens, they become convinced that being a persecutor is a good thing. They may actually experience a power high, so they come to the conclusion that it is their *right* to coerce others into complying with their dysfunctional rules by manipulating them – mentally, emotionally, spiritually, or even physically.

Persecutors will try to diminish the spiritual connections of others because they are fearful of any new thoughts or ideas that might come from a personal connection with a Higher Power. They try to make everyone conform to their ideas and surround themselves with people who think and act as they do – so they won't be so lonely. (This is often the reason that destructive cliques, such as gangs form and so much self-righteousness is displayed in rigid religious denominations.) Clinging to only those who agree with them is an unsatisfactory solution to their sensations of isolation; because even though they are surrounded by a horde of people who agree with them, they are still aware of their lack of connection.

Some people show a form of fearful respect toward persecutors, because they believe that persecutors are strong and victims are weak. Persecutors often seem more confident and are usually more outspoken and willing to compete with others to get what they want. Unfortunately, their competitive attitudes may spring from their strong belief in maintaining the VPR Cloud and not out of true confidence or the originality of their ideas.

Persecutors often become very angry with people who won't follow their rules. They often consciously, or unconsciously, believe that they have the *right* to be "the boss." People, such as these, have often been raised to believe that there are only two types of people – winners and losers – *controllers* and *control-ees*. Newly fledged persecutors, in particular, may believe that anyone who isn't willing to be controlled by them is resisting them, because that person actually wants to control *them*. So, they struggle very hard for dominance.

As long as they uphold the values and beliefs of the VPR Cloud, their new persecutor state of mind may, for a time, give them a temporary high and the illusion of security. They may conclude that they have finally found the perfect environment/mate/career/religion, etc., to distract them from their pain. This so-called solution, however, is, in fact, an illusion, a story or script that they have created to deny their sensations of disconnection and may continue to cloud their judgment. They have simply created the illusion of a secure environment, because, on a deep level, they are still afraid of the outside world and they recognize their inability to control their environment. They lack the skills to cope with daily challenges, so they sequester themselves behind delusions.

Persecutors use a variety of control dramas whenever other people hold their ground or don't immediately comply with the persecutor's wishes. They may become more manipulative or aggressive, or even reject people by shutting them out of their lives. They don't understand that *real* power comes when we no longer believe that we have the right to control others and we learn to be comfortable, relaxed, and fair in our dealings with other people.

People who are in the persecutor state of mind often become proud or self-righteous, because they are no longer victims; however they are usually lonely, desperate individuals. Even though they rant and rave about the irresponsible behaviour of others and the injustices in our society, they blame everyone and everything for their problems – except themselves.

Some persecutors eventually get tired of always being disliked and lonely, and tired of being constantly angry with others. These are the people who become creative and believe that they can do something to *fix* the problem – and of course, "the problem" is that other people aren't playing by the rules of the VPR Cloud *properly*. Unfortunately, because their whole life has revolved around the clouded perception of the VPR Triangle, and their role models have all been victims, persecutors, or rescuers, they usually move directly into the rescuer state of mind.

Transition Time from Persecutor to Rescuer

When persecutors begin to take on the rescuer state of mind, they go through another transition. This transition time usually coincides with some sort of education, in which they learn new techniques, such as how to use a softer tone of voice and gentler words to manipulate others. They become rescuers by learning ways to *fix* the people in their lives, so they can feel good about themselves and keep everyone inside the perimeters of the VPR Cloud. They believe that, if everyone stays within their roles, everything will be in alignment and their world will be safe.

The transition from persecutor to rescuer thinking is similar, in some aspects, to the transition from victim to persecutor thinking. It also causes a great deal of stress, because such individuals are moving into a different mind-set or perspective – adjusting to a different role. It may be a different "flavour" of stress, but they are again experiencing an identity crisis. They are struggling to change their old habits and patterns of relating to their environment. Since they are a persecutor-turned-rescuer, they have previously been seen as *angry rebels,* and now they are asking people to believe in their gentler way of being, as well as follow their lead. They are letting go of the projected anger and softening their image. Consequently, this change causes a great deal of chaos and confusion in their environment.

Some of their associates view this change in personality as a terrible *defection,* while others view it as a wonderful *conversion.* Because the new rescuer has previously played the aggressive or bossy role of persecutor, most victims will see this transformation as an *improvement.* The new softer, more sophisticated behaviour is easier to accept, and, in reality, they have been looking for a rescuer all along.

Whereas the victims hated the people who persecuted them, they usually approve of the change in attitude that the new rescuer exhibits. The change is, therefore, encouraged and praised by those who will benefit from this attitudinal shift. However, other victims may now be upset and confused, because their scapegoat or persecutor is now being *nice* and may actually be trying to *help* them. Initially, they may be cautious or afraid to trust this new behaviour, due to the abuse that they have previously suffered at the hands of that person.

Established rescuers are usually threatened, because there is now a "new kid on the block" who believes that he or she "knows something." This attitudinal shift challenges the authority of the resident rescuers who are afraid that their followers will stray away from their domination and follow the new "authority figure."

The Rescuer State of Mind

People who function mostly in the rescuer role have developed skills that have changed their own lives and they assume that those same skills will also *fix* others and solve their problems. Because they have learned gentler and less offensive ways of manipulating and controlling the people within their circle of influence, they are on a temporary high and they feel good about themselves. In our present culture, rescuers are the most highly respected group in the VPR Cloud. They demand this respect, because they were formerly victims, and now they no longer believe that they are helpless, nor do they "stoop" to behave as aggressively as persecutors. They become self-righteous, because they believe that they have invented *better* scripts to follow. They may have invented better scripts, but they are still living within the VPR Cloud.

Some people who function mostly in the rescuer state of mind have come to it quite naturally, because they lived in a family in which one parent played the persecutor role, while the other parent played the victim role. In such a setting, most children automatically try to fill in the missing component in the VPR Triangle and try to become the *saviour* of the group – the rescuer. If they succeed in diffusing dangerous situations, they become proud of their ability to "keep the peace" in the family or group. They may rush to the scene whenever someone is being abused or in pain – believing that they are able to help. They might even be willing to risk their own safety to rescue someone, even if it is unlikely that they will succeed.

Rescuers want to reflect a persona of authority into society, so they must learn skills that give them a position of superiority. Some doctors, ministers, teachers, therapists, alternative health practitioners, and counsellors, have chosen these professions – not because they are actually motivated to be of service to others, but because they want to be important: plus, it suits their rescuer role. These professions traditionally have the reputation of being saviours, so even the professionals, who are not rescuers, are often *expected* to play the rescuer role of the VPR Triangle. Unfortunately, many professionals unconsciously support this type of dysfunctional relationship, because it furthers their agenda, strokes their egos, and reinforces their false perception of superiority.

Victims are automatically attracted to people who have developed rescuer skills and may eagerly give away their Personal Power to anyone whom they believe is willing to *fix* them. This leads to an unhealthy parent-child relationship, even though both people are adults. We are naturally attracted to the same type of energy as the people who raised us, and, if we are in a confusing environment, we look for the same type of energy that was missing in our parents. We may believe that our new "parental figure" will fix the problems in our lives, but in reality, they just make our confusion greater.

The greatest problem with trying to *fix* other people is that *fixers* always assume that they know what is *right* for others. This is seldom, if ever, true. If the *fixers* are successful in manipulating others into complying with their "prescription" for how to *fix* things, the other people become robots or carbon copies of the *fixers'* perception of reality. Therefore, when victims, or *fix-ees*, encounter the next difficult situation, they are faced with the same kind of confusion without the necessary skills to think through the dilemma and come to an appropriate solution on their own. They may then run back to their rescuers/advisers or *fixers* and again give them the power to choose what is *right*. When this happens, the *fixers* are enabling the *fix-ees* to stay in the helpless victim role; but the victims are also enabling the rescuers to continue to believe that they are superior.

All rescuers have to be extremely careful not to become co-dependents. When rescuers meet up with a chemically-dependent individual, such as an alcoholic or drug abuser, for example, they automatically try to *fix* the addict's life. Because rescuers have only been exposed to the rules of the VPR Cloud, they have learned only unhealthy methods of controlling the other person's addictive behaviour. Therefore, they will usually try to rescue the chemically-dependent person by repeating the previously "successful" methods of control they have learned in their unhealthy environments.

This "rescuing" disempowers the addict even further. Nothing changes and the energy of the rescuers disappears down a bottomless hole. In reality, these rescuers are being used and abused, not only by the person that they are trying to rescue, but also by themselves, because they become convinced that they have to try harder. In essence, they have fallen back into the victim position. However, because they have previously managed to climb up to the rescuer perception, they often become indignant, resentful, frustrated, and angry to be back in the victim state of mind, so they rebel and become persecutors. If they wish to leave all of those dysfunctional roles behind, they must climb a different ladder – one that, hopefully, leads them completely out of the VPR Cloud.

Unfortunately, many romantic relationships begin in the haze of the VPR Cloud, because both individuals are embroiled in the unhealthy belief that we *need* to have a partner to rescue us and help us *feel better* about ourselves. This unhealthy pattern of relating may have been created in early childhood, causing us to believe that this expectation is normal or even the best way to achieve happiness.

Another common example of the rescuer dynamic is when one parent rescues a child by taking the child's side against the other parent or other authority figures. Rescuer parents often interfere with the natural consequences of their child's behaviour. Common scenarios of this include: preventing one's partner from appropriately disciplining their child; blaming a teacher for their child's poor grades; or giving their child money to *fix* his or her problems. Eventually, over the years, the *fixing* behaviour escalates. The rescuer parent pays for a speeding ticket; bails their child out of jail; or sets their child up in a business, for which the child is not adequately prepared, or keeps their child prisoner in a family business.

All these acts have a seemingly benevolent motive, because our society sees this type of parent as a *good* parent. Unfortunately, however, underneath the apparently charitable act is the belief that their children are incapable of making appropriate decisions. Unfortunately, this is often true, because the parents have not taught their children healthy coping-strategies or appropriate, problem-solving techniques. These young adults are crippled even further, because their parents continue to prevent them from learning from their own mistakes. The parents disempower their children by not letting them grow up and become responsible adults, who are accountable for their thoughts, feelings, words, and actions. *Fixing* problems for others simply disempowers them and leaves them believing that they are always going to be inadequate – helpless to solve the next problem.

If you have lived in the dysfunctional thinking of the VPR Cloud all your life, very probably you have formed patterns of relating that automatically click into place each time you are faced with a new or threatening situation. Once you realize this, you have become consciously aware that something is clouding your thinking. You are then in a position to rethink and change those patterns. You are then on your way out of the VPR Cloud. During this period of transition, however, you must consciously stop your dysfunctional patterns and create new, healthier, and more functional choices.

Other Dangerous Habits that Support the VPR Cloud

Making Excuses

People who don't take responsibility for their thoughts, feelings, words, or actions often become creative in inappropriate ways. They invent excuses – illusions or unreal scenarios in their minds to deny their responsibility and justify their unhealthy thoughts, feelings, words, and actions. They are often so convincing with their stories that they may eventually convince themselves of their innocence.

Some people become so adept at making excuses that all their creative energy is channelled into that one direction. Persecutors, for example, often excuse their aggressive behaviour by justifying what they have done. They often pretend that the violence began with the other person, so they believe that they are responding appropriately. They do this so they won't be held accountable for causing the conflict and they can revert back to the perception of themselves as helpless victims. They often believe that they couldn't help themselves – they just "had to" act that way, because the other person *forced* them, through *their* actions.

Such individuals often claim that there was a *logical reason* that they acted in aggressive and violent ways. They stubbornly hold onto their *reason* and vehemently claim that they wouldn't have had to do what they did, if the other person hadn't done what *they* did. They may deny their aggression and argue with the others involved, attempting to convince their victims of their innocence by trying to prove that everyone else is *wrong*.

One very aggressive man was so adamant about his innocence that he vehemently stated during a counselling session that he "would rather be dead" than believe that he was a violent person. This intensity of passion could have been because he couldn't comprehend the idea that he had actually done something wrong, or simply a ploy to deflect attention away from being responsible for his behaviour. However, such intensity is usually caused by the belief that people who live in the VPR Cloud are *never* responsible, no matter what they do. They say things like, "She deserved it;" or, "He was asking for it!" These excuses may have worked for them in the past, because our society often supports the VPR Cloud by excusing irresponsible behaviour.

The clouded thinking of the VPR Triangle also supports the unconscious belief that we are *all* victims of something –

meaning that we are powerless to change our thoughts, feelings, words, or actions. The belief that you are powerless is a lie. You may have initially used it as an excuse when you didn't want to be accountable for your thoughts, feelings, words, or actions. Eventually, it became a way of life.

If you wish to move into your Personal Power, you must move out of this erroneous belief into the realization that you are part of the Creative Force of the Universe. This awareness requires, however, that you stop making excuses for your behaviour and accept your responsibility to make healthier choices in the future.

Mistakes

One of the most common misconceptions in the VPR Cloud is the belief that it is always *wrong* to make mistakes. Therefore, it is a topic requiring careful consideration. Whenever you initiate a thought, word, or action, you become the creator and director of an experience, situation, or circumstance. In some cases, the effect or outcome of that initiative is a pleasing one – one you would label as "a success." In other cases, the effect produced by that initiative is a disappointment. When the latter is the case, you think of it as "a mistake."

> *Every choice that creates a disappointing result (a mistake) is caused by thoughts, feelings, words, or actions that are lacking in intuition, insight, intelligence, adequate information, or sufficient planning.*

If you carefully examine *how* and *why* you have made a mistake, you will be able to understand the unconscious elements that contributed to that particular choice. Perhaps, you made your choice by following an unhealthy habit – one that has developed over the years, but has never worked. Perhaps, you unconsciously replayed traditional family scripts – memories in which your father or mother handled situations in a specific way. Perhaps, you were being selfish or inconsiderate and you were only considering what you wanted, excluding the possibility that others would be adversely affected. Whatever the case, *you* are responsible for making your choices, and, if you don't achieve your desired outcome, *you* are responsible for making amends and creating more appropriate choices in the future.

Movie directors have learned from experience that it may be necessary to make several attempts to produce the results they desire. So, each attempt to produce a scene is called a "take." The producer calls out "Take 1," or, "Take 2." When we dissect the word "mistake" into two parts, we have "mis-take." So, every mistake is simply a *missed take* or a failed attempt to produce a desired result.

People who are raised in confusing environments are seldom encouraged to try new things, because there is already so much chaos that they are discouraged from making more. This is often the source of fixed solutions. So, when children try new things, if their attempts to produce the desired result fail, it is often implied that there is something inherently wrong with *them*. It is implied that *they* are *bad* for wanting to have their needs met or wanting something that the family, culture, religion, etc. is unwilling to allow or respect.

If you have learned that you are *bad* or *stupid* whenever you make a mistake, subsequently, you may assume that every failed attempt (mistake) is due to your deficiencies or inadequacies. This belief very quickly devolves into a state of doubt and fear, in which you act out the unconscious scripts that you have previously stored in your clouds. When this happens, you are no longer accessing the logic in your Mental-Body and you have diminished your connection with your Spiritual-Body that holds your curiosity and creativity. When these connections are restricted or repressed, you will automatically fall back into the victim role.

This unhealthy perspective also allows you to entertain the idea that an outside force (a god, a devil, fate, etc.) has prevented the desired outcome – leading to the belief that you are a victim and unworthy of what you desire. You may conclude that you *deserve* punishment for being *bad* or *stupid*. This perversion of thought promotes self-flagellation and stifles your creativity to manifest a better way of life.

Whenever you make an attempt to do *anything* in a different way, you *always* run the risk of making mistakes. You also risk disapproval from others. On the positive side, however, if you pay attention to your mistakes, you can accumulate a list of failed attempts – methods that have not worked. This information can be a valuable asset when you would like to try again. The old adage, "If at first you don't succeed, try, try, again," could be rephrased to say, "If at first you don't succeed, try something different."

If you honestly and carefully look at each situation that you have called a "mistake," you can understand the underlying reasons of how and why you created it. Then you can think of ways to change your behaviour in the future, until you find a method that works more efficiently.

When you view your life choices as opportunities to try different approaches to achieve your goals, or as a series of attempts to get it *right*, you will consistently engage your Spiritual-Body and activate your curiosity and creativity. Whenever you are brave enough to try something different, every new attempt comes from your creativity and stretches your boundaries into an unknown territory. If you wish to expand your thinking and create new experiences, you must take risks. If you are afraid of making mistakes, it is almost impossible to learn anything new.

Many wonderful inventions were by-products of so-called "mistakes." When we keep in mind that everyone makes mistakes, we can become less fearful and more adventurous. Then our true genius has a chance to emerge.

When you give yourself permission to make mistakes and learn from them, you are no longer living in the VPR Cloud. You are following the pathway to your Personal Power. You will also stop the people who are still living in that dynamic from having power over you. You are breaking the cycle!

If you believe that the suggestions that others make are *wrong* for you, the challenge before you is to hold your ground. It is important to learn how to say no to people who want to control you. It is possible to do this lovingly by saying, "I realize that you really want me to…, but I would appreciate it if you would respect my right to do it this way and let me learn from my mistakes, if necessary."

Good judgment is an essential ingredient in our healing process. When we take responsibility for our previous choices, we can accept that our past decisions may have been poor choices – mistakes. Good judgment often is the product of our previous bad judgments. Good judgment involves taking the time to thoroughly consider the potential outcome of each of our decisions. Therefore, it is essential for each of us to learn from our mistakes and forgive ourselves for making them. We run the risk of making mistakes every time we try something new;

however, unless we try new things, we aren't growing and evolving.

The Need for Secrecy

Secrecy is a prominent element in the VPR Cloud. People who have been abused have often been conditioned to believe that secrecy is necessary to cope with, or at least survive in, their confusing environments.

When you believe that you need to be secretive in order to cope, you may be afraid that more abuse could occur, if the truth were revealed; you may have been subjected to abuse when you expressed yourself in ways differing from the rules of the VPR Cloud; or when you act in ways that are out of the "norm" of your environments. The resulting punishment may be expressed in a variety of forms – from disapproval, criticism, or rejection, to physical abuse.

> *Fear of further abuse causes people to hide their authentic-self in the closet of secrecy.*

You will only believe that you need to be secretive *IF* you are worried about approval from others or fear their judgment or abuse. Honesty is the only way to fully connect with others and build healthy relationships. Secrecy creates prisoners of us all! Only "the truth shall set you free."

The Scapegoat

The scapegoat archetype is a fundamental dynamic of the VPR Cloud. The word "scapegoat" was coined to describe an ancient Jewish tradition. On the Day of Atonement, the high priest confessed the sins of the people over the head of a goat – then let it "e-scape." (In reality, they chased it from the city.) It was believed that the goat took on and carried away the sins of the people, much like the ancient tradition of shedding the blood of an animal to atone for one's sins. One of the most common names given today for the scapegoat archetype is "Satan" or "The Devil" who is traditionally depicted as having cloven hoofs and horns like a goat.

Over the centuries, this tradition eventually developed into the scapegoat archetype even though an actual goat is no longer used. Humans use this archetype to continue to avoid responsibility for what they have created in their lives – upon the erroneous belief that it is possible to project their so-called sins, faults, or responsibilities onto another.

Dysfunctional families often create an "official scapegoat" – someone who will be the *fall guy* for the more dominant members who don't want to take responsibility for their thoughts, feelings, words, or actions. Looking for a scapegoat reveals a lack of personal responsibility and prevents you from being accountable. Blaming others gives away power that could possibly be used to improve your situation and allows clouded thinking and behaviour to continue.

The dominant members of dysfunctional families often develop a formula/script for survival and insist that the members comply with this fixed set of behavioural rules. It is believed that everything will run smoothly *IF* those scripts are followed to the letter. Therefore, whenever something happens to prove the inefficiency of those rules, rather than looking at the possibility that it is necessary to revise or discard them, one person or group of people must be blamed.

The person who is designated as the "official scapegoat" or the "black sheep" of the family is usually the one who has previously rebelled from, or challenged, the status quo. It may start with something as simple as a child's inappropriate attempts to gain attention. For example: Jimmy may have felt left out, so he acted out. Jimmy's parents may have then cancelled a family outing, "because Jimmy was a *bad* boy." Before long, the whole family is reinforcing the message that Jimmy is *bad*.

Soon Jimmy learns to believe that everything *bad* that happens in the family environment is his fault. He then begins to act in ways that are appropriate for someone who is *bad* and it quickly becomes easy to blame him for *everything* that goes wrong in the family. A vicious downward spiral has been set in motion, in which the outcome may be that Jimmy believes that he is the cause of all the trouble and pain occurring in the family. He has finally and totally accepted the title of "official scapegoat."

This sets a dangerous precedent in place. When one person is blamed for *everything* bad that happens in the family, that person is actually being told that they are the *only* creator in the family. Inevitably, the scapegoat learns that he or she is only capable of creating bad things, not good things. The scapegoat gets no credit for the good things that occur. Someone else gets credit for those things, so that person begins to believe that they can do no wrong. Other family members are abdicated from all responsibility and can therefore act irresponsibly. This leads to a distorted perception of Personal Power and confusion ensues, anchoring the VPR Cloud, and making it denser and more prominent.

The VPR Cloud in Daily Life

In fairy tales, movies, and romance novels, the female is often portrayed as the *helpless* victim who the male rescues from an impending disaster, so they can live happily ever after. In real life, however, the person, whom the woman believes to be her "knight in shining armour," often becomes the villain/persecutor when he doesn't precisely comply with her wishes. This dynamic is played out often when individuals, who frequently play the rescuer role, become overwhelmed by external stress, the expectations of others, or their own unconscious rebellion from the role that they believe they *should* perform.

The person who has previously played the role of the rescuer may have had a long, hard day and not want to rescue *anyone* at that particular moment. His or her resulting frustration is seldom expressed in appropriate ways and additional confusion ensues. It is also common for rescuers to become so frustrated by their lot in life that they hide in their addictions (sports, career, alcohol, drugs, entertainment, etc.).

This scenario was obviously the case of a young couple who came for counselling. Christine complained that Robert was "always criticizing" her, and "when he isn't yelling at me, he is watching some sports program on television." She saw herself as a victim and Robert as a persecutor whenever he criticized her or neglected her by watching his sporting events. (This is an example of how people use a variety of methods of control to confuse and ultimately manipulate others. In this case, verbal attacks were interspersed with rejection and avoidance.)

During our counselling session, Christine talked about her dreams of being "a perfect little wife who would stay at home and look after the house and kids," and said, "I want to greet Robert at the door in my sexy outfit at the end of the day." (This is showing that Christine wants to play two conflicting roles-the nurturing mother and sex-goddess.)

Robert, on the other hand, complained that he had to "work hard all day, while Christine just lies around the house." He justified his criticism with the statement: "She never does anything right. Why, just the other night, I came home to find her in her usual mess, and she had even burned the damn potatoes." This had been "the last straw," so they had spent the evening arguing and accusing each other of a great number of wrongdoings.

Upon further questioning, it became evident that Robert had already been upset when he arrived home from work, because his boss had reprimanded him for "making some stupid mistake." Robert had felt like a victim on the job, but repressed his frustration. Then, he had inappropriately inflicted it upon Christine by yelling at her for burning the potatoes (he became a persecutor).

There was, however, an even deeper issue at the core of their problem. It was caused by the conflicting beliefs, which they both held. They both believed that Robert "should be the provider" (rescuer), because he was "the man" and therefore, more "adequate." Robert accepted that role, because he thought he "should," but he resented it. He resented the belief that only he could support the family – a burden that he didn't want to carry alone. Christine resented it, because it implied that she was not as competent as Robert and couldn't contribute "anything of *real* value" to the partnership. Even though they both knew on some level that this was illogical, it revealed a deep unconscious belief that "man's work is more important than woman's work." They had both internalized this erroneous belief from early childhood and had agreed upon it when they began their relationship. They had decided that it was "only right" for Christine to quit her job when she got pregnant, because Robert "had to work and *somebody* had to look after the kids."

It became obvious that the patriarchal, marriage archetype (a prominent cloud in our society that supports the VPR Triangle) was firmly set in place before they married. So, instead of their working as a team to accomplish a happy, healthy, family environment, their conflicting beliefs became destructive stress in their lives.

The situation was exacerbated when Christine complained to her friend Carol, telling her how "cruel" Robert had been to her, "just because I burned the potatoes." Carol commiserated with Christine about how unfair life is, because of her belief that, "all men are mean, insensitive scum." This asserted that Robert had actually been a persecutor all along. At this point, Carol took on the role of rescuer by pretending to *help*. She filled the classic, rescuer role by giving unhealthy advice to Christine about the "best way to cope with men."

Typically, a friend, family member, neighbour, or counsellor, who tries to control the energy dynamic, plays the rescuer role and offers suggestions about how to cope with a particular situation. Eventually, however, the rescuer must suggest, if he or she is going to conform to the rules of the VPR Cloud, that there is *nothing* the victim can do about the situation – except stay and suffer. By continuing to listen to the complaints, however, the rescuer is affirming that it is "alright to complain about it." This is because, if the victim doesn't ask the rescuer's advice, the rescuer would be out of a job.

Granted, we feel better when someone listens to our complaints, because we don't feel so alone. So, Christine experienced a moment of relief by talking to Carol; however, there was no expansion in Christine's thinking or any resolution to her problem. (In that moment of so-called "relief," however, there were two addictions at play. Christine was addicted to being miserable in the victim role and felt confirmation from Carol. Carol was addicted to being in control as a rescuer, and she felt the *high* of being powerful, because she had controlled Christine's behaviour, affirming her importance and dominance as the rescuer.)

Unfortunately, by acquiescing to Carol's opinions, Christine didn't learn how to understand, address, diffuse, or avoid Robert's verbal abuse. She didn't even learn that it *was* abuse. It was implied that Robert was *normal* for his gender and was also, like the rest of his gender, "a jerk" and therefore, incapable of change. Consequently, since there was nothing that could be done, the message was that it was a hopeless situation. The VPR Triangle was kept firmly in place and that clouded thinking continued to cause misery in their lives.

Robert, on the other hand, didn't have an opportunity to become responsible for his own thoughts, feelings, words, or actions. He also didn't see how inappropriate it was to vent his frustration by being abusive to his mate; nor was he able to understand how it had adversely affected his relationship with Christine. He didn't have an opportunity to learn new ways of expressing his frustration, nor, on a deeper level, to address what had originally caused the frustration. All the scripts in the VPR Triangle would have been replayed at regular intervals, causing pain to all concerned, had the couple not sought professional help.

Let us now look, hypothetically, at how the roles played by Christine, Robert, and Carol could easily be switched within the context of this VPR drama. Let's keep the character, Carol, in the rescuer role for the moment. Carol has been on the fringes of Christine and Robert's relationship for years. She had often been Christine's "shoulder to cry on." Let's pretend that suddenly Carol changes her daily routine. She takes up jogging after work every night and isn't at home to hear Christine's woes. Christine now has no one to complain to. She becomes frustrated and begins to nag Robert, instead of venting to Carol. The energy flow has turned. Robert now sees Christine as a nagging shrew (a persecutor) and himself as a victim.

Robert now complains to Carol. Carol knows the validity of his complaints, because Christine has been venting to Carol for years. Carol can stay in the rescuer perspective simply by agreeing with each of them in turn, becoming the rescuer for them both, and thinking that she is capable of becoming their therapist. Or, she could shift her perception of who is the *real* victim and who is the *real* persecutor. If she decides that Robert is the *real* victim, she will let him complain about Christine. This could lead into a friendship or even a romantic connection in which Carol becomes "the other woman" and is perceived by Christine as another persecutor. Now, Christine could shift her position to see *both* Robert and Carol as persecutors and look for someone to *rescue* her from them.

Another variation of the same Triangle dynamic might be, if, before Robert becomes close to Carol, Christine repeats something to Robert that Carol has said about him. Robert might then perceive Carol to be an instigator or persecutor, to the point where Christine feels sorry for Robert and tries to *rescue* him.

It is also possible that Carol could fall into the persecutor role by simply telling Robert that he is the one who is at fault. This would lead to a conflict between them, because Robert doesn't want another person treating him like a persecutor. He will probably look for someone else to *rescue* him. We now have all the ingredients for the typical soap opera.

Whenever anyone changes his or her mind-set and shifts roles within the VPR dynamic, anger, frustration, resentment, blame, shame, and guilt are frequently expressed by all parties. It is also important to note that, if an authority figure plays the rescuer role, an entirely different drama ensues. It is common knowledge that, when the police are called into a violent domestic scene and they try to *rescue* a victim, the parties quickly change roles. If officers try to subdue the person they perceive to be the abuser or persecutor, the victim often attacks the police officer.

This dynamic is due to the unconscious belief that police are a higher authority than the person who was originally the aggressor in the dispute. Both the original players unconsciously believe that the higher authority must be the one who is the *real* persecutor. The so-called victims switch to different positions in the VPR Cloud energy by placing police officers in the role of persecutors, and shift their perception to *protect* or *rescue* the abuser, who has become the lesser threat.

People, who are firmly entrenched in the VPR Cloud, as were Robert and Christine, are able to deftly switch roles and mental states at a moment's notice. If however, a victim complies with a persecutor's wishes, there is no overt conflict. If a victim quietly suffers, whines, or complains ineffectively to his or her persecutor, or simply complains to a rescuer, there is also no hope for healing or change.

Hope for change needs to come from a greater understanding than is present in the conflict. This greater understanding can be accessed when you have the courage to see beyond the present mind-set and realize that you have the power to change your life. You will then be able to view the situation from a new perspective. Often, a third party is able to rise above the mindset of the problem or challenging situation and is able to introduce a new perspective to the mix.

Robert and Christine learned how to review and change their conflicting beliefs. They learned how to stop themselves from engaging in their old patterns of relating. They learned that they are each responsible for their thoughts, feelings, words, and actions. They learned that by observing the effects of their thoughts, feelings, words, and actions, they now feel more connected with themselves and each other. They learned new ways to interact in their relationship. They are now able to communicate in ways that bring them to greater levels of understanding – ways that empower each person. Instead of repeating inappropriate patterns of relating, they are able to consciously choose to communicate their needs in healthier ways. The reason that they are able to do this is because they have removed some of their bad habits and self-limitations that were previously held in their clouds. They now are able to hear the messages of their authentic-voices, instead of repeating the old scripts of their phony-voices, which were developed to protect them from abuse. Now, they can pause to consider their options, before they respond to each situation, instead of relying on their old reactions.

As Robert and Christine found out, we cannot change our past. We can, however, learn from it and change our perception and opinions about what has happened. In so doing, we can change our opinions about past experiences, rethink and release our unhealthy scripts, and make better decisions about how we would like to act in similar situations in the future. This choice causes a spontaneous shift in perception – out of the VPR Cloud. Then our present and future automatically changes.

When you no longer see your life from the clouded perception of the VPR Triangle, you are free to examine your full list of options and become creative as to how and what you wish to choose. You are then able to accept the fact that you are a unique spark of the God Force who makes decisions. Whether your decisions are unhealthy or healthy is totally up to you. If you wish to make healthier decisions, you must release your old scripts and your old patterns of relating and choose what is best for you. Then, you will step more fully into your Personal Power. Each healthy choice takes you further along the *Path to Wholeness*

Possible Repercussions When You Step Out of the VPR Triangle/Cloud

Even though it is much healthier and self-empowering to live outside the VPR Triangle, there can be many challenges when you choose to step into your Personal Power. It can be a challenge to stand alone in a world that functions mainly within those dysfunctional parameters.

You may begin to feel alone and unsupported because those around you try to convince you that the VPR Triangle is the only way to live.

In some cases, the people who are left playing the game may gather in agreement that you are a rebel, a trouble maker, or essentially "bad" – in other words a "persecutor." They don't want to consider that *they* could possibly be "mistaken," so they make you "wrong."

In other situations they may attempt to put you back into the VPR box by demeaning you with labels such as foolish, stupid (ignorant of the facts of life) or even crazy (mentally deranged) – trying to put you back into the Victim position, so you can be controlled again. They usually look to others to reinforce their judgment of you and then conclude that, because they have found other dysfunctional people to agree with them, they are correct in their assumptions.

Another common sub-conscious game that thrives in the VPR Triangle is the success/failure dynamic. When people are stuck in the VPR Cloud, they always see the world from a win/lose perspective. Because they are viewing the world from a very limited perspective, they cannot consider the possibility of a win/win scenario. They believe that the only way they can win is when someone else loses.

For example: Let's take a fictional person, called Petra, who is still stuck in the VPR Cloud, but she wants to be successful. Petra sees Sarah as someone who is already successful and wants to be just like her. Petra attaches herself to Sarah to learn about what she has accomplished, thinking that, if she can copy Sarah's values, mannerisms, and techniques, she can achieve what Sarah has.

Petra insinuates herself into Sarah's life by offering her support, telling her that she will help her achieve her goals. If Sarah is feeling the least bit insecure about her ability to succeed on her own, Petra can hook Sarah into the belief that she could be much more successful with Petra's help. Petra will then begin to do little things for Sarah, with the hope that Sarah will eventually believe in Petra's value. She may have skills that are actually useful and she may become a valuable asset to Sarah and her endeavours.

Petra will offer her support, with little to no payment, to prove to Sarah that what she is doing is "out of the goodness of her heart." You've undoubtedly heard the old adage, "When something seems too good to be true, it usually is"? In this case, that statement is very apropos because there was always a hidden agenda. Petra was simply playing by the rules of the VPR Triangle to achieve her goal – her desire to be "important." She was "rescuing" Sarah from her feelings of inadequacy; however, there is always a price to pay for being rescued. That price is to lose one's self-esteem and independence.

Gradually, Petra will take over other aspects that are essential to the operation of the project, making her indispensable to Sarah. However, she will hoard her knowledge, making sure that she is the *only one* who has access to this information or knows how to do these tasks. She will never teach Sarah (or anyone else) how to do them. By keeping this essential information to herself, she begins to see herself as more "important," necessary, or valuable to the operation than Sarah. (Often, the things that people like Petra suggest are non-essential to the overall success of the operation. They have been introduced solely with the intention of making them "look good.")

At this point, Petra will begin to undermine Sarah, believing that she has to step on Sarah "to reach the top of the heap." Remember, Petra thinks that there is only one winner in this game. Petra wants what Sarah has, so she thinks she has to undermine, demean, or diminish Sarah's value to step over her.

This is a subtle, but common dynamic in the VPR Triangle. Petra has insinuated herself into Sarah's life, because Petra had observed or sensed, either consciously or unconsciously, that Sarah felt inadequate in some way. Consequently, Sarah has been sucked into Petra's game. If Sarah should push back in the slightest, Petra can very easily turn the tables to pretend that she is the victim, by saying, "I was only trying to HELP." In truth, they both have lost their way.

In reality, even though Petra has mastered the manoeuvres of the VPR Triangle, she will always feel ashamed deep down, knowing that she has not earned her position: she has stolen something that is not hers. Unless she steps out of the manipulative behaviour that is so common in the VPR Triangle and becomes honest with herself about her own feelings of inadequacy that drive her to *pretend* to be "important," she will never understand how she has been limiting her potential. Only then will she become aligned with her true, authentic-self and walk the path of her Personal Power toward her true destiny.

On the other hand, unless Sarah re-establishes her direction by stopping the game and stepping out of the VPR Triangle by taking back her Personal Power, she loses her self-respect and self-direction – her connection with her life-purpose. If she is brave enough to reclaim her life-path and purpose, she will re-establish her connection with her destiny. It is not an easy process, but it is the only way that both people can be in alignment with their own Personal Power. Once Sarah stops the dynamic, Petra may choose to examine what her intention was in using and abusing Sarah in an attempt to scrabble to "the top of the heap;" thereby, stepping out of the VPR Triangle and finding her own true path.

Each of us has a destiny that is unlike anyone else's. We are each a unique spark of the Divine. There is no duplication in nature. Every form of life, whether it is an insect, plant, animal, or human, is unique in its own way and has its place in the Universe. When we find our true niche, there is no competition … only the fulfilment of the contract we made when we came to this planet in this lifetime.

Chapter Three

Emotional Elements in the VPR Cloud

To begin this section, it is important to define some terms I will be using throughout. The words "reaction" and "response" are often used interchangeably in everyday conversation; however, whenever I use the word "reaction," I am referring to an automatic, *unconscious* way that you think, speak, or make a movement to reflect how or what you are experiencing in a given circumstance. On the other hand, a "response" is a *conscious* choice about what you will think, say, or do. When you *respond*, you think things through and consciously choose what is right for you before you take action and you are willing to take *respons*ibility for that choice. Responsibility is the ability to respond consciously.

Following is an analogy that can be used to understand the difference between a reaction and a response. When any object, even something as small as a speck of dust, *unexpectedly* comes close to one of your eyes, you automatically blink. This is an unconscious reaction to protect your eyes from harm. This reaction has been programmed into your autonomic nervous system as a method of keeping your eyes safe.

However, if we were playing a game with a ball, you would *expect* a ball to be coming toward you at some point. Then, you would have a choice as to how you would *respond* to that approaching object. Because you know that the ball is a part of the nature of the game, you are *conscious* of the possibility that it will come near you. To succeed at the ball game, you know that it is up to you to do something with the ball. For example: If you are playing baseball, and you are at bat, you would be expected to hit the ball; or if you are in the field, you would be expected to catch the ball. So, because you have chosen to play the game, your expected *response* would be one of those two choices. If, however, you are convinced that you can't possibly hit it or catch it, an appropriate response might be to duck or move out of the way.

It is easy to see that your automatic reaction of just blinking would be foolish in that situation. Therefore, it is important to see that many of your automatic reactions may be just as foolish. In this chapter, we will be addressing your dysfunctional, automatic, emotional reactions that you may still have – the ones that don't work well for you – the dysfunctional ones that reflect the beliefs and scripts that make up the VPR Cloud. By understanding that your typical, automatic, emotional reactions are simply a by-product of the programs that you are running in your subconscious mind (the "computer" in your Mental-Body), you will become more conscious of what to expect; then you can rethink and take responsibility for your automatic *reactions* and choose how you would like to *respond* to your future challenges.

Your emotional reactions are the automatic products emanating from your unconscious beliefs about your world. You may not understand many of your reactions, or, they may not even be rational. Many of your automatic reactions were learned when you were very small, because you simply absorbed them from the cloud that enveloped your early environment. Therefore, you may have no conscious recall of the experiences that caused them. Some were conclusions that you came to when someone reacted inappropriately to your words or actions, or to situations in your environment. Keep in mind that some of *their* reactions were conscious and deliberate, but others may have been totally unconscious to them, because they had been internalized early in *their* lives.

Some of your emotional reactions are defensive-mechanisms that you learned during your early years, when you were totally focused on ways to keep you safe in your environment. The type of reaction that worked well for you at four years-of-age may no longer be appropriate at your present age. You may need to consider how your reactions will affect your life from this point forward.

It is now important to consider whether the way you are expressing yourself emotionally is in your best interest. If you have chosen to read this book, it is possible that you have some emotional reactions that could be keeping you in a cloud of misery. Now, you may wish to make conscious choices about whatever is "thrown at you" by the circumstances in your life. Therefore, the intent of this chapter is to help you become conscious of your emotional reactions and accurately label them. Only through a deep level of honesty will you be able to examine your deep-seated, unconscious triggers. This has the potential to dissipate your previous clouds, and allow you to respond differently to the stimuli in your environment in the future.

When you react automatically – without any conscious thought – you are acting like an unconscious robot or puppet. You become distracted by your scripts, causing you to lose your focus. As was shown in the illustration on page 23, when a cloud was formed between your Mental and Emotional Bodies, your Total-Self was weakened, because you no longer were in contact with the light of truth from your Spiritual-Self. Your natural defence system was weakened, because you had less connection with your integrity – your healthy boundaries.

The process of healing your clouds includes defining what you are reacting to and understanding why it has caused you to react in a specific manner. It is then possible to release your dysfunctional reactions and decide how you would like to respond differently to future situations. This engages your Total-Self by activating your Personal Power to choose appropriately in the future.

Now, let's look at some other words that may be confusing. Many people use the words "thinking" and "feeling" interchangeably. They often say, "I feel that…," but they actually mean, "I think that …" Usually, when we say, "I feel *that* …", it is the expression of a belief, but we try to soften it by inserting a reference to an emotion. When we are expressing an emotion, we will always say, "I feel sad/lonely/unhappy, etc." There is no "that" in the sentence. An "I feel that …." sentence is seldom a true expression of what we are actually experiencing emotionally.

When I ask clients, "How are you today?" they usually say one of the three labels – "good," "bad," or "okay." Many people use the word "okay" when they can't identify what they are actually experiencing; so it isn't an accurate answer. When they say that they are "okay," it is often because they don't know what to say, so they are implying they are okay; or, it may actually be a defensive-mechanism, because they don't want to tell me what they are actually experiencing on an emotional level.

I have come to the conclusion that there are actually only two emotional categories – emotional sensations that we experience as *good* or *bad*. This conclusion may be a corollary to the belief that there are basically only two categories of emotions – love and fear. Love and fear are said to be the only true emotions; all other emotional reactions are simply different layers of these two emotional categories.

Becoming consciously aware of what emotional state you are actually experiencing, will assist you in defining your emotional states efficiently and effectively. Putting labels on your emotions increases your awareness of what you are actually experiencing and increases your ability to express yourself in appropriate ways. This practice will also assist you in understanding your underlying beliefs.

Most people who have grown up in unhealthy environments have difficulty identifying their emotions accurately, because they have learned to doubt their ability to accurately assess the energy in their environments. You may have developed automatic reactions to ordinary situations that may be based on false information, because you are not sufficiently connected with your intuition. You may try to cover up your reactions and pretend that you are "okay" to hide the fact that you are actually upset or even terrified. If this pattern of relating is firmly in place, it may take conscious effort on your part to find a more in-depth or a more accurate definition of your external and internal environments.

You may have also developed defensive-mechanisms to prevent *others* from knowing what you are actually experiencing. These may have become so unconscious that you automatically activate them in the hope that others won't notice that you are being affected. For example: You may be experiencing fear; but you have developed a habit of holding your face in a fixed position to not reveal your true emotional state. Or, you may have developed unconscious habits to prevent *you* from experiencing the pain of your true emotions. This habit may have become a conditioned reaction, so you could have a temporary respite from experiencing your pain. Unfortunately, you may have become so *numb* to your true emotions that you have difficulty defining or labelling what you are actually experiencing.

Some emotions are more prominent, depending upon whether you are playing the victim, persecutor, or rescuer roles; whereas others are common in all three positions.

In the beginning of your exploration into your emotional reactions, it may seem impossible to carefully and honestly examine your sensations when you are engaged in an emotional situation. You may be confused by the variety of reactions that you are experiencing. When you are in the beginning stages of your process, it may be helpful to focus on remembering the experience as closely as possible, so you can replay it afterward and understand it. However, if you can stay conscious during the experience, it is helpful to pay attention to the specific sensations that you are experiencing in different parts of your body while your emotions are being triggered. Remember, being totally honest with yourself is a crucial part of becoming aware of what is actually happening.

Different emotional reactions will be described in the following pages, so you can put specific labels on the various emotions that occur in your daily life. It is important to put a specific and accurate label on each emotion when you wish to understand your reactions and have the power to change them into conscious responses. Labels activate the left brain – your logical side, your Mental-Body – and consequently, labels assist you in disengaging from your automatic emotional reaction to a given stimulus. This practice will allow you to explore your beliefs and understand which scripts have previously clouded your judgment and created that specific reaction.

Try to not give a vague label to your emotions, such as "upset" or "confused." For example: You may be in an emotional turmoil, because you have been given a speeding ticket. If you label your emotional reaction to this experience as "upset," you won't get to the actual emotions lying beneath the surface. It is essential to take the time to decide the true emotions that you are experiencing. Perhaps, you are experiencing the emotion of *shame* about your lack of awareness of your surroundings. Perhaps, you believe that you were *stupid* to have been so unconscious of your environment, which may be self-judgment, self-criticism, self-flagellation, or internalized anger. Perhaps, you are experiencing *vulnerability,* which is a form of fear; because now you know that you were not in control of your vehicle. Perhaps, you are experiencing *anger,* due to your resistance to authority. Or, perhaps, you are experiencing *arrogance,* because you believe that you can do no wrong. Whenever you define your specific emotional reactions, you have the opportunity to rethink, revise, and reverse your dysfunctional patterns of relating or reactions.

The following list is designed to clarify the variety of emotional reactions that we all experience. It may also help you discern whether a different label is more accurate for what you are experiencing than the one you have formerly used. A specific set of emotional reactions is expressed whenever you are operating within the VPR Cloud. The list below shows many of these emotions. Take time to say each word out loud to see what sensations are triggered.

Fear	Anxiety	Worry
Blame	Shame	Guilt
Anger	Frustration	Lack
Unworthiness	Loneliness	Resentment
Need to Control	Unfounded Hope	Insecurity

Fear

It is natural, and in some cases, very appropriate, to experience fear when we are in new, unknown, or threatening situations. Fear is a constant companion, however, for those who live in the VPR Cloud. This is because the unknown is a much larger territory and more frightening to people who have lived in confusing or unsafe environments. They may have come to believe that the entire Universe is an unsafe place. Fear is expressed very differently by people who live in each position in the VPR Triangle.

Victims are often afraid of everyone and everything. They didn't learn how to create healthy boundaries around their Total-Selves, so they fear for their very existence. This is most evident, when they believe there is a possibility that they might lose even yet more of their Personal Power. They have a mile-long list of things that instil fear in them. Fear may have become such an automatic way of life that they have shut down their ability to recognize it. They may have suppressed it to the point where they may even deny its existence, to prevent it from coming to the surface of their conscious awareness to constantly plague them.

Victims usually assume that the worst is going to happen any second. They have little or no faith in the God Force as a source of good in their lives. They are in a constant state of fear because they have such a strong belief in *lack*. They have been conditioned to believe that there isn't enough to go around. Therefore, they are constantly preoccupied with trying to find someone, or something, to distract them from their pain. This is how all addictions are born.

Persecutors don't usually admit to being afraid. They have learned to suppress any expression of fear. They don't want others to realize how vulnerable they truly are, because the others might try to control them. They are convinced that everyone is looking for their weak spots, with the sole intent of using that information as a way to abuse or control them. They often cover up their fear with anger or aggression.

Rescuers are very easily hooked into other people's fears, because they are only pretending to be *strong* and *helpful* to others. They pretend that they are never afraid to give the impression that they are able to *fix* every problem. Rescuers cover up their fear with self-importance, self-righteousness, or even arrogance. Rescuers believe that their ability to control others determines the amount of safety that they experience. They express what they call "justifiable anger" at the system when they are afraid – so others won't see their fear.

Rescuers are also afraid that others won't respect or agree with them, or that they won't be able to rescue *all* the so-called victims of the world. As a result, they are afraid most of the time, but they have learned to put more sophisticated labels on their fear. They self-righteously claim that it is their moral obligation to be caring and concerned about the welfare of others. They don't see, however, that their caring and concern is motivated by a self-serving desire to control others and keep them within the VPR Cloud.

How to Reduce Fear in Your Life

The simplistic solution to this dilemma is to replace the fear with love-because love and fear can't live in the same heart or mind. This isn't easy to do, however. All fear, with the exception of the fear of falling, is a *learned* behaviour. You learned your specific fears through your experiences. It is a logical conclusion that the only way to *unlearn* your fears is to live in a safer external environment. In some cases, this might be a good idea; however, in most cases, this solution is also too simplistic, because it is impossible to avoid danger and it is important to learn how to respond appropriately to those unsafe environments.

Hopefully, you will be able to see each situation that arises as an opportunity to learn about the clouds that have previously dimmed your consciousness. You may then find that you no longer attract the people or circumstances that have previously triggered your fears. You will begin to choose healthier external environments and learn alternative methods of satisfying your needs. You are then in a position to reprogram your internal, fearful scripts and create more positive self-affirmations, such as words that express self-love and your willingness to receive healthy love from others. You will then be living more fully within healthy boundaries around your Total-Self and be able to find more appropriate responses to situations in your external environment – responses that express self-love and loving kindness toward others.

Anxiety and Worry

People who live in the clouded thinking of the VPR Triangle are anxious and worried most of the time. They may have felt unsafe so often, in their early years, they believe that their world is *always* an unsafe place to be. They believe that they need to be on guard constantly to ward off impending danger. Anxiety is constant, if you believe, either consciously or unconsciously, that you live in an unsafe world.

Anxiety may also come from a belief in lack, a fear of loss, or a lack of self-confidence. It is often caused by the repression of our individuality due to abuse in tightly controlled environments. Anxiety is always a natural by-product if we have given away our Personal Power to others. When we are totally dependent upon others for all our needs, we will naturally be worried or anxious that our needs won't be met.

Many people who have lived in confusing environments excuse their worry by renaming it "concern." This is a form of denial – a way to put a pretty mask over their unconscious belief in an unsafe world. Using another word allows them to pretend that it is okay to be concerned, but it doesn't really allow them to relax and be free to trust their environment. Their anxiety is simply called by a different name. Each role in the VPR Cloud manifests anxiety in different ways.

Victims are usually in a constant state of anxiety – on edge about most things in their external environment, because of their self-limiting beliefs and their lack of self-confidence. They believe that the natural state of the world is unsafe – to the point of being dangerous. They believe that they are inadequate or unable to cope with that unsafe environment, because others have controlled them to the point where they don't know how to make their own decisions. Their lack of connection with their Personal Power prevents them from thinking of better ways to cope with any of life's challenges.

Persecutors seldom admit their anxiety in overt ways, but they often exhibit it in a variety of aggressive mannerisms. They want to present a powerful front; but their main source of anxiety comes from their fear that people won't comply with their demands. So, they often express their anxiety by increasing the volume of their control tactics – even before they find out whether or not those tactics are necessary.

Rescuers will often find a fancy label such as "concern" to camouflage their anxiety, so they can continue to pretend that they are all-powerful and they are only anxious about the welfare of others. They instil fear by teaching victims to be on guard against persecutors with dysfunctional scripts about others being *bad,* or "out to get you." They often generalize individual concerns to global proportions – "*all* men/women are mean" or "*all* employers are greedy," or "*all* people are out to get us."

Rescuers constantly worry that their vulnerable position will be exposed and others will find out about how inadequate and confused they truly are. So, they create scripts that are excuses or justifications for their anxiety. They say, "It is natural for all people to be suspicious of others;" or, "There is a good reason that we are all anxious." This is, of course, an expression of their underlying erroneous belief that we are all vulnerable in an unsafe universe.

How to Reduce Anxiety and Worry in Your Life

Anxieties, worries, and concerns are all based on the belief that you are incompetent or incapable of coping with the situations that arise in your environment. This is usually because you feel disconnected from everyone and everything around you – especially the God Force. Whenever you are anxious, you naturally believe that you won't be given what you want or need, or even worse, you will only be given what you don't want or need.

Worry has been compared to the whirring sound that a wheel makes when it spins in the same place. When you worry, you go over and over the same unhealthy scripts, which prevents you from accessing the light of truth from your Spiritual-Body and creating an appropriate solution to your dilemmas. In reality, however, you can't stay in the same place and time – time and circumstances are constantly changing. Consequently, if you focus your energy on anxiety and worry, you actually waste precious time and energy by wallowing in uncomfortable emotions, reinforcing your self-limiting beliefs and making your clouds denser and more prominent in your thinking.

To reduce your levels of anxiety and worry, the first step is to stop trying to control other people and situations in your environment and pay attention to what *you* are thinking, saying, and doing, instead of wasting time thinking of ways to criticize and control others. At first, this may be a difficult task, especially if you are associating with people who insist on doing dangerous or violent things. Your only choice in this type of situation may be to remove yourself from their company. This separation may allow you to gain perspective and begin to eliminate the controls that they have previously had over you. Then, you will be able to love yourself enough to make healthier choices.

There is a very distinct difference between worrying about the possible outcome of a choice and the careful planning of the necessary steps that you will need to take to achieve your goals. Worrying simply reruns or regurgitates your old fears; while planning a success-strategy engages your creativity and opens your consciousness to the truth of your Total-Self.

The Blame, Shame, & Guilt Triangle

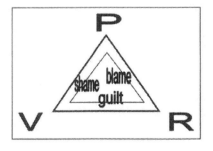

The Blame, Shame, and Guilt triangle seems to be the glue that holds the VPR Cloud together. It has been so successfully used to control people for so many years that it seems to be the normal way to live. Consequently, it is necessary to pay very special attention to understanding blame, shame, and guilt and stop using the accompanying scripts that perpetuate that dysfunctional energy.

Let's begin by examining the words, "blame," "shame," and "guilt," because these words are so commonly used in our culture. In order to put this topic into context, it is important to understand that the same words are used to describe huge principles as well as minor misdemeanours. For example: The word guilty is used to describe a person who is guilty of murder as well as who is guilty of leaving the milk on the counter after breakfast.

When we look at this issue from the greater perspective, we begin to see that our culture has devised a system of order, designed to create a harmonious and safe environment. This system of order contains rules of conduct that, as citizens, we agree to support. Our judicial system is designed to enforce these rules and punish those who break the rules. Originally, the punishment of individuals who stepped outside the law was designed to not only hold the perpetrator accountable for his or her misdeeds, but also to demonstrate the power of that judicial system, so others would see the consequences of breaking the rules. In the early years of "civilization" as we know it, there were public demonstrations of floggings, mutilations, and even hangings. Those public demonstrations were designed to instil fear into the rest of the population, so they wouldn't attempt to break the rules of the established order.

A similar system is used in most family environments. Parents create a system of rules that children are expected to follow. In healthy, functional families, those rules are designed to create a safe, harmonious environment. The rules are clearly explained and enforced in healthy, appropriate ways. However, in dysfunctional families, rules are often less clear and more convoluted, as well as frequently changed. The ensuing punishments may be inconsistent or even demonstrated in violent outbursts that may include inappropriate use of force.

A healthy system, or social structure, holds us accountable for our deeds and there is potentially a lesson to be learned, an opportunity for growth, as well as an opportunity for redemption. In the Blame, Shame, and Guilt Triangle, however, there is no opportunity for education, evolution, or redemption. A downward spiral of energy takes us into a perpetual state of misery. The dysfunctional energy of the Blame, Shame, and Guilt Triangle creates a self-perpetuating state of self-flagellation. Whether the environment is a family unit or society-at-large, the energy of blame, shame, and guilt is directly linked to the belief that it is always *wrong* to make mistakes.

Whenever we view the act of making mistakes as a *bad* thing, we automatically fall into a chaotic energy package where there is no hope for change, evolution, or growth.

Instead of allowing ourselves to explore our reality as curious children, we may try to avoid punishment by pretending, on one extreme, that we are not responsible for anything, because we know nothing; or, to the other extreme, where we pretend that we know everything about everything. This happens because we have been conditioned to be fearful of being judged or receiving serious repercussions whenever we fail to achieve our desired goals or make choices that we don't wish to be accountable for.

Blame

Blame is always a projection of wrongdoing. "You are to blame for ..." The underlying message is that, because you have made that choice, you are wrong/bad/inadequate/stupid, etc. It is true that you may have been the causal factor that initiated the energy that is being judged; however, you may have had good reasons for making that choice.

Some people confuse the energy of blame with taking responsibility for one's actions. They say things like "You were to blame for that mistake," even though that may not be true. However, those two energy packages are actually very different. Just because someone blames you for a choice that you have made, it doesn't mean that you need to accept shame or feel guilty, because you made that choice. You may believe that your choice was a good one or the only choice that you could have made under the circumstances.

Blame is always an energy package that we project toward others as a method of manipulation. Some people use the blame energy to maintain or achieve a position of superiority by making other people feel *wrong* for their choices. The main script is, "It was your fault that … happened, so now I can be angry with you." People who have developed the habit of using blame to control others are either trying to manipulate them into doing what they want them to do, or, to make them feel inferior, so they will be more easily controlled in the future.

In some cases, people project blame toward others simply because they don't want to accept responsibility for creating the mistakes or chaos in their own lives. They don't want to be seen as inadequate or incompetent, so they project blame for their mistakes onto others. They are trying to divert that *bad* energy away from themselves, because they are afraid of the consequences of their actions. Or, they already feel so *bad* inside that they can't accept more misery.

Instead of using their creativity to solve problems in an efficient, effective, or harmonious manner, they choose to project blame toward others. Sometimes, they do this, because they hope that no one will notice that they, in fact, initiated the process that led to the chaotic end result. They don't want others to see their inadequacies, so they quickly project blame instead of being accountable for their words or actions.

Shame

We experience shame whenever we internalize the blame energy that has been projected toward us. Whenever we feel shame, we must relate to that energy in some way and believe that we *deserve* to be punished for our actions.

Whenever we accept blame, it is usually because we already have a cloud in our consciousness that matches the energy package being projected to us. If we have previously created a similar situation for which we felt shame, we will most likely believe that we are to blame for other, similar situations as well. In this case, accepting blame has become our pattern of relating to our environment. We automatically assume, "It must have been my fault." Subsequently, we conclude that we are also to blame for the current situation.

It is important to distinguish the difference between shame and regret or remorse. Regret and remorse will be addressed at length in Chapter 5, but suffice it to say at this point, that shame is unproductive, leaving the individual in the hopeless and helpless state of victim consciousness, while regret and remorse allow for positive change.

If you were abused with blame, shame, and guilt as a child, your Total-Self was adversely affected – creating a cloud of confusion between your Mental and Emotional Bodies.

Your Personal Power was diminished because the people that you trusted to guide and protect you had betrayed that trust and you became confused. Your natural perceptions of safety or danger were questioned – diminishing your level of trust in your Emotional-Body. The messages you were receiving from your Mental-Body were also put into question – reducing the clarity of your logical processes. Consequently, your connection with the light of truth from your Spiritual-Body was dimmed or extinguished.

Without solid connections to these aspects of your Total-Self, your Personal Power to make healthy decisions became weakened or even non-existent. Because you were dependent upon your parents or caregivers to nourish you mentally and emotionally, as well as physically, this kind of abuse would have conditioned you to believe that you will always deserve this abusive energy, setting in place a downward spiral of addiction to shame.

In your attempt to cope with this abuse, you may have focused all your attention on a variety of self-protective patterns of relating. If you have internalized the blame/shame/guilt energy package into your Total-Self, your scripts will continue to give you those messages. This unconscious habit allows you to absorb the projected blame and you automatically experience shame, so you carry guilt with you wherever you go.

This unconscious pattern of relating not only makes you live in a cloud of misery, helplessness, hopelessness, and powerlessness, it wastes precious time and energy. If you waste time making yourself *wrong* and listening to the scripts of shame, you constantly reinforce the power of that cloud in your Total-Self.

Guilt

Guilt is what we carry away from the blame and shame experience in our little "suitcase of self-punishment." On the surface, it may seem that we are accepting responsibility for a mistake, but every guilt energy package contains scripts that are rife with self-judgment and self-flagellation. When we carry guilt, we are so busy with self-flagellation that we seldom take responsibility for how we contributed to the problem, nor do we fully realize that we have the power to choose differently in the future. Instead, we have sunk into the victim state of mind, thinking that we are hopeless, helpless, and powerless; because we are running the scripts that we are *stupid* or *inadequate* in some way.

Guilt has a residual effect. We may carry it for days, months, or even years. If, however, we don't want to change our behaviour, we may divert the responsibility for the specific action toward another and project blame toward them. This action completes and perpetuates the Blame, Shame, and Guilt Triangle. Depending on which position you are operating from in the VPR Triangle, the Blame, Shame, and Guilt Triangle is manifested differently.

Victims are so accustomed to living in blame, shame, and guilt that it becomes a normal way to live. They accept the blame, shame, and guilt; because they are conditioned to believe that everything that goes wrong in their world is their fault. They may even accept blame for things that have nothing to do with them. These people may have been, as children, falsely accused of creating problems in their family environment and they accepted the scapegoat role.

People who live in the victim state of mind also have their own unique ways of projecting blame toward others. They often suffer in silence, while giving their persecutor dirty looks. Or, they may try to shame others by whimpering or whining to let their persecutors know that they have been hurt. They are passively or aggressively attempting to manipulate their presumed persecutor into a rescuer position, so the VPR dynamic can go the way they believe that it is "supposed to." They do this so they can revert back to the illusion of safety in the VPR Cloud – with a protector or rescuer.

Persecutors use blame in a more aggressive manner than victims. They often use it as a method of intimidation to constantly confuse and "muddy the waters," to keep their victims under their control. A person who lives in the persecutor state of mind often uses confusion to create stress, which will throw those in the victim state of mind into chaos, so they can be more easily manipulated.

They believe that they have the right to blame others, if anything goes *wrong,* because they never admit to making mistakes. Because they are able to redirect the blame energy through deceit or dishonesty, it prevents the original creator of the action from becoming accountable. Also, this effort to boost the persecutor's ego often becomes an addiction, because they experience a temporary "power-high." This "power-high" comes from having succeeded in manipulating the situation and it reinforces their belief in their right to manipulate others to get what they want.

Rescuers believe in their *superior* ideas and abilities to make the *right* decisions for others. They often discount, discredit, or diminish the value of anyone who doesn't agree with them. They project blame and shame toward others in an effort to manipulate them into doing what they believe is the *right* thing. Because they are trying to *fix* the other person's life, they always assume that they are justified in using blame, shame, or guilt to control him or her. They try to make victims feel guilty by shaming them, suggesting that they don't know the right way to be. This may be because they have invested their time and energy into fixing the victim's life. They expect compliance and they become resentful and frustrated when that doesn't happen.

How to Reduce Blame, Shame, and Guilt in Your Life

Rethinking how you have been shamed or blamed in the past is a very important step to move out of the VPR

Cloud. When you realize that blame or shame is always meant to diminish or distract you from your Personal Power, you will be able to see it as a "power grab" and choose to do what is right for you.

Once you identify blame as a manipulative tool, you have developed a coping-strategy that will allow you to deflect unwarranted blame away from you, automatically. Then, you are able to stop the dynamic of blame, before it becomes shame, and not let yourself sink into guilt-scripts.

Once you have fully rethought this dynamic, you won't be as likely to accept blame or shame from others or harshly blame yourself when you make mistakes. You now know that it is important to be courageous enough to risk making mistakes whenever you wish to learn new things. Instead of choosing to be a helpless victim, you are now able to say *no* to any suggestions that aren't in alignment with your integrity and create healthier boundaries.

When we respect each other as human beings who are always growing and learning, we allow each other to make, and learn from, our mistakes. This attitude of personal accountability creates balance in our Total-Selves.

Anger

Anger is an aggressive energy package that is projected toward others that is designed to control them – to have power over them. There are basically two reasons that we use anger to control others. We are either trying to protect ourselves in this moment, because we actually feel threatened; or we have the belief that it is necessary to always protect ourselves, because *everyone* will try to control us, if we let them.

Whenever we feel angry, it is because we have been threatened and our primitive urge to snarl at our attacker is engaged. Anger is the expression of a primitive natural defence against people who are threatening to us. (Note how the word "anger" is inside the word "danger.")

However, anger may have also become an automatic, defensive-mechanism that we use to cover up more vulnerable emotions that are buried deep within our clouds. In this case, anger has become a protection that we believe will keep us from experiencing further abuse, or hide the fact that our fears, insecurities, inadequacies, or vulnerabilities have been, or *might* be, triggered.

Whenever we use anger as a cover-up reaction, it implies that we do not feel safe enough in our environment to express our actual emotional states. In this case, we are using anger to *pretend* that we have more power than we actually have. Our angry outbursts have become a camouflage or defensive-mechanism to confuse people and prevent them from knowing about the fear that we are *actually* experiencing. Our angry mask may have fooled some people in the past; therefore, because it was effective, it reinforced the idea that it was a *good tool*. Eventually, we internalized it, until it became an automatic reaction that we use whenever our triggers are activated.

The expression of anger toward another is *always* abusive. It is like a "stick" that one person uses to hit another. In every expression of anger, you are either the one who is using anger to abuse someone, or they are using anger to abuse you. In most cases, whenever you are arguing with another person, you are taking turns being abusive and hitting each other with the "anger stick."

Whenever you perceive that someone is being abusive to you, you will always experience fear. If you cover-up that fear with an expression of anger, you are actually being dishonest and you are creating a denser cloud of confusion. Unless you are able to catch yourself and become honest, you will probably feed the "fire" with more abusive "sticks."

Often, when you are expressing anger, it is because you have been triggered by painful memories from past experiences that you don't want to deal with. But instead of taking the time to realize that you are actually experiencing insecurity, you get out your automatic, angry, defensive-mechanism and yell at the other person. Unfortunately, this is usually someone whom you claim to care for, because most people refrain from yelling at people they don't know or trust. The script that accompanies this kind of thinking is usually, "They know me, so they 'should' know what I want;" or "I can be myself with the ones I care for. So, I can yell at them to control them;" or, "They won't listen to me unless I yell at them." Persecutors and rescuers call this "justifiable anger," because they believe that they are justified in using anger to control others.

Subsequently, the other person's painful memories are triggered also; but instead of taking the time to realize that they are also experiencing vulnerability, they get out their automatic angry, defensive-mechanism and yell back. Their scripts are, "If you are going to try to control me, I'll show you that I have a bigger voice/stick/more power than you do." Or, "I can yell louder than you can." The real truth is usually that you don't want them to know about your fears or insecurities, so you yell at them in an attempt to protect your ego position. Arguing is seldom the path to resolution, because neither party is actually listening to what is being said.

Our angry reactions to others could also be a way of punishing them for previous wounds, or an attempt to control them by making them *wrong*, because they haven't done what we wanted them to do. In both of these cases, we are trying to intimidate them and instil enough fear in them, so we can manipulate or change them and they will do what we want in the future. So, our expression of anger may actually be an overt attempt to manipulate them into complying with our wishes.

Angry reactions could also be a way of pushing away something that we don't want to hear about ourselves.

Perhaps, we could sense that the other person is telling the truth about something that we do not want to take responsibility for, because it was something that we are ashamed of. It can be our way of saying, "Don't tell me that I am not perfect! I don't make mistakes!" Therefore, anger can be an automatic defensive-mechanism that we utilize to protect ourselves from an uncomfortable truth.

Anger can also become an addiction that "numbs-out" our pain, but it also "numbs-out" our ability to cope successfully with life. Remember that "every addiction is the belief that we will feel better if …" Therefore, anger becomes an addiction to distract attention away from our other emotional states. We believe that we will *feel better*, if we can confuse or control the other person, instead of experiencing our *actual* emotional state, because those emotions make us feel too vulnerable – like a victim. In this case, even though anger is used to confuse the other person, it also confuses us.

These defensive-mechanisms were probably learned in early childhood when we learned that our truth was not accepted, supported, appreciated, or, in many cases, heard. We learned that it was not safe to express our real emotions, so we learned to create a cloud to deflect them, stuff them, or cover them up. This cloud not only confused others, it also confused us and hid the real issues behind a cloud of deception.

Sadly, little boys are seldom told that they shouldn't express anger. Anger is an "okay guy thing to do." It is even encouraged in competitive sports, in which the aggressiveness of anger is used to compete with the "enemy" and "score points." Consequently, some males develop the habit of using it to cover up a variety of other emotions, such as fear. They have been told that they must not express fear or hurt; they shouldn't cry or whine. The script is, "Don't be a wimp! Suck it up and be a man!" They are being trained to be persecutors.

Girls are often told the opposite story. "Little girls aren't supposed to get angry." However, it is all right to be afraid and express their fear by whining or crying. The script is, "Be nice and everyone will like you," or, "It's not ladylike to raise your voice." They are being trained to be victims or rescuers.

Erroneously, it has been assumed that this different approach to the expression of anger is a natural distinction between the sexes. It has been proven that both sexes have the capacity to experience the same emotions; however, they are socialized to express them differently.

When little boys are told to repress their fear and express their anger and little girls are told to repress their anger and express their fear, this dichotomy naturally leads to an inability to communicate effectively; and it ultimately causes chaos between the sexes. When a woman expresses anger, she is seen as "a bitch." When a man expresses fear, he is seen as "a wimp." These cultural stereotypes further separate the sexes and prevent the type of communication that could lead to a resolution of the kind of issues that crop up in relationships.

When we are fully conscious of our feelings of anger, it has the potential to be a very powerful, motivational force to remove us from unjust, threatening, or dangerous situations. It may encourage us to seek professional support or motivate us to move away from abusers and abuse, allowing us to take back our lives and live in harmony with our integrity.

The projection of anger affects all relationships – between spouses, partners, friends, parents, children, etc. Whenever one person expresses anger, the other becomes afraid of disapproval, or even abuse or abandonment. If the second person expresses those fears, it is likely to spark more anger from the aggressor, because aggressors often use anger to cover up their vulnerability – sensations of helplessness, hopelessness, inadequacy, their fear of being misunderstood, rejected, or abandoned. Or, the aggressors may be ashamed that they have expressed themselves in an inappropriate way, that caused fear in their partners; but they don't want to know that fact about themselves. They don't want to know that they have the capacity to deeply hurt the ones they love. They may try to cover up this awareness with more aggression. The roles can switch between the two people, depending upon their tendency to automatically resort to anger.

You may have been hurt in the past for expressing anger when injustices were perpetrated upon you. You may have been told to "be quiet" when you were expressing thoughts that your parents didn't want to hear. Your parents may have become more aggressive, if you told them that they were being hurtful. You may have concluded that anger was the best way to respond to abuse, because you observed that people didn't stop abusing you when you just cried or told them that they were hurting you.

To get along in your family environment, you may have gradually learned to make excuses for your parents' or caregivers' abuse, neglect, or inadequate support. You may have concluded that it was easier to suppress your anger than to take the chance that you might be punished, rejected, or even abandoned. You then began to build an imaginary world around the idea that, if you were a really scary monster, people wouldn't try to control you or hurt you. So, anger became your weapon of choice. It was a case of you trying to have the biggest "stick" to protect yourself.

You may have unconsciously copied the unhealthy scripts of the abusers in your environment and learned to utilize angry, abusive statements. "Don't be such an idiot!" or "If you do that again, I'm going to punch you in the mouth!" "Get out of my way, or I'll run you over!" Actually, these scripts may be defensive-mechanisms, but they are also designed to make other people so afraid of you that they won't hurt you. If these scripts are the ones that you have used to cope with the challenges in your environment, you need to understand that they are all aspects of dysfunctional behaviour, meant to confuse others. They may seem to work temporarily; but they don't work well in the long run.

When you acknowledge that your projected anger may be simply covering up fear, you can access your Personal Power to refuse to be hurt again or hurt others with your anger. As soon as you acknowledge your fear, you can avoid reacting to abuse with anger. If you stand strong in your truth, it will allow you to access your Spiritual-Body and say, "I'm a divine-spark. You can't treat me that way." Your honesty about how you have given away your Personal Power in the past will give you the courage to make the necessary changes to live in harmony with your integrity. It will prevent others from interfering with your choices, your commitments, your dedication to your goals, and ultimately the expression of your highest good.

Unresolved angry thoughts can eat away at your self-confidence; reduce your effectiveness and productivity; adversely affect and limit your circle of friends and eventually destroy your physical health.

Anger is one of the most frequently experienced emotions in every position of the VPR Triangle; however, it is experienced in different ways and has an entirely different outcome when we are operating from each of the three states of mind within the VPR Cloud.

Victims seldom express anger openly to avoid additional punishment, rejection, or abandonment. They quickly stuff, suppress, or swallow their anger, internalizing the energy, which exacerbates the belief in their helplessness and hopelessness and reinforces their scripts of self-flagellation. By repressing their anger, victims lose a source of potential power that could motivate them to explore creative thoughts, feelings, words, and actions, or give them the courage to move away from abuse. Self-inflicted or internalized anger is common in the victim state of mind, because they hate themselves when they make mistakes or reveal their vulnerability or humanness.

Persecutors usually have no problem projecting their anger outwardly. They use their angry stance to exhibit an impenetrable mask, so they are inaccessible to any feedback from others. This stance allows them to avoid the resistance or confrontations that would be the natural effects of their aggression. Their use of anger has become a valuable tool they use as a weapon – a sword that they use to control the "battlefield." It can also be used as a shield, a protection, so they don't have to take responsibility for their behaviour, or, so they won't experience vulnerable states.

Rescuers are more likely to use anger as a general expression of disdain that encompasses most of humanity; therefore, anger is justifiable in their minds. They may see *all* children, women, poor people, animals, etc. (anyone who has been stereotyped as an underdog) as victims who need to be rescued, and, subsequently, they will blame *all* parents, men/women, a race, a religious denomination, etc. for the problems in the world. Even though this type of unreasonable, unjustified generalization is judgmental, abusive, and separative, it is used to justify their anger.

How to Reduce Anger in Your Life

As you can see, the use of anger is very common within the VPR Cloud. Because it is an emotional reaction that is either the overt or covert way of manipulating others, it is often seen as the cause of problematic situations. However, as is demonstrated in the above examples, it is not usually the root cause of problems. The root cause of our angry outbursts is usually that we are not being honest about what we are *actually* experiencing, so we use anger to cover up our true, emotional states.

The best way to reduce the type of anger that is a cover-up is to become aware consciously of each of your emotional states. When you can give an appropriate label to your emotions as you are experiencing them, you will become able to accurately identify the underlying emotions that you may be trying to cover-up.

However, if you happen to find yourself engaged in the anger energy, stop immediately – take the time to make a conscious choice about how to deal with it – a time out. Then, take a moment to become honest with yourself about what other emotional states you were actually experiencing or what you were trying to cover up with your angry outburst.

If anger is being projected toward you, it is possible to take a moment to label that energy objectively, without becoming embroiled in conflict. You may be able to rise above your usual reaction by realizing that the other person's outburst may not have anything to do with you. That person may be having a bad day (or life). From this objective perspective, you have a distinct advantage. You can take a moment to decide whether it is prudent to sidestep the situation or confront it directly. If you have developed a script that says, "I have to defend myself by pretending to be strong," you'll give yourself permission to project anger toward the other person. If you have developed a script that says, "I'd better not say a word, or I will just make it worse," you'll probably stuff your anger and delay any resolution.

If you wish to take back your Personal Power and choose a healthier way of expressing yourself, you must take complete responsibility for your thoughts, feelings, words, and actions. This won't happen, however, if you choose to blame the other person for your angry reactions, which is actually a denial of your personal responsibility for having a part in the creation of the situation.

Once you have become accountable, you must quickly make restitution. This could be in the form of an apology and a request for forgiveness; but ideally, a true apology must be accompanied by a commitment to guard against the possibility of ever falling into that old habit again. If you are in a close relationship with the person, it may be helpful to be honest with him or her about what triggered your reaction. This will allow a greater level of understanding between you both, and you will also achieve a greater level of intimacy with that person.

Whenever you repress or "stuff" any emotion, or you don't express yourself honestly and appropriately, you won't be satisfied by the interaction. You will be confused and you will also confuse the other person. The relationship is wounded by your dishonesty. Unless you express yourself honestly and appropriately, people who have been abusive toward you don't get the necessary feedback that could stop them from initiating further abuse. You haven't given them the clear message that you are aware of their inappropriate behaviour or the message that you won't tolerate their abuse in the future. Your lack of honesty is actually enabling them to continue abusive patterns of relating – to you as well as the others in their circle. You haven't drawn the proverbial line in the sand and claimed your right to be honoured and respected for the divine being that you truly are. When you aren't honest, they don't have a chance to get to know the real you.

If you suppress your anger, repress it, or control it in unhealthy ways, you will ultimately become angry with yourself and turn it into self-abuse – become your own persecutor and continue to experience the clouded thinking of the victim state of mind. Because you know that you have acted in a way that disempowers you and separates you from your Total-Self, your scripts surface. "I should have told him or her…" or "I wish I had said…" "I'm such a loser for not standing up for myself."

If you wish to find the root cause of your habit of repressing your anger, you may need to explore your early childhood environment. Your habit may have started as an attempt to keep you "safe." If you were raised in a confusing environment, you probably built an illusion of safety around yourself, so you could survive. This didn't happen as the result of one incident; it happened gradually, over the years.

If you wish to reduce anger in your daily life, you must be willing to follow your chosen path and not give others the power to make your decisions. If you respect the opinions and ideas of others and don't try to control or interfere with their lives, you have the right to expect the same from them. If you don't respect others, you can't expect them to respect you. Your angry thoughts, feelings, words, scripts, and actions will dissipate as soon as you are fully walking your own unique path and you are expressing your Total-Self in an integral way.

Frustration

Frustration is a form of anger. Sometimes, people use the word "frustrated," because they don't want to *admit* to being angry. So, when you say that you are frustrated, it may be because you want to control another person and they aren't co-operating; or, you may experience frustration when others aren't living up to your expectations, whether or not you have expressed those expectations to them; or, you have a desire for a specific outcome that hasn't materialized; or, the Universe hasn't supplied what you believe you *need* to be happy. You may also experience frustration whenever you repress your true thoughts and emotions.

Victims most often experience frustration, because they believe that they can't get out of their misery. They also experience frustration when they expect someone to *rescue* them and that person or situation doesn't perform to their satisfaction.

Persecutors most often experience frustration when others don't obey their commands and demands. They expect to control every situation through manipulation, intimidation, or aggression and are frustrated when their control tactics don't work. Here again, the envisioned scenario was not played out to their satisfaction, so frustration is the result.

Rescuers most often experience frustration when people don't follow their advice or believe in *their* solutions to life's problems. In other words, the person won't be *rescued*. A rescuer's advice always has conditions around it. If someone refuses their advice, the VPR Triangle is threatened, so the rescuer is frustrated.

How to Reduce Frustration in Your Life

Our frustration is usually projected outwardly; but if we look deeply enough, we are often frustrated with ourselves for not being able to control other people. The key to eliminating frustration from your life is to realize that you do not have the right to dominate the will of anyone else. This is because they are just as much a divine-spark as you are. They have free will. When you are expressing anger or frustration toward them, you are actually trying to take away their right to choose and trying to force them to do whatever you want them to do. By acknowledging that they have free will, you will also realize that they are responsible for their own decisions. If you respect their right to make their decisions and learn from their mistakes, you won't be frustrated by their behaviour. Frustrations are a direct result of expectations; consequently, letting go of your expectations of others automatically eliminates frustration.

The Belief in Lack & That You are Unworthy

The belief in *lack* is rampant in the VPR Cloud. It is based on the worldview that there is a finite/limited supply available to satisfy our physical and nonphysical needs. The script, "There's not enough to go around," becomes the mantra of lack. There are many reasons that you could have developed a belief in lack. Perhaps, during your childhood, there was actually a lack of food, shelter, or physical support; perhaps, there was a lack of affection or acceptance; or perhaps, there was a lack of appreciation for the qualities that you had to offer – your unique gifts to share with the world. Whatever the root cause of the belief in lack, it was definitely man-made. It was introduced into your life by people who had learned to believe that we live in a limited Universe. They had moved away from the light of truth from their Spiritual connections and their lack of appreciation for their heritage as divine-sparks.

Let's begin by discussing physical lacks. In primitive times, people either lived in tropical climates where there was a constant supply of food, or they lived a nomadic lifestyle where they followed their food supply and ate whatever was available to them in a specific location at a specific time of year. Survival depended upon co-operation. Everyone had a specific role to play and each role was valued. The children were valued as the hope for the survival of the tribe. Adults were valued as the workers and hunters that kept the tribe functioning successfully. The elders were valued for their wisdom. It was their job to guide the tribe and teach the younger people how to live successfully.

The tribe depended upon the wisdom of the elders to keep balance. The elders used their intuition, or knew through previous experience, how to send the hunters in the right direction to bring back food. The women gathered and stored food in times of abundance. If there wasn't enough food to go around, usually, it was due to inadequate planning, lack of appropriate leadership, or abnormal weather conditions. However, because they knew that they needed each other to survive, it was not normal for people to take more than their fair share of the natural resources. Their motto was, "Share and share alike." In addition to sharing the natural resources, they were also supported mentally, emotionally, and spiritually by the balanced structure of the community.

In dysfunctional family environments, there is always an imbalance of power. In today's society, young people often start to raise families, before they have learned how to live successfully and independently. They often disconnect from their family and reject the wisdom of their elders. Then, they become self-absorbed, believing that they are more important than others and that their wants and needs must come first.

This may also lead to an imbalance of physical resources to satisfy everyone's needs. This may be because one or more family members take too much of the available resources to feed their addictions. Perhaps, too much of the family's money is used to buy drugs or alcohol, or even junk food. Perhaps, one member is irresponsible enough to gamble away the food money. Or, perhaps, the problem lies in even greater social causes, such as when there are inadequate natural resources in an area to support the number of people who live there. Due to the misuse or mismanagement of natural resources, there actually *is* a limited supply, so the natural assumption is to believe that lack is natural. It is not. This is a planet of abundant resources and there would be an adequate supply, if we were able to correctly manage those resources.

Young children believe that the world revolves around them. When they are consistently abused or neglected, they assume that there must be something lacking in *them*. They conclude that it is their fault that their needs are not being satisfied, so, they begin to believe that they are unworthy. This is a lie, and on some level, they know it; so, they soon develop scripts to convince themselves that their specific addictions will "numb the pain in their brains," keeping them from being conscious of their feelings of inadequacy. Nevertheless, their deeper emotional state of unworthiness is triggered again and again, because their old scripts and beliefs are unconsciously controlling their thoughts.

Victims believe in *lack* and their unworthiness to such a degree that, whenever they are offered unconditional love, support, or encouragement from others, they automatically reject it. They say, "Oh no, I can't accept that! I don't deserve that!" Or, they may believe that the giver is just another persecutor who wants *all* of their Personal Power, so, they twist the offered energy to fit their worldview.

Persecutors have learned that they have to force others into giving them any energy – physical, mental, emotional, or spiritual. Their belief in a limited supply causes them to demand more than their share of everything, because they believe that they aren't naturally worthy and they are under the delusion that "things" or "attention/power" will make them "feel better." It has become an addiction.

Therefore, when persecutors are offered any form of love, support, or encouragement from others, they may reject it, because if they were to believe it, it would make them feel afraid of becoming a victim again. As well, they may accept the energy as their due; but their script says, "I tricked them into giving that to me." So, they don't value it as part of the abundance of the Universe.

Rescuers demonstrate their belief in lack by thinking that they have *earned* the love, support, and encouragement of others by *helping* them. However, when they receive any kind of appreciation, their script says, "I'm entitled to that. I worked hard to earn it!" They see any form of abundance as always due to *their* efforts. They never give any credit to any source outside themselves. This makes them feel superior and powerful, but very isolated and alone.

Whenever people have accepted the beliefs that they are unworthy of love, support, and encouragement, a strange thing happens: even when they are surrounded by abundance, they automatically reject the support that *is* available to them. It also becomes difficult for others to give them any of these offerings in an unconditional or functional way, because they usually don't trust the intentions of the giver. When their belief in *lack* is strong, it is manifested in many ways into their environment, keeping them deeply entrenched in the VPR Cloud and disconnected from every type of support.

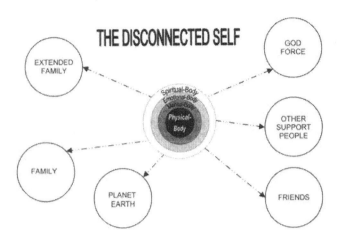

This illustration shows the distance that could have been formed between you and aspects of your natural support systems. The broken lines illustrate how your connections may have been damaged or broken.

Even though your connections with your natural support systems may have been diminished or clouded by the thoughts, feelings, words, or actions of *others*, you may have come to the conclusion that your disconnection was through some fault of *yours* – that there was/is something intrinsically missing in you – a flaw – a lack. This could cause you to believe that you are unworthy of the love, support, and encouragement of the Universe. Also, you may have observed that others were getting what you were not – deepening the belief in your lack of self-worth. You may have assumed that, if you hadn't been *inadequate* in some way, you would have received the same kind of support as those people.

You may have had good reasons to mistrust the people who were your core support system. Family, friends, and others in your environment may have acted inappropriately toward you – causing you pain and imprinting beliefs of separation on your psyche.

Children may also learn that they are disconnected from Mother Earth by watching adults carelessly pollute, by dumping their trash or refusing to recycle. Children learn that they are disconnected from the God Force by dysfunctional religious beliefs about a distant, inaccessible deity that is waiting to punish humanity for every infraction of the "rules." Dysfunctional systems, such as fundamentalist religions and dictatorships, are often held in place by individuals who have a vested interest in maintaining a belief in *personal lack* and *individual unworthiness*; because, unless people hold these two beliefs they don't stay in unhealthy relationships.

Often, children are damaged emotionally when they are ridiculed or rejected by other children. They may believe that they *must* accept abuse from their peers to be included in a group. Children who have been abused or neglected in their home environment are far more likely to accept abuse on the street. Because they haven't learned healthy boundaries in their home environment, it makes them easy targets for bullies. Some of them even join street gangs in an attempt to fit in. However, the gang dynamic is often a replication of the dysfunctional home environment.

The belief in unworthiness creates a false dependency upon people or possessions. This may lead you to believe that you "can't live without" a partner, no matter how they treat you, because you don't deserve love and respect. You may become so attached to a particular lifestyle that you think you can't live without any number of things. These erroneous beliefs are held in place by your unconscious belief in your inadequacy or unworthiness.

How to Release Lack and Unworthiness in Your Life

The easiest way to release your belief in unworthiness is to examine nature. When you look out your window, do you see the sun shining or the rain falling on certain people and not others? There is no discrimination in nature. The sun would be shining, or the rain falling, on the worst criminal or the greatest saint on your street. The only factors that come into play are the perceptions of the individuals. Some people are looking up and appreciating what nature is giving to them, while others are complaining about the same things. The same is true with worthiness. Some people take for granted that they are worthy of the *best* and some people insist they can't have it because they don't deserve it. Their perception of their worthiness is always the product of their conditioning as children.

If you were conditioned to believe that you are unworthy, due to your exposure to unhealthy values, you must rethink that belief by accepting that the God Force does not discriminate. Whatever is available, you have free will to either reject it or accept it – the choice is yours. You have the same ability to create a successful life as everyone else. You just have to consider the possibility that it is available to you. You will then be able to open your mind to the truth that you *are* every bit as worthy of the love, support, and encouragement of the Universe as any other being. If you have learned to believe that you are unworthy, you now can rethink your position. Then you can begin to build the healthy connections as illustrated below.

This illustration shows how we can have healthy connections that overlap the essential components of our

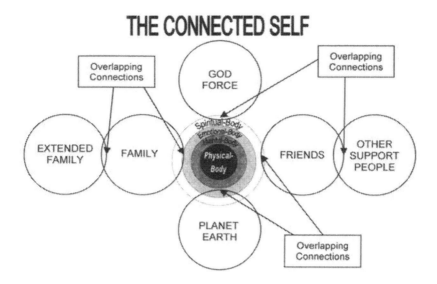

environment. The overlapping areas are solid and strong. They create harmony and balance in every direction, allowing us to experience the love, support, and encouragement of our environments.

To fully release a belief in lack or unworthiness, it is also necessary to understand the nature of the flow of abundance. This is a planet of balance. There is night and day. There is birth and death. What goes up must come down. This is the natural flow of energy. This is the natural flow of the abundance on this planet. What you give out to your environment comes back to you. When you are willing to give from your abundance, you will receive in kind.

There is also a natural energy flow that happens whenever goods or energy are exchanged. When things are flowing naturally, there is an equal amount of energy flowing in both directions. An analogy for this would be when you pour liquid out of a bottle. As the liquid comes out of the bottle, air has to go in to replace it. When the liquid is not flowing naturally, there is some blockage that prevents that flow. The belief in lack and unworthiness is similar to a cork in the bottle that blocks the path of the energy – preventing it from flowing. Your scripts about lack and unworthiness may say, "There is only so much of … and I certainly don't deserve it;" or, "Someone else might need it, so I'd better not accept it;" or, "There is only so much available, so I must grab it quickly before the supply runs out." These are the corks or clouded beliefs that block abundance from flowing freely in your life.

Desire is the awareness of lack. When you want something, you desire it, because you have become aware that there is an unfulfilled need or something in missing in your life. Desire is always increased whenever you have an awareness of scarcity or *lack*. You may have noticed that, whenever you have an abundance of a natural substance, there isn't as much emotion attached to having it: it isn't as appealing as when that substance is scarce. You may even lose your desire for the substance when there is plenty of it.

You may even begin to take it for granted and find that you aren't as interested in it anymore.

When there is an abundance, we are satiated, relaxed, and we experience no sense of lack. This is also true for the many aspects of love, support, and encouragement that a healthy family provides for a child. That natural abundance of attention provides a level of comfort that the child takes for granted. This is missing in dysfunctional families, in which children's natural desires for love, support, and encouragement from their parents and siblings are often stifled or completely blocked. Gradually, children invent substitutions that partially compensate for their lacks, but a strong awareness of the emptiness, which the lack represents, is imprinted on the child's mind and heart.

When this awareness is accompanied by the belief that the lack is due to some intrinsic deficiency or fault of their own, their belief in their unworthiness is born. This belief eventually prevents children, and subsequently adults, from believing that they deserve to have *any* of their needs met.

Whenever your wants or needs are accompanied by the self-limiting beliefs of lack or unworthiness, you will act in one of the following ways:

1. You will put your desires on hold and dream that perhaps your dreams will magically manifest someday – without any effort on your part.

2. You will assume that you aren't worthy of having your desire, so you change your focus to an addiction – try to substitute an addiction for the original desire and settle for second best.

3. Or, you will push past your self-limiting beliefs and their accompanying scripts, and take the necessary steps to achieve the specific end result that will satisfy your true desire.

You now have the opportunity to rethink the beliefs that you have learned about scarcity and lack, and replace those beliefs with the light of truth from your Spiritual-Body. If you are able to do this, soon your patterns of relating to your environment will change, allowing the abundance to flow freely into your life. A healthy state of worthiness is the ability to accept the abundance of the Universe without any resistance or limitation.

Loneliness

Loneliness is a very common component in the lives of people who live in every position of the VPR Cloud. Loneliness is a natural by-product of dysfunctional family environments. Whenever children are consistently neglected by the people to whom they look for sustenance, shelter, or support, they soon learn to believe that they can't trust anyone, so they feel disconnected. Consequently, when they go out into the world, they naturally assume that no one will offer them the love, support, and encouragement that they need. They have learned to believe in separation and disconnection from other people, Mother Earth, and the God Force.

Victims experience loneliness, because they have learned to believe that no one loves or cares about them, from past experiences. They may have learned to believe that their needs are not being met, because they are stupid, bad, ugly, worthless – inadequate in some way. They have learned these lies from observing the inappropriate reactions and behaviours of people in their environments. They then assume that everyone else will, of course, agree with their perception of their inadequacy. They conclude that no one will love them for themselves, so they automatically reject any overtures of friendship, because it would be necessary to rethink their perceptions of themselves.

Unfortunately, when we believe that we are worthless, others often treat us that way. We create what we believe to be true, especially if our beliefs are unconscious. Therefore, victims usually attract other unhealthy people who are willing to keep them in the clouded thinking of the victim state of mind.

Persecutors frequently experience loneliness, because they become adept at running abusive scripts to control others; so, healthy people stay away from them. The only people who will associate with them are still playing by the rules of the VPR Triangle. Persecutors are accustomed to being rejected, because they believe that everyone is out to hurt them. The rejection started when they dared to step outside the bounds of their previous victim position. Their ideas, words, and actions have been labelled as "rebellious" and they were told that it is always *wrong* to "rock the boat."

Eventually, they come to believe that the way to survive is to stay away from people who can't be controlled. They don't want to be rejected again, so they only associate with victims. However, they aren't *actually* connected with the victims, because they know on some level that their victims don't enjoy the association. Persecutors avoid rescuers, because the persecutors know that the rescuers will judge them. Persecutors call rescuers "do-gooders" or meddlers. They become obsessed with a particular set of defensive-mechanisms, until very few new people are allowed to enter their sphere to challenge their protective walls.

Nevertheless, they may join groups of other persecutors such as gangs of bullies to gain some semblance of a peer group. This ploy may keep their false sense of security intact, but it also isolates them from people who could offer alternative solutions.

Rescuers are usually surrounded by victims, because rescuers do such a good job of feeling sorry for others and pretending to *help* them. Rescuers, however, usually experience a deep sense of loneliness – even in a crowd. They seldom achieve the level of support and security that they want and need, because they don't accept support from others. That would make them feel like a victim, in their worldview.

They also have the habit of surrounding themselves with people who expect more from them than they are willing or able to give in return. They often complain, "I do so much for others, but where are they when I need them?" One reason that they are so lonely may be that emotionally healthy people don't want to be treated like victims, so they don't like to associate with rescuer types who offer unsolicited advice.

How to Reduce Loneliness in Your Life

Your loneliness will gradually dissipate as soon as you begin to entertain the idea that you actually *are* connected on different levels. You may realize that some of those connections are already strong and healthy and some of them need further nurturing. As you begin to feel better about yourself, you will attract healthier people who bring with them healthier levels of acceptance and support. Learning to love and accept yourself can be challenging at first, but once you accept your true value, it will become easier. Then, you will be able to appreciate others who may be willing to truly love and accept you.

It is important to note here that it is also common to feel isolated and alone when you initially step out of the VPR Cloud, because the people with whom you have previously associated could choose to stay in that way of being. Also, you are walking on an unknown path. It is important to be patient, however, because this is an adjustment time for you and you may need time to solidify the changes that you have chosen to make in your environments.

If this is where you are at the present time, don't worry. You will soon begin to attract people who have also made that quantum leap in consciousness and you will begin to form new friendships. This is because, as you start to really love yourself, you will begin to attract more loving people. This will gradually become a way of life that will satisfy you in new and healthier ways. However, keep in mind that you probably won't find worthy friendships in the same old environments that you have previously frequented; so you may need to spread your wings and explore new places where people gather. When you begin to practice the tools of loving yourself unconditionally, you will automatically be more receptive to the unconditional love of others.

Resentment

Resentment is experienced by people who live in every position of the VPR Cloud. Resentment is often the awareness that life is not meeting your expectations. It is usually a build-up of your own angry energy, because you realize that you have allowed someone to control you; or a by-product of unsuccessful attempts to control other people or situations.

People who don't feel capable of making healthy decisions, often use control tactics to get what they want or need, or they may give away their power to others in the hope (perhaps unfounded) of receiving what they want and need. If either is the case in your life, you will feel resentment often, because you will probably find that other people will not always comply with your wishes, or you will blame them for taking away your right to choose.

Resentment is also the by-product of the script that it is "a good thing" to sacrifice ourselves to the wishes of others. This script has created the tendency in our society to revere martyrs. They are set upon a pedestal, because others, who are still living in the VPR Cloud, are looking for a hero/rescuer. Resentment is the most common emotional reaction to martyrdom. One of the most unconscious stereotypical martyr roles is the traditional mother position in the family unit. It is common for women in many areas of the world to believe that they have to take on *all* the care and nurturing of a family, without expecting the father to carry his share. They are often expected to be on call twenty-four hours a day, seven days a week, without any time for themselves. When women do a good job of martyring themselves, they are often called "saints." However, they are overburdened and eventually resent their families for the unfair distribution of power. Often when this happens, the mother quickly shifts from one position in the VPR Cloud to another.

The martyr may experience a fleeting moment of the illusion of power and self-importance, because they are "being of service;" but they resent being taken for granted and always resent being the only one who *helps.* They may have been trained to believe that they will *feel better* or be seen as a *good person* by sacrificing themselves; so they suppress any resentment that might arise – but resent they do. They may find that their position as peacemaker is a thankless job, but they seldom question or examine it, because the martyr role has become a crucial part of their identity.

Resentment is always the product of giving away our Personal Power and doing what others say we "should." This will be thoroughly discussed in Chapter 4.

Victims most often experience resentment when people don't rescue them. They always resent persecutors who make their lives miserable. They may also experience resentment when healthier people tell them that they don't have to be victims, or refuse to treat them like victims. In this case, they resent that individual because they don't want any interference. They have used their victim status to draw attention and energy to themselves; and, because they believe that is the only way to stay safe and in control.

Persecutors most often experience resentment when people either refuse to be controlled or try to turn the tables to control them. They have come to believe that they are the only ones who should be in control; so they resent anyone who challenges their position of authority. Also, their expression of resentment may be expressed as exasperation or distain, which will be a form of manipulation – to regain control.

Rescuers most often experience resentment when people challenge their intelligence, skills, superiority, etc., because they have worked so hard to develop those abilities. They expect people to accept their authority, unconditionally and believe in their views and opinions. Consequently, they will resent anyone who questions them or offers alternative solutions to problems.

How to Reduce Resentment in Your Life

The easiest way to let go of resentment is to accept that you have the right to make your own decisions – and so do other people. When others resent you, it is because you have tried to control them. When you resent others, it is usually because you have allowed them to control you by telling you what you "should" do.

If you don't give others your Personal Power, they can't take it. It is useless to blame them when they take it, because most people believe that the only way to be powerful is to take it from other people. Keep in mind that resentment only occurs when you are not being totally in control of your thoughts, feelings, words, and actions.

You may find that, if you look deeply enough, when you are experiencing resentment, you are usually angry with yourself for being unable, or unwilling, to make more appropriate choices and more fully express your Personal

Power. So, if you look beneath your resentment, you may be experiencing the emotional state of powerlessness. Your perception of yourself as powerless is the product of your belief that you are so inadequate that you can't change your environment. When you are so busy resenting and blaming others, you don't give yourself the opportunity to change the direction of your life. When you connect with your Spiritual-Body, you will find the motivation to make healthier choices, and you will experience much less anger and resentment; thus creating a space for self-empowerment.

The Belief That You Need to Control Others

Children who are raised in confusing environments learn unhealthy methods of asking to have their needs met; so they often use control tactics in the form of emotional reactions (such as temper tantrums) to control those in their environment. The script is, "If I yell and scream long enough or loud enough, I will get what I believe I want." The old saying, "Negative attention is better than no attention" applies here. It is important to keep in mind that children who have their needs met in healthy ways, usually do not have to use control dramas or threats to control their environment.

When parents consistently deny their children's requests, children learn to believe that the parents have all the power to control their environments, and, in many cases, this is true. Most dysfunctional families consistently give messages that diminish the intrinsic value of each family member and often belittle or diminish the value of their children's needs.

Therefore, these children gradually begin to believe that, if they wish to have *any* of their needs met, it is necessary to use the same control methods that their parents have used on them. Subsequently, it often becomes necessary for them to use devious methods or manipulation to satisfy their simplest needs. If their needs still aren't adequately satisfied, after all their attempts, they try to find alternative methods of artificially satisfying their needs – through addictions.

Victims have learned to believe that their choices are very limited. They usually believe that they don't deserve to have their needs met at all, but they continually hope that their misery will inspire others to give them a few crumbs. They seldom do anything to improve their situation, however, because they assume that they are unworthy to have their needs met.

Victims constantly experience lack of control. This is due mainly, because as children, they didn't learn how to think independently or learn appropriate ways to solve their problems. Therefore, they believe the lie that other people have all the power – but they don't have any. They usually believe that there is an external power (a force such as a god or a devil) that is "out to get them" – to prevent them from having what they want. They seldom take responsibility for having created the difficult situations they find themselves in. They usually create excuses or find a scapegoat – something or someone to blame for their difficulties.

Victims also control others by pretending to be helpless or fragile. They react emotionally to so many different stimuli that the people around them are conditioned to "walk on eggshells." This defensive-mechanism may have been successful in the past to maintain some semblance of safety, so they continue to utilize it; however they don't realize that it also keeps them in the prison of the victim state of mind.

Persecutors fight against any system that tries to control them, but they are also very capable of using control and manipulation to get what *they* want. They might use anything, from sarcasm, to verbal or physical abuse to get their way. They may walk away from a situation in frustration, if they aren't able to control other people, but persecutors will usually give the impression that they are rejecting the others because they are *wrong*.

If people want to be accepted by persecutors, they must be willing, on some level, to take the abuse of being dictated to. If they don't want to continue to be controlled, they must be brave enough to risk a persecutor's rejection by giving him or her honest feedback. It will, of course, immediately change the relationship dynamic and may even terminate the relationship.

Rescuers control others in much more subtle ways. They have learned techniques that are designed to gain the confidence of others. They are very polite and diplomatic and try to be non-threatening with their manipulation. They have learned to *pretend* to be very *helpful*, but the information they give is always disempowering – instead of actually being helpful. It is specifically designed to manipulate the point of power toward the rescuer, rather than to encourage others to think about their choices or solve their own problems.

If an individual makes a stand and expresses an original thought in the presence of a rescuer, the result will usually be a put-down of the idea. Any original idea, clarity, or solution threatens the clouded perceptions within the VPR Cloud and the individuals who are addicted to playing by its rules. Rescuers may see a chance to twist their own fear of change into a "gentle" warning to the person with the original thought. This is designed to control others and keep them within the "safe" limits of the VPR Cloud.

How to Reduce the Need to Control in Your Life

People who believe that they have the right to control others are still playing by the rules that have been established within the VPR Cloud. The best way to stop wasting your time trying to control others is to focus your attention on building your own life and living according to your integrity. The best way to stop the control that comes from others is to step out of the VPR Cloud and become fully conscious of your ability to make healthy choices and develop healthy boundaries.

People who set themselves up on pedestals of power are so busy maintaining their false persona of authority and finding ways to control others that they seldom have time to examine their own thinking and behaviour. This addiction to control is a defensive-mechanism to avoid personal responsibility. Also, the temporary *high* that they get from that moment of power becomes their addiction of choice.

Your own thoughts, feelings, words, and actions are the only things that you have the power to control. Therefore, if you wish to let go of your addiction to control, you must realize that you have no right to anyone else's life. If you wish to have full power within your own life, you must start by realizing that others have no right to *your* life. Therefore, the opinions of others may have nothing to do with you – they may be totally irrelevant to you. They are simply their opinions! Whenever others express their opinions to you, you don't have to agree with them. However, you must respect their right to their opinions, if you want them to respect yours. Subsequently, when you respect the opinions and choices of others, you don't waste time trying to change or control them.

If you are filling your own needs in appropriate ways, you will have no need to manipulate or control others. The people, who wish to be with you, will be with you; and you will be with the people you wish to be with. This doesn't mean that you won't try to change your circumstances or be unconcerned with the rest of humanity, but you will take responsibility for how you create your circumstances and you will take every opportunity to learn from your experiences.

Unfounded Hope

Hope springs eternal in the minds of individuals suffering in the VPR Cloud. Hope for a better tomorrow that includes creative action is healthy; unfounded hope is not. People who believe that they must "never give up hope," even though there is no real evidence that their hope will ever be satisfied, create a confusing environment of unproductive, wishful thinking and waste a great deal of time – "wishin' and hopin' and prayin' " – as the old song goes.

The illusions that are created when we focus on unfounded hope can become so "real" that we can't see the issues in our own reality. This prevents us from being creative and seeing other, more practical solutions to our challenges. Because unfounded hope can't satisfy us, it keeps us prisoners of addictive habits and unhealthy beliefs.

A common example of unfounded hope is when one partner is consistently doing something, such as being inconsiderate, neglectful, or unfaithful to the other, and the person who is being neglected or betrayed keeps hoping that his or her partner will change, even though the partner has shown no willingness to do so.

Victims, persecutors, and rescuers all live in a constant state of unfounded hope. It is a main ingredient in the lives of all addicts and co-dependents. It is based on the belief that there must be something, somewhere that could change their environment, so the challenges in their lives will magically disappear. It is true that there is "something, somewhere;" but it can't be found within the clouded perceptions of the VPR Triangle.

How to Reduce Unfounded Hope in Your Life

If you wish to reduce or release unfounded hope from your life, you must be willing to step outside the VPR Cloud and allow the light of truth from your Spiritual-Body to penetrate your thinking processes – by internalizing original, self-nurturing, self-empowering thoughts, feelings, words, and actions. When you let go of unfounded hope, you have the opportunity to look at the reality of any situation, logically. When you find yourself hoping that other people will change, ask the following questions:

1. Have they expressed any desire to change?

2. Have they made any movement in a new direction?

3. Have they made any commitment to that change?

4. Have they actually made any changes?

Also, you might ask yourself the following questions about your behaviour:

1. Have I clearly asked to have my needs met?

2. Are my goals realistic/attainable?

3. Have I made a firm commitment to achieve my goals?

4. Have I taken steps to make changes in my life?

If the answer is no to any of these questions, hope for change is probably unfounded. Creative hope includes belief in your abilities, the commitment to transform yourself, and an action plan to achieve your goals. Without a realistic goal, an attainable plan of action, and a firm commitment to do whatever you need to do to achieve your goal, unfounded hope is a waste of time and energy. Goal setting, planning, commitment, and action are necessary for healthy changes to take place.

Insecurity

Insecurity is simply the belief that we are not safe and that we are not capable of coping with the challenges in our environments. It is the natural by-product of all fearful reactions to our environments. It is quite different from the natural reaction of wariness whenever we are exploring new territories. While we are experiencing insecurity, we lose our connection with our Personal Power, so we can't access our creativity to make healthier choices. We lose touch with the people in our environments, the God Force, or Mother Earth. While we are experiencing this disconnected state of mind, it causes us to be afraid of the possible outcome of every situation. Because we feel so isolated and alone, we move into the victim state and feel hopeless and helpless.

Insecurity can take many forms and has many labels, dependant upon in which area we are experiencing insecurity. Jealousy is the most common form of insecurity. We may compare our lives with others and become jealous of their accomplishments. We may focus our attention on what they have that we don't – causing us to believe that we are inadequate or inferior to them. We may be jealous of the attention others receive – causing us to withdraw or act in pushy or aggressive ways to gain attention. If we are insecure in a relationship, we may feel that something is missing – that our needs are not being met due to some fault of our own – even if we haven't asked. So, we may feel jealous when our partner gives any attention to another person, or when he or she exhibits any signs of independence.

Insecure people usually believe that everyone else is *better* than they are in some way. People who are insecure about money may be nervous, worried, or concerned about any changes in the economy. People who are insecure about their looks may spend excessive amounts of time and money to make themselves look more attractive. They may go on crash diets to lose weight or try to compensate with food and gain tremendous amounts of weight; either extreme will serve to make them more insecure and diminish their self-worth.

When you are insecure about your physical environment, you naturally believe that there is not *enough* to go around. You may be afraid that someone will take away (steal) something from you or you may be afraid of disease or disaster. You might be afraid that your partner would prefer to be with another, because you are "not good enough;" or, that your boss would prefer a better employee; or, that your children would be better off with a more perfect mother or father. Every insecure thought reinforces your fearful pattern of relating to your *unsafe* environment.

How to Reduce Insecurity in Your Life

Whenever you are in an insecure state of mind, such as experiencing the belief that you are "unsafe," "out of control," "inadequate," "inferior," or "vulnerable," you are actually living in a state of *disconnection* – from yourself, others, the God Force, or Mother Earth. Therefore, the best way to move out of your insecure state is to take the necessary time to reconnect. Use your logical mind to assess your *actual* human connections. Think about all the people that you associate with on a regular basis. Think about the people that you care for, and the people who care for you. Make a list of the people with whom you could connect more fully, if you were to make the effort. This will allow you to be more cognizant of your human connections.

Moving out of your insecure state may take a conscious effort to resolve core issues in your life. You may need to find a competent mentor or counsellor to hold the light of truth for you. You may need to learn how to stop comparing your life with the lives of others. You may need to realize that you can only bring to the table what you have to offer and that others can only do the same.

Adopt an attitude of gratitude for your connections. Remind yourself moment-by-moment that you are in the right place at all times for your highest good. Pay attention to the unexpected treasures that happen, such as a smile from a stranger, or better yet, a loved one; or an unsolicited gift of love, support, or encouragement from others. Pay attention to the natural gifts that are given to you on a daily basis, such as when you find a beautiful flower; hear the song of a bird; feel a cool breeze on a hot day; the warmth of the sun on a cold day; or observe how the night sky allows you to see the stars and rest quietly in the darkness.

Take time to meditate. When you take time to get to know your higher connections, you will find that gradually your sense of disconnection will lessen. When you are going through a difficult time, remind yourself that it is just your *perception* that you are alone or vulnerable; you are still a divine-spark and your connection with the God Force cannot be broken. Even though you may be walking through a terrifying situation, you are still connected in many ways – physically, mentally, emotionally, and spiritually. Call on those connections and trust them to the best of your ability. Each time you do, your feelings of connectedness will increase.

When you trust your connection with your Spiritual-Body, Mother Earth, and the God Force, and you follow the guidance of those connections, you will be able to carefully choose which other people and situations to trust. You can then relax and trust that everything happening in your life is *right* and *good* for you in some way.

All addictions are attempts to bring about a sense of security; however, addictions only give us a false sense of momentary comfort that simply distracts us from our sensations of insecurity. Our addictions also inhibit our ability to change and grow, because they postpone the healing process and squander precious time and energy that could be used more wisely.

If you make a commitment to heal your addictions and you want your clouds to be penetrated with the light of your truth, it is necessary to be totally honest about the subtle energies that cause every addiction. False security is one of those subtle energies. There are many addictions that are commonly used to create false security.

In today's society, money is one of the most common measures of security. Traditionally, men were the "bread winners" *rescuing* the family from *lack*. Women previously took on a more submissive role, being dependent upon a mate for financial security. This dependence may have, at one time, led to a sensation of security for both partners; because the "bread winner" could count on "the wife" to support him/her in making a comfortable home environment. In our present culture, however, it is often necessary for both partners to work outside the home to achieve their chosen lifestyle. Many females have learned to believe in their own value and don't want to forfeit their dreams for an illusion of security; however, those raised in confusing or unsupportive environments may still believe that they *need* another person to provide financial security and safety.

The fear of loss of financial security often keeps people in unhealthy relationships. In an affluent income bracket, fear of downsizing the family home, selling the summer cottage, or giving up a luxury car may keep people living in toxic environments. For others without the same financial resources, it may be the fear of being unable to find shelter, food, or protection. In both of these cases, there is a belief that it is *safer* to remain in their *familiar* setting, even though it is unhealthy, instead of taking a risk and beginning a new life. This decision is often based upon fear of the unknown and scripts about their inadequacy or low self-worth.

Another root of false security is the belief in materialism – the more *things* you have, the more secure you are *supposed to* feel. Marketing techniques are designed to appeal to people who want to *appear* successful and secure. In reality, the purchase of non-essential items usually leaves them feeling emptier. The purchases of these *things* are attempts to deflect their attention away from their clouds; however, the desperate feeling of emotional lack can't be filled by material possessions.

The drive for material goods has led to technological advances that are designed to enhance our lives and help us feel more secure. The need for external security is always based in fear. A confusing environment helps perpetuate fear by designing security systems to protect us. Mass media supports this fear of abuse by bombarding us with images of violence and crime. People carry cell phones in fear of some sort of emergency. It is now common for Global Positioning Systems (GPS) to be inserted in vehicles as a navigational device while others purchase them to give them the illusion of safety and security. All these so-called security measures are based in fear – and the solutions are a form of false security.

While it is true that computers have opened up vast amounts of information and have greatly increased levels and convenience of communication, they have also created other problems. Sometimes, they are used to serve humanity; other times, they are used to control humanity and free will is stifled. Many people are becoming more and more dependent upon the internet and emails to connect with other people; while others have become disconnected from society by hiding behind a computer screen. This has created the illusion of connection, when, in reality, it creates more disconnection and isolation.

To create a complete sense, instead of a false sense, of security, it is necessary to build inner security. When we are honest about what we want and what we expect in our lives, we will lay the foundation to become balanced within our Total-Selves. When we are honest about what we want in relationships, we have the potential to build more solid ones – ones that are based on honesty and integrity. When we have inner security that is based on the belief that we are always provided for in the way that is in our highest good, we will never want for anything, because our lives will be filled with abundance. Abundance isn't based upon material wealth or the acquisition of goods. It is based upon the belief that we have the inner resources to create a secure, loving environment, in which all or our needs will be met.

Emotions Specific to Each Position

There are some emotions that are most commonly experienced in a specific position in the VPR Cloud. These are defined in the lists below. However, there is some overlay in all of the emotional reactions, because the people who live by the rules of the VPR Cloud often feed off each other's emotions.

All persecutors and rescuers were once victims. Therefore, many of the emotions in the victim position are also frequently experienced by people who live in the persecutor and rescuer positions. Nevertheless, victims don't usually experience many of the emotions that are experienced by the persecutors and rescuers, because they haven't yet moved into those emotional ranges.

Emotions Specific to the Victim State of Mind

Self-Pity	Depression
Unhealthy Remorse	Lack of Control
Unworthy	Disappointment
Despair	Self-Critical
Low Self-Esteem	Helpless
Hopeless	Powerless
Needy	Envy
Inadequate	

Self-Pity, Helplessness, Hopelessness, Inadequacy, Powerlessness

Self-pity is the emotional state that is most frequently experienced by people who live in the victim position. It is experienced to a much lesser degree by persecutors and rescuers, because they are much more creative and tend to project blame for most situations toward someone or something outside themselves. Self-pity is a natural result of living in the victim state of mind, because victims believe that they have no choices and are *never* going to get out of the mess they are in.

Victims wallow in self-pity and believe suffering to be their lot in life. It is actually a form of self-flagellation and it reinforces their sense of worthlessness. Self-pity is a state of mind that is very closely linked with helplessness, hopelessness, and inadequacy. These emotional reactions are a logical progression, because victims believe the scripts saying that they aren't good enough, or capable enough, to deserve a better life. These scripts create more self-pity.

Self-pity becomes a *normal* way of processing the victim's perception of reality, but it wastes time and energy that could be used to make healthier decisions – decisions that could lessen stress and create the potential for change. Self-pity is a reinforcement and reaffirmation of powerlessness. It creates a downward spiral of emotional pain. It is designed to evoke sympathy and guilt in others with the hope that someone will offer assistance. Consequently, a victim will automatically see any individual who offers assistance as a potential rescuer. However, those who don't offer the type of assistance that victims want are usually seen as persecutors.

The best way to reduce self-pity is to count your blessings. While you are engaged in the victim state, there is no opportunity to become creative; so by turning your attention away from what you don't have, to what you do have, you will automatically shift your state. The next step is to determine what you *actually* want and engage your creativity to set achievable goals to attain your desire. As you work toward achieving your desires, you won't waste your time in unproductive activities and gradually, you will feel that you are accomplishing something worthwhile. Your success will become your new focus.

Disappointment and Despair

Disappointment and despair are the natural by-products of unrealized or unrealistic expectations, fear, anxiety, worry, and the addiction to control. Disappointment may be present when people don't fully comply with our wishes. This is natural when we have set our minds and hearts on attaining a specific goal. When we are unable to achieve that end result, we are disappointed; however, different people process disappointment very differently.

People who were raised in unhealthy environments seldom had their needs met in appropriate ways. Consequently, disappointment was a constant in their early years. They were programmed to believe in specific solutions to every situation, so they expect specific outcomes *IF* they play by the rules that support the VPR Cloud. When people in their environment don't comply with those rules, it confuses them. They seldom have sufficient problem solving skills to adjust to a different way of thinking or behaving that would allow them to solve their dilemmas.

Victims often perceive disappointments as a punishment from an unfair person or Higher Power. They wallow in self-flagellation and self-pity, because they don't allow their disappointments to change their thinking, engage their creativity, or accept responsibility for the process that has caused an undesirable result. Subsequently, they may find ways to punish others for not complying with their whims, but they seldom alter their approach to create a different end result.

All expectations have the potential for disappointment and frustration, because every person in our environments has free will. We can't control them. When we disrespect the tastes and preferences of others, we will always be disappointed. When we are closed-minded enough to demand that other people comply with our tastes and preferences, it is not only unreasonable, it is unhealthily selfish.

If you accept responsibility for your part in the creation of every situation, you will use it as a learning experience. If you respect the choices of others, you will accept their right to choose what they contribute to each situation. If you like what others share or contribute, you will be in harmony with them. If you don't appreciate what others share or contribute, you can either work to change your perception or judgment of them, or you can choose to be with other more like-minded individuals.

You may be disappointed, because life hasn't given you what you believe you want. Many people live their entire lives wishing that they could be different. If they are short, they want to be tall. If they are dark, they want to be fair. If they have curly hair, they want straight hair. If they are poor, they want to be rich. The list is endless. This kind of disappointment is not only unrealistic; it is a waste of precious time and energy.

When you fully accept the idea that you have chosen to be on this planet, at this time and in these circumstances, to learn valuable lessons and fulfill a purpose, you will be more fully in your Personal Power, capable of growth, and able to accomplish your goals. Situations arise constantly that give you opportunities to explore new realms of consciousness. Sometimes the adventure is pleasant, and sometimes it is not. If you see each new situation as a learning experience, your life becomes a continual adventure, so you won't be focused on what you don't have.

If you find that you feel disappointed on a consistent basis, you may need to ask yourself whether you have unrealistic expectations of others, or what it is that your environment is trying to tell you. If you don't observe the natural feedback coming toward you and you ignore the messages that are offered, eventually you may be overwhelmed by disappointment and despair. Life is too short to be wasted on unrealistic wishes. Consciously living in the lesson of the present moment places your focus and perspective into your place of Personal Power – your alignment with your integrity. You then have the power to choose differently in the future.

Depression

People who are living in the victim state of mind are very susceptible to bouts of depression, because of their inability to sift and sort their reactions to their environment in healthy ways. They are constantly anxious, worried, or concerned about the choices of others. They worry about how other people's choices will affect their environment – whether their environment will change or become threatening to them. They seldom adequately process their emotions, because they haven't learned how to cope with the issues/triggers that cause stress in their lives. They perceive chaotic or confusing experiences as adding to their "pit of despair" in which they have no options. They are seldom capable of making choices, other than the ones that they have previously made. Consequently, they have many unresolved triggers that further their misery.

Depression is the accumulation of unresolved emotional reactions. When you don't completely resolve an issue, you keep it stored in your "box of stuff" from the past and you believe that you can't change your situation – making you feel hopeless and helpless. When you carry your "box of stuff" along with you, and keep adding to it, until the box is bulging at the sides, you will naturally become overpowered by it. This overwhelming chaos is called "depression."

Unfortunately, a very self-limiting and self-destructive addiction has become a common way to deal with depression – that is the use of antidepressants. It is thought that those pills will "make you feel better." That isn't true. (See the illustration on page 38 The Cycle of Addictions.) There is adequate scientific research to prove that antidepressants work no better than placebos (sugar pills). Unfortunately, antidepressants cause many serious side effects that the placebos don't. The saddest part of the addiction to antidepressants is the number of young children who are being taught to numb their emotions with medication. The use of antidepressants for young children has more than doubled in the last few years.

The idea that you should avoid your issues is irresponsible at best. The use of a pill to "numb the pain in your brain" is no different than the use of alcohol or illegal drugs. However, many people resort to escaping their reality, because they have been influenced to believe that that is the best way. We only have to research the statistics of the number of violent episodes, murders, and suicides that are directly linked to the use of antidepressants to understand how dangerous they are. (If you are presently on medication and you wish to wean yourself off or stop your medication, it may be necessary to seek professional help.)

The best way to start on the pathway out of depression is by resolving one issue at a time. When you shift to the perception that you *may* be able to find a solution to a problem, you engage your creativity and this attitudinal shift usually leads to a solution, or at least, to a new way of coping with the challenges in your life.

Emotions Specific to the Persecutor State of Mind

Rebelliousness	Defensiveness
Competitiveness	Judgmental
Hostile	Critical of others
Impatient	Greedy
Need Control	Disappointment
Misunderstood	Capable of Dominating Others

Rebelliousness

Feeling rebellious is a natural state for persecutors. They rebel against any association with victim consciousness. It is good that they are no longer a victim; but, when they become persecutors, instead of moving directly out of the VPR Cloud into their Personal Power, they remain inside the VPR Prison. In the persecutor position, they live in fear that they will become a victim again, so they become an aggressor.

This aggression often builds in persecutors, until it becomes inner rage that they use as a weapon to appear as if they are in control of the people in their environment. Persecutors want to give the impression that they are more powerful than anyone in their world. They alter their personality by wearing a macho mask – acting, dressing, walking, and talking differently than before – to give the impression that no one can "push them around."

Dysfunctional families often excessively restrict children who become rebellious in an effort to prevent them from breaking away from dysfunctional patterns within the VPR

Cloud – the established "order" of their culture. Whenever a person moves out of victim consciousness into the persecutor or rescuer roles, it always entails some sort of rebelliousness. Healthy rebelliousness is your soul calling you out of the clouded thinking of the VPR Triangle.

Therefore, not all rebels are persecutors. It is the *intent* of the rebel that determines whether or not they are trying to control others through their rebelliousness. The difference is: if your intent is to stop external control, so you can have Personal Power in your life, you might be justified in rebelling. If your intent is to take control over others, your rebelliousness will have a different flavour. For example: If you have previously been bullied at work and you now stop responding to the control tactics of the bully, this would be a form of healthy rebelliousness. If you begin to aggressively take control over the other people in your workplace, you are a persecutor.

Sometimes persecutors get in the habit of rebelling against everything. If you find yourself automatically rejecting the ideas of others, you may have allowed rebelliousness to become a way of life. This may have become your defensive-mechanism to prevent others from controlling you, but it can limit your growth and prevent you from finding and expressing your highest potential. You could be "cutting off your nose to spite your face," as it prevents you from seeing the opportunities that are offered to you from your environment.

People, who are still living in the VPR Cloud, might even call *you* rebellious when you are no longer willing to play the game of life their way. So, some rebelliousness may be necessary if you wish to stretch and grow. When you view your creativity and the expression of your creativity as healthy rebelliousness, this may even release the guilt that was previously used to control you whenever you didn't conform.

Defensiveness

Defensiveness is a reaction to a perceived threat. People who live in the persecutor state of mind often have what is called a "chip on their shoulder." It is also what persecutors hope will be a "scary mask" that they hope will protect them. They lash out at anyone who challenges their authority. They hope that their display of aggression will stop any challenges that could potentially undermine their fragile position, so they are protecting their fragile hold on their territory.

They may actually believe that they are defending the progress that they have made out of their previous victim state of mind. Unfortunately, they believe that it is essential to protect their new way of being with defensive-mechanisms. Their values and beliefs are so fragile that they very quickly jump on anyone who challenges their new way of coping with their environment.

The refusal to comply with the wishes of others is often a necessary step out of the structure of the victim consciousness; however, there are many ways to resist their control, other than defensiveness. For example: If someone says something that is offensive to you, something designed to put you down or criticize your decisions, it may be important that you tell them in no uncertain terms that they do not have the right to control you. This may be an important step in regaining your Personal Power; however you can do it in a clear, inoffensive way. You might say, "Thank you for your suggestion; but I have decided to do it this way." You don't even have to give a reason, if you don't want to. But, if you do, you might say, "because it makes sense to me" or, "it makes me happy."

Competitiveness

Persecutors become competitive because they see the possibility of gaining "an edge" in their intended "power grab." The accompanying aggression, hostility, defensiveness, criticism, and judgments are a natural outcome of their shift in focus. Instead of believing, as victims do, that there is no way out, persecutors believe that they are the only ones who can rise above the old way. This type of creativity can be somewhat beneficial, because they begin to consider alternative solutions; however, persecutors often get stuck in dysfunctional patterns by "doing unto others what others have done unto them." They move into the "alpha-dog mentality." Once they perceive a weakness in their opponent, they quickly pounce to take advantage of their "edge."

To move out of the VPR Cloud, it is necessary to be creative enough to stop competing with anyone! There is no other being on this planet exactly like you, with the same qualities, personality traits, talents and abilities, or interests. Acknowledging your unique place and purpose, and valuing your unique contribution to this planet, lifts you out of the desire to compete with any other being.

Emotions Specific to the Rescuer State of Mind

Superiority	Arrogance
Disrespect	Fatalism
Critical of Others	Judgmental
Highly Skilled	Self-Sacrificing
Overly Sensitive to Others	Self-Righteous
Need to Control	Capable of Controlling Others

Superiority, Arrogance, and Disrespect

Rescuers pretend that they are superior to *everyone* in their circle of influence. They set themselves *above* others, because they have become skilled in certain control tactics and have gained a sense of superiority. Rescuers have worked hard to become skilled in the rules of the VPR Cloud; therefore, they believe that it is their job/duty to look out for others who are *beneath* them or *less fortunate*.

When we set ourselves *above* others, we lose sight of their divinity, but we also lose our connection with our own divinity. We have also lost our true connection with others, our appreciation of what they have to offer, so they can't teach us what they know.

Because rescuers set themselves above others, they believe that they are justified in being disrespectful, so it is acceptable behaviour to discredit or diminish others. They also believe that it is their *right* to prevent others from exploring something new, because they are "just preventing those people from making mistakes."

It is always arrogant and disrespectful to try to take responsibility for the choices of others. It is an illusion to pretend that one person can be responsible for the thoughts, feelings, words, or actions of another. When we are focused on analyzing what others are thinking, trying to figure out why they are reacting in a certain way, or manipulating them into thinking, speaking, and acting the way we want them to, we have no room in our minds for genuine honesty with, or responsibility for, our own thoughts, feelings, words, or actions.

To move out of the belief in superiority and the resulting disrespect, it is necessary to understand that we are all "special" in our own unique way. We all have gifts to present to the world, our own brand of genius. Just because a person is lacking in knowledge in one specific area, doesn't mean that they can't have a major contribution to make in another.

Self-Righteousness

Rescuers present themselves as self-righteous, so they can dupe others into believing that the rescuer has greater value than others. They are proud of the fact that they are highly skilled in living by the rules and scripts of the VPR Cloud. They have learned many techniques to become competent within its structure. They experience an artificial type of security within the perimeters of the VPR dynamic, so they are eager to keep others in it also.

Because rescuers have learned that there is only one solution to every problem area, their self-righteousness soon develops into advice-giving or preaching about the validity of that solution. Unfortunately, their perception has become so narrowed that they have "tunnel vision," so they have to constantly expand their creativity to find new ways to convince others that their solutions will work. Unfortunately, what they suggest is actually a defensive-mechanism that they have learned in an effort to keep them safe, or, a projection of what they believe *they* would like to have or do, if *they* were in the other person's position.

We constantly see people on news reports who have been violent toward other people, simply because they believe that those people are wrong or bad or inferior in some way. We have seen how white people were violent toward black or native people, erroneously believing that the colour of skin was enough to judge people as inferior. We have seen protestors bombing abortion clinics due to their self-righteousness about saving the lives of foetuses, but not caring about the lives of the people who work in those clinics.

We have seen people of one religion killing people of other religions, because they believe that those people are wrong in their beliefs. We have seen reports of men trying to control what women are allowed to wear and do, because they use the words in some ancient text to define their beliefs. We have also seen heterosexuals claiming that it is "a sin" to be homosexual, bisexual, or transgendered, by using words in other ancient texts to define their beliefs.

It is very common for these self-righteous people to selectively choose parts of the text from their source, taking it out of context or forgetting to mention the other parts that would make their claims seem ridiculous. They often reject the rest of the message and distort the overall message, just to prove their point and support their prejudices. Their self-righteousness is usually a defensive-mechanism, because they are threatened by the diversity of other ways of being. They don't want to think of the possibility that those differences have value. Perhaps, they have never met a person of a different race or sexual orientation and they have learned prejudices about how those people would hurt them in some way; so rescuers try to maintain the status quo.

They don't consider the fact that their beliefs haven't really satisfied them, nor have they resolved anything. They continue to feel isolated and alone, because they are being judgmental toward others. They continue to preach that judgmental information to anyone who will listen, because they want to feel important, and they want to validate their position in life. They feel self-righteous, because they are protecting the boundaries of the VPR Triangle; and they think that is a good thing.

Fatalism

The belief in fatalism is a very important ingredient in the VPR Cloud. Fatalism is based on predetermination – the belief that there is an external power that has predetermined the outcome of everything. People who believe in fatalism believe that an external force has made the rules with which we must comply. And of course, the rules are the same rules that hold together the VPR Cloud. The script says, "It has always been this way. So, that's the way life will always be. I have no choices in life, so neither do you."

Rescuers are so convinced in the validity of their role in the VPR Cloud that they say, "My parents/society/God wants me to be this way, so this is the way I have to be." Rescuers perpetuate unhealthy scripts by saying, "Everything will turn out the way it is supposed to;" or, "There is simply nothing anyone can do about it." It is the internalization of these restrictive scripts that perpetuates a belief in the VPR Cloud. These clichés are the tools of the trade for rescuers. Fatalism holds people in the prison of unhealthy thinking and behaviour, because there is no hope for positive change.

The main problem with the belief in fatalism is that we cut off all connection with our creativity and our personal responsibility. If we believe in fatalism, we can do nothing to influence our environment, so we also think that we are not responsible for our thoughts, feelings, words, or actions. We think that we are not accountable; but that is not true. By believing that everything is predetermined by an outside force, we limit ourselves and feel like "a puppet on a string." When we believe in a limited Universe, we limit our potential.

When we believe in an unlimited Universe, we have no limits; our potential has no boundaries except those that are self-inflicted. As soon as we move out of the clouded perceptions of the VPR Triangle, we begin to explore the Personal Power that is inherent in our Spiritual-Bodies. We are then able to let go of our self-inflicted limitations and reconnect with the Source of our being – the God Force.

Overly Sensitive to Others

Many adults, who are very sensitive to the emotions of others, learned this skill as small children. Because their environment was often unsafe, they learned that it was wise to keep their antennas up to be constantly on guard against danger. These children become very sensitive to the emotions of others, carefully gauging the mood of those around them to determine whether they should just keep very quiet, or if it would be better to hide or run away. Because they haven't been taught how to have healthy boundaries, they are often deeply affected by the thoughts, moods, or attitudes of others – subtle energies.

This unsafe environment caused them to stay focused on the external stimuli coming from the people who were close to them. These children were so intelligent that they learned the rules and scripts of the VPR Triangle at a very early age. They realized that it was no fun to act like a victim, so they soon became persecutors. They found that role to be even less fun, so they quickly moved into the rescuer role and found ways of caring for and pleasing others. These children often become parents to their most unhealthy parent – usually the one who is playing the victim role. They have turned their intuitive skills toward others to *help* them, but the way they are *helping* them is by keeping them firmly entrenched in the VPR Cloud.

As these people grew up, they concluded that the only way they could be safe was to control their external world, so they became adept at rescuing others and fixing their lives. They don't want to, or perhaps they don't know how to, deal with the natural stress that occurs in their environment, so their pattern of controlling everyone else seems to be the best solution. Gradually, controlling the others in their environment becomes their main goal in life.

Instead of staying focused on their own thoughts, feelings, words, and actions, and expecting others to do the same, some of them developed a defensive-mechanism that was designed to control everyone in their environment. They pretend to be *helping* others, but in reality, they are doing this so *they* can feel safe in the rescuer position. Unfortunately, they don't realize that by controlling everyone else, they are actually reinforcing the energy of the VPR Cloud and keeping themselves prisoners of it.

Many very sensitive children take their self-protection to the next level. They learn to anticipate what will happen by learning how to read the signs that will lead up to an explosive or dangerous episode. They learn to predict the behaviour of the people in their environment. Because they are aware of the dangerous nature of their environment, they learn the four D's of dysfunctional families – how to duck, diffuse, divert, and deny.

These children begin to be known for their predictions, because they are so clever in avoiding difficult situations. These talents are often called psychic abilities and are, in some cases, applauded; in other cases, punished. However, because their intuition is so finely tuned, they are more likely to be wounded by the more subtle energy dynamics in the family environment. Therefore, they are also learning to be constantly on guard or fearful of criticism, judgment, rejection, abandonment, and all forms of physical, mental, emotional, and spiritual abuse.

In some cases, their fine-tuned sensitivities may lead them to being judged as *too* sensitive in the eyes of the people in their environment. It is usually the very insensitive people, or the ones who are totally engrossed in their addictions, who make this type of judgment call; but the end result is usually that these "special" children learn that there is something "wrong" with them. Their connection with their Spiritual-Body is diminished through this abuse.

Several different types of people would have a vested interest in stifling the sensitivities of such children. If such children know, ahead of time, that bullies or persecutors are going to attack them, they can be somewhere else. They will know how to hide or protect themselves in some way. If a parent or teacher, for example, wants to control them, the authority figure wouldn't appreciate it if the child were smart enough to be somewhere else. When children are able to tell when someone is lying, they are a threat to dishonest people. Therefore, many people try to stifle these talents for their own convenience, or out of selfishness, or the simple desire to be in control at all times.

Gradually, the natural intelligence and intuitive abilities of such children may be stifled or diminished by others in their environment, so they quickly learn the rules of the VPR Cloud to survive. They learn to hide their natural abilities behind a dysfunctional script, such as, "I'm crazy. I don't know anything. It's impossible to know what is going to happen;" or, "I'm stupid. No one likes me, because there's something wrong with me;" or, "I'm a loser. I'm just overly sensitive. I can't cope, so I give up."

Because these children are very intelligent, they often quickly create defensive-mechanisms to protect them from possible further abuse. They use their intelligence to gain achievements in school – they become the "nerds" or "computer geeks" – to pretend that it isn't important for them to "fit in." Or, they channel their talents and abilities into ways of entertaining others – become jokesters, comedians, musical or artistic performers, or sports pros. These activities seem like ways of "fitting in" or getting the attention they crave, but accolades of praise will never penetrate their clouds.

There will never be "enough" praise to satisfy them, so they are constantly looking for new ways of "showing off" their intelligence. They may choose a career that exhibits their talents or their ability to tune into others, so they will gain appreciation. They may become addicted to climbing the ladder to success. However, whatever they do, it is "not good enough." They never achieve a level where they believe that they are "important enough" to feel safe in this world. This state of mind can be seen by others as unreasonable; so the idea that they are *too* sensitive is reinforced.

If people have told you that you are *overly sensitive*, it might be helpful to consider the possibility that it is *a good thing* that you are so sensitive. You can use your sensitivities to tune-in to deeper levels of awareness and become totally honest about what has disconnected you from others, the God Force, or Mother Earth. It is important, however, to make sure that your direction takes you out of the VPR Cloud; because your early childhood conditioning (that the only way you will survive is by "fitting in") may drag you back into the VPR Cloud. This belief actually stifles your Spiritual-Body and diminishes the value of your Total-Self.

Instead of constantly using your intuition to tune-in to the people in your environment, because you are afraid for your safety, you can create a safe environment where you can use your intuition to tune-in to your Spiritual-Body, listen to your inner knowing and reconnect with your will to make healthier choices. This refocusing of your intuitive connection leads you away from dysfunctional thinking and behaviour, forms a pathway out of your past patterns of relating, and opens a world of possibilities.

The false identity of each of the roles expressed in the VPR Cloud creates layer after layer of denial and keeps people from using their natural curiosity to find their true identity, their creativity, their spontaneity, their unique value and their special contribution to society. There is no hope for change within the boundaries of the VPR Cloud; there is only misery and separation from other people, Mother Earth, and the God Force. The potential is within each of us to be free of our unhealthy emotional reactions by looking at the past with different eyes, understanding how we have created our unhealthy thinking and behaviour and making a choice to step out of the VPR Cloud into our birthright as sparks of light of the God Force.

Chapter Four

Rethinking the Beliefs in Your Clouds

We all have beliefs that are successful and healthy; however, in this chapter, we will focus our attention on the confusing or unhealthy ones – your self-limiting or even self-destructive beliefs and your unconscious scripts.

As was mentioned in Chapter One, your beliefs are stored in energy packages that are held between your Mental and Emotional Bodies. If the belief is not in your best interest, it is called a cloud, because it dims or extinguishes the light of truth from your Spiritual-Body. Many of your clouds have become unconscious over the years; therefore, when you honestly delve into your beliefs, you will uncover the root causes of your thoughts and emotional reactions. This takes courage and strength of character. It also takes patience and enough self-love to follow the curiosity and creativity from your Spiritual-Body into the recesses of your Mental and Emotional-Bodies. If you are vigilant in your search and curious enough to follow where your Spiritual-Body leads you, you will find many opportunities to expand your thinking into a new and healthier way of life.

Your beliefs are simply a grouping of ideas – conclusions that you have come to during your life experiences. You believe them simply because you have attached an emotional value to them, so you've probably created a story to justify your conclusion – a script. Even though you may have little or no data to substantiate your conclusion, you say, "I believe this to be true!"

This process is similar to when a small child has dreamt that there is a monster under his bed. He is convinced that the monster is real and he may be actually experiencing sincere emotional trauma as the result of his belief. His parents may try to convince him that it was only a dream, but until he is in a fully awake state and able to actually look under his bed, he is not convinced.

It may be helpful to consider that most of your beliefs and scripts developed during your formative years, while you still believed that your parents controlled your behaviour because they loved you or wanted to protect you. If their desire to control you was based on an intention to keep you safe, healthy, and happy, they meant well; however, some of their values may not have supported or encouraged you in the way that you needed – then, or now.

If you were not safe and secure in your early environment, you have very different beliefs from the children who were actually safe. Therefore, unless you are totally happy and secure at all times, you are probably still being influenced by self-limiting, unconscious beliefs that are diminishing the expression of your highest potential.

Beliefs and scripts are simply energy – like a dream – either a good or bad dream. The dream seems real, but it is not. The only person for whom it is real is the person who has formed an emotional attachment to a specific belief. When we think that our conclusions are accurate, we often assume that they are a universal truth. However, your conclusions may have been limited by your mindset at the time. For example: If you were in the victim mindset, you would have concluded that everything was your fault; if you were in the persecutor mindset, you would have concluded that everything was someone else's fault; or, if you were in the rescuer mindset, you would have concluded that everything was society's fault.

If your emotional attachment to your conclusion becomes deeply embedded, it becomes an addiction, because you are basically saying, "I can't live without my belief." Keep in mind that every addiction is based on a belief that, if you act on your belief, you will feel better. However, the opposite is always true. Whenever you act upon your addictive beliefs, you may temporarily feel "high," but you will eventually feel worse than you did before you made your choice.

When beliefs are repeated in your mind and played out in your external environment, they wear "grooves" in your thinking – like a lightning bolt that shoots into one of your clouds. Your beliefs become pathways that your subconscious mind automatically follows – unconscious patterns of relating to your environment. Metaphorically speaking, your habits follow the same pathway as the original lightning bolt.

When you start making changes in your life and you start to adjust how that energy flows, you will naturally experience a certain amount of discomfort for a time. It is necessary to be gentle with yourself as you gradually withdraw from your old habits and develop new ways of living your life.

Consider that whenever you experience any thought or emotional sensation, it was preceded by a series of connections in your brain, called neural pathways, which had previously been imprinted through the repetition of certain events or circumstances in your past. Those thoughts and emotional sensations travel at the speed of light – like a lightning bolt. Some researchers suggest that our subconscious thoughts travel 40,000 times faster than our conscious thoughts.

If you allow yourself to become conscious of your ideas and emotional sensations while you are experiencing a belief, you will slow down the process, until you can observe the deep groove of similar emotional sensations that have travelled through your conscious awareness a multitude of times. You may be able to see that in actuality, that particular emotional sensation is simply a memory of similar situations that caused similar emotional sensations in your past. This process was unconscious, so you have been unaware, until now, of how the preceding linkages have caused your emotions to either dip or soar. Now, as you honestly assess your ideas and emotions, you can follow your process backward to dissect and define the beliefs that are at the root cause of your emotional reactions.

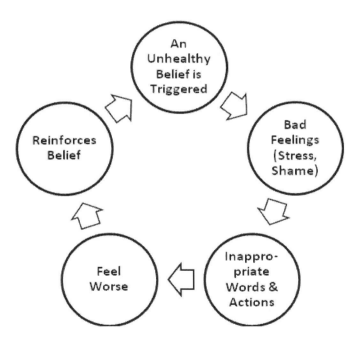

Every self-limiting belief creates its own set of automatic, emotional reactions and one or more accompanying scripts. When you activate an unconscious belief about yourself on a regular basis, it begins to take on a life of its own. As soon as your belief is unconsciously triggered, the script automatically flies through your mind faster than the speed of light. (Remember that beliefs and scripts are energy! They actually do move faster than the speed of light!)

Whenever an unhealthy belief is triggered, you automatically feel fear and assume that you are unsafe, so you run fear scripts – such as "something is going to get me." This state of fear creates a high level of stress and confusion, so you can't think clearly. This state of chaos is reflected in your choice of thoughts, feelings, words, and actions. You blunder along doing things that are not in your best interest – usually the same things that have proved unsuccessful in the past. You see the result of your choices in the reactions of others. Then you feel worse. This reinforces your belief that you are an inadequate or bad person. This completes the cycle. All this chaos has reinforced your cloud.

The cycle of reinforcing unhealthy beliefs can be broken! By being consciously aware of your reactions – your automatic thoughts, feelings, words, and actions – you will expose your underlying beliefs and scripts. This gives you the ability to consciously intervene in the repetitive cycle of creating situations that reinforce your clouded beliefs. To create significant change in your life, you must patiently examine your thoughts and emotional reactions – moment-by-moment. You then have the power to choose a healthier response to external stimuli.

The Belief that You Have to Struggle to Survive

Your beliefs around survival were probably the earliest ones that you developed – while you were still a tiny baby. You realized at that time, on a deep primitive level, that you would not survive, unless you had the support of the people around you. This was very true when you were a baby and completely dependent upon others for your care: As an adult, however, it is important to rethink your areas of dependency. While you no longer need as much support, you may not feel capable of completely taking care of yourself, because you didn't learn those skills.

If the people in your environment were not safe and secure in themselves, they may have given you the impression that you would *never* be able to survive on your own. For example: Some girl children learn to believe that they are so inadequate that they will *always* need a man to support them; some boy children learn to believe that they will *always* have to struggle to make ends meet; therefore, it is imperative to have a "good job" or they might starve or be homeless.

Many children learned that they must *always* follow their family values or they would be rejected, punished, or even abandoned. They believed that they wouldn't be able to survive without the support of certain things, substances, or people. At this point, an addiction was born, because they believed that they wouldn't be able to survive without that support. It became a perception that continues to cloud their ability to be self-sufficient and independent.

You are no longer a child; but you may not be fully in control of your life, because you learned unhealthy patterns of relating in your early environment. As an adult, you are now capable of making different choices and developing different belief systems – ones that will work more effectively for you – ones that will empower you to be responsible for your choices – ones that will free you to reach your highest potential.

The Belief that You are Powerless

Children who are raised in confusing environments are often led to believe that they have no choice but to *agree* with the people in power. They are seldom, if ever, encouraged to think independently or question the established rules of their family unit or culture.

It was natural that you began to believe that you were powerless, if your needs were not met emotionally as a child. Perhaps, it was as far back as the first time your mother or father left you while you cried in pain. Whenever it was, you felt unsupported by your caregivers, and it created the sensation of desperation and aloneness that eventually created a belief in *alienation* or *separation* from your parents.

It is also possible that your perception of a *specific* situation may have caused you to view your environment in a *generalized* way that exaggerated its true meaning and a universal cloud was created in your Total-Self, instead of a specific one. For example: If you were bullied by an older, stronger child – a brother or sister, your perception of that specific situation could be generalized into a belief that you are powerless in many other types of situations with other people, rather than only to that specific individual. If it was your brother who was the bully, you may have concluded that *all* boys/men are naturally aggressive and not to be trusted. Or, if it was your sister who was the bully, you may have concluded that *all* girls/women are naturally selfish or bossy.

You may have developed the persona of a weakling to avoid further abuse. Or, you may have packed on the pounds or trained as a body builder to make sure that you would never appear to be powerless again. But, underneath your new persona may be the unconscious belief that you will always be "a loser." That clouded belief must be penetrated with the understanding that this universal perception is untrue. It is important to realize that at one point, you actually were smaller or weaker, but now you are an adult who has the right to make your own choices.

The belief that you *need* something or someone to survive is at the core of all addictive thoughts and behaviours. The idea that some people have power and you don't is just a script from your phony-voice. You have the right and ability to choose – therefore, you are powerful! Practicing your ability to choose differently increases your sense of Personal Power – and your connection with your Spiritual-Body.

The Belief that You Need to Escape

You may possibly have the belief that you need to get away from your environment. This belief is very similar to the previous belief about survival; because, if you want to run away or escape, you probably believe that you can't survive in your present environment. You could actually be threatened – physically, mentally, emotionally, or spiritually – or, you may simply believe that you are. Hope for a better environment, one that you can control, perhaps, motivates you to remove yourself physically.

This conclusion may be true, if you are unsafe in that environment, but running away from every challenge in your life is a very bad habit to get into. It is important that you consider whether you are contributing anything to the situation that needs to be changed. Perhaps, you have been contributing unhealthy habits into interactions that were unsuccessful. Perhaps, you have not been speaking your truth. Perhaps, you have been enabling the other person to continue their unhealthy habits. Whatever you have been doing, it is important to take full responsibility for your thoughts, feelings, words, and actions, even if you decide not to participate in that environment in the future.

Often, the first step of recovery is to remove oneself from dangerous environments. However, you can't escape from yourself. Wherever you are, you take yourself with you! You can't run away from the source of your problems – you! Your real problem may be how you perceive yourself, other people, the God Force, or Mother Earth. If you believe that you can only survive in a different environment, you disempower yourself, because you are blaming the outside environment for your dependency or desperation.

The Belief that You are Too Stupid to Choose Well

Another common core belief that plagues people who are living in clouds of confusion contains the script that they are lacking in intelligence. If you have any doubts about your ability to learn concepts that will help you attain your highest potential, examine your beliefs and scripts about your intelligence.

Do you believe that you are smart and can accomplish whatever you set your mind to? If you can't say an unequivocal "Yes!" to this question, explore your past and think about where you began to believe that you lacked sufficient intelligence.

This is another area where our reaction to specific situations can grow into generalizations. For example: As a young child, you may have failed a grammar test and felt stupid. However, you mistakenly assumed that you were stupid in general, instead of understanding, that just because you had problems with the English language, it didn't mean that you were inadequate in every way.

An erroneous belief or pattern of relating to your environment may have been formed to protect you from further pain. You may have scoffed at the English language and developed a habit that showed your disdain for proper grammar. This habit may be a temporary diversion from your scripts about your inadequacy, but the truth is that your improper use of language may, in fact, lead others to the conclusion that you actually are lacking in intelligence. It becomes the proverbial "shooting oneself in the foot."

If you have any doubt about your level of intelligence, stop and think about how that clouded thinking affects your life. When did you start to doubt your intellectual abilities or your ability to solve problems? How did you become convinced that you couldn't make healthy decisions on your own? What rules were set in place due to that cloud? Do you stifle your opinions because you have an underlying doubt of your level of intelligence? If so, it is most likely that you were very young when you developed this cloud. If you can't remember a specific situation, think about times when the message was implied, because it was a common theme in your environment.

It may be helpful to consider that the individuals who taught you that you were lacking in intelligence, probably had been taught the same thing as children, so they thought it was the right thing to teach you. Consider also, that it is easier to control someone who doesn't believe that they are adequate, so it may have been somewhat deliberate.

It is also important to consider that you are likely the product of an inefficient educational system that compartmentalizes children. If you were deemed to be inefficient in a particular area, you may have learned to believe that there was no hope that you could succeed in life. You may have been grouped into a special category, or singled out because you didn't do well in a particular subject. This type of unfair system has made many people equate their inability to do certain things with lack of intelligence. You may have assumed that there was something lacking in your intelligence, instead of realizing that you were just less talented in that specific area. We all have things that we are good at. Explore the things that you are good at and give yourself credit for doing them well. Realizing this will anchor a new belief about your actual intelligence and you can build on that foundation.

When you believe that you are intelligent, you will take the time to think carefully about what you are going to say and do before you speak and act. This pause allows you to check with the rest of your consciousness – aligns you with your integrity, and opens the gates to your creativity, so you can explore the many options that are potentially available to you. This will affirm your connection with your Spiritual-Body and reinforce the belief that you are intelligent enough to cope with the challenges that occur in your environment. You may actually be a genius in some areas of your life and not even realize it.

"Shoulding" on Yourself or Others

The words "should," and "shouldn't," represent strong beliefs. They always contain the desire to control. If they are expressed internally, they are attempts to control our thoughts, feelings, words, or actions. If they are expressed externally, they are attempts to control the thoughts, feelings, words, or actions of others. They always contain an opinion about what is the "right thing" to think, say, or do. Therefore, whenever a person expresses their thoughts about what they want you to do, they are actually saying that they are superior to you in some way – either they actually have more information or insights into a specific area of your life or they just think they do.

"Shoulds" that are consistently repeated each have a story attached to them to justify that particular opinion. Eventually, they become internalized as beliefs that become our story and we automatically express them through the corresponding scripts that we have invented to justify those opinions. These scripts often become unconscious rules of behaviour.

When you were a young child, the words "should" and "shouldn't" were used to show you the rules of conduct that others wanted you to obey. Those people may have had good intentions and simply wanted you to fit into your environment; however, the words that they used were designed to control your behaviour. Those opinions may have been labelled "morals," "good values," "manners," "etiquette," or "social graces." They were not necessarily universal truths, but they were designed to ensure your acceptance in your culture and to prevent your deviation from the status quo – to prevent you from "rocking the boat."

When you heard the same messages repeated and repeated in your environment, you eventually internalized them into automatic reactions or unconscious rules of behaviour that, even now, you may continue to use to create your life. It may now be necessary to contemplate your choices and make healthier decisions, IF you want to take back your ability to control your life; develop healthier rules to live by; and build your integrity.

Whenever someone says that you should do something, the best way to cope with it is to realize that the advice is well-intended and think of it as such – advice – someone's opinion. It is simply an idea that was projected toward you, which you can either accept or reject, depending upon your desire in the moment. However, it is a really good idea to pay close attention when you quickly accept or reject a "should suggestion;" because this means that you have a subconscious cloud that was automatically triggered.

There may be several reasons for your reaction. It may have been a memory that was triggered that included information about that particular suggestion. Previously, you may have tried that option and had a bad reaction. You may, however, be triggered by much more subtle sensations: the tone of voice or behaviour of the individual, or, you may have unconsciously picked up their desire to change you. You might even be afraid that they want you to be just like them.

It is also important to consider that their suggestion may also seem threatening to you, because it expands your worldview, out of your comfort zone, or has the potential to change your perception of reality. Therefore, you may need to take a moment to consider whether you would like to embrace that action. Actually, it may be a gift to you, if your desire is to be more consciously in control of your thoughts, feelings, words, and actions.

There are three ways you can respond when people say you should do something:

1. If you automatically say, "Yes, I will follow your advice," you may be blindly complying with the other person's suggestion, because you have previously followed that suggested path many times in many similar situations. However, if you automatically comply with their wishes, you give away your Personal Power and dim your connection with your Spiritual-Body. Whenever you automatically comply, you forfeit your freedom to choose

what you want to do, or what is right for you. You may have been conditioned to "be nice" or "be obedient," so you automatically follow their advice, because you are afraid of disobeying them or hurting their feelings. It may take awhile, but the eventual product of your compliance will be resentment, because we always feel resentment when we give away our power.

2. If you were to immediately say no to the suggestion, the emotional reaction you would experience is usually rebelliousness, hate, or anger. This causes you to feel disconnected from the person; because when you reject their suggestion, you believe that you are also rejecting the person, causing you to feel isolated/alone. There is also another by-product of this automatic reaction that may actually be even more important than the previous one. If you reject their suggestion too quickly, you don't give yourself the opportunity of exploring that particular suggestion for value. You may actually be rejecting that idea due to an old dysfunctional and internalized belief that may no longer have any value in your life. Also, if you repeatedly remove items from your list of options, you eventually run out of options and are imprisoned by your own restraints.

3. Whenever you hear someone say the words "should" or "shouldn't," it helps to mentally insert the word "could," into the suggestion. When you do this, you retain your power to say, "Maybe I will, or maybe I won't. I'll think about it and make my decision at a later time." If the

suggestion is one that you have not previously considered, it has the power to expand your list of options; yet you still maintain the power and right to make your own choice.

There is, however, a challenge in following the last option. You have to be willing to take responsibility for your choices. You have to think! You can no longer project blame toward others if the idea doesn't prove to be successful. You must be willing to say, "I am doing this, because I want to! And I will take the consequences." By taking this approach to challenges, you give yourself permission to make your own choices, even if they turn out to be mistakes. In the eventuality that what you choose isn't the best choice for you, you take full responsibility for learning from that choice and you retain your ability to try something different in the future. On the other hand, if your choice is a good one, this allows you to take full credit for your successes. This builds your self-confidence and encourages you to consider all your choices, before you make them.

With this kind of adventuresome spirit, you take back your Personal Power and your right to choose whatever is right for you. The "should prison" is soon replaced by the freedom to express your Total-Self and you automatically expand your creative potential.

We all have absorbed "shoulds" from our environment. Some of them actually enhance your life, but it is essential to examine your inner thoughts for the "shoulds" that unconsciously prevent you from expressing your individuality. Whenever you hear a "should" in your thinking process, Stop! Ask yourself where that belief (opinion/story/rule/script) came from. Ask yourself if you actually believe that it is the best way to handle the situation, or, if it is an unhealthy script that has been automatically controlling your choices.

Processing my internal "shoulds" was a very healing experience for me. Many years ago when I first began this process, I found hundreds of inappropriate shoulds lurking as clouds between my Mental and Emotional Bodies. As I diligently processed them, one-by-one, I began to be less and less controlled by my past conditioning and freer to live my life the way I saw fit.

I became fairly smug, thinking that I wasn't "shoulding" on myself any longer, until one cold, drizzly, November day, when I was waiting in my car for my daughter to conduct some business at her bank. I was very relaxed as I lazily watched the scene in the parking lot before me. I observed as a car pulled into a parking spot and a young woman jumped out wearing a bulky knit sweater. She ran for the door of the bank. As I watched, I noticed her breasts bouncing up and down beneath her sweater and the thought popped into my mind, "She should be wearing a bra!"

I was shocked awake! Not only was I shocked that I was thinking about what the woman should be doing, I was also shocked, because this script didn't match my present value system. I hadn't worn a tight bra for years! I had developed a belief that tight bras have an unnatural effect on women's breasts and the restrictive nature of a bra could possibly lead to a blockage of lymph flow in the breasts, eventually causing a variety of health problems – even cancer.

As I became aware of the dichotomy of the two opinions, I began to laugh at myself. I realized the "should package," which had popped into my mind, wasn't even my voice, but the voice of my grandmother. It had been buried there for over thirty years. This example shows how important it is to be diligent as you weed out your old shoulds and shouldn'ts, because they may represent unconscious scripts that you automatically say to yourself that may not be your own opinions or even correspond with your present worldview.

Pay attention to your internal dialogue – your self-talk. Watch diligently and observe whenever you entertain thoughts that include the words, "I should" or "I shouldn't," or, "he or she should or shouldn't," or, "they (the general population) should or shouldn't." Stop the process! Realize that those thoughts came from an unconscious script that could be floating around in your consciousness. That cloud may have been automatically controlling your thoughts and preventing the light of truth from penetrating into your daily life.

It is now your responsibility to consider whether that script needs revising or releasing. Ask yourself if you want those beliefs and their subsequent scripts and rules to control your life. Activate your will to consider what is best for you in each situation and allow others the same privilege.

The Belief that You Have to Be "Nice" to Get What You Want

"If you are good, you can have a treat." This type of bribery creates a false persona in the parent – and in the child. The parent is placing him/herself into the role of an unfair dysfunctional god who only doles out treats to the ones who are compliant – the so-called good children. Children, who live in this type of environment, and comply with their parents' rules, inevitably give away portions of their identity. The resulting "treat" – sweets, a bonus (watch an extra movie/play a video game, etc.), an expression of approval or "a pat on the head," teaches children that the only way that they can gain approval is to comply and forfeit their own personal needs. It may actually be a reward for inappropriate behaviour that was a betrayal of the child's individuality.

The children suspect, at least on an unconscious level, that they have tricked the parent into giving them the treat, by lying to them. This then, also reinforces the belief that they aren't really good, which was instilled in them by previous judgments. They hope that the treat will replace the chunk of their identity that was taken away by the judgments; but it never does.

Remember, nothing artificial can ever penetrate your clouds or satisfy your deepest needs. If you have to coerce someone to give you what you think you want, you are never truly satisfied by the acquisition. A true gift, given freely from the heart, is much more satisfying. However, if you have become accustomed to substitutions, you may believe that second best is all that you deserve. If you learned to believe that you would only get a reward IF you were good or nice, you probably now believe in lack instead of abundance.

If you believe that it is only possible to get what you want by being nice, it creates another problem. It is the belief that, if you ask other people nicely, they will automatically give you what you want. This belief becomes a rule or script that says that others are supposed to comply with your demands, if you ask them nicely. One of my clients believed in just such a rule. It became evident in counselling that when he asked his wife nicely to do something, she was supposed to always comply with his wishes. He used this rule to justify his domineering behaviour by saying, "She should have done it, because I asked her nicely." Even when she repeatedly told him she didn't want to do a particular thing, he insisted that she comply with his wish – just because he had cleverly asked nicely. He couldn't comprehend that she had the right to refuse him, if he asked her in that way.

He was unwilling to consider the possibility that his "nice request" was really a demand that was candy coated. The assumption that she was obliged to comply with his wishes, if he asked her nicely, had been internalized in his early childhood. He had only been allowed to have his needs met IF he was polite and nice. As an adult, whenever his wife refused him, he thought that he was justified in punishing her with his anger or even using force to make her comply with his wishes. His behaviour was coated in a nice wrapping, until she made a choice that was different from his established rules. Then, he became more aggressive to force her to comply with his wishes. This couple learned that he had to rethink his belief that he should be able to get whatever he wanted, just because he asked nicely; and she had to keep a constant message that being nice doesn't necessarily mean that you get what you want.

This example shows how essential it is that you take responsibility for yourself and take back your right to choose what is right for you. As you accept responsibility for the choices that you make in your life, you will start to decipher new data as it comes into your awareness; consciously choose what is healthy; and know how to throw out what is harmful.

The Belief that You Have to be "Clever" to Have Your Needs Met

If you were not supported and loved unconditionally when you were a child, you probably concluded that you would never have your needs met unless you learned "clever" ways to manipulate the people in your environment. You may have learned how to use fairly repetitive, simple, and yet devious measures, which were a reflection of your immature mind. Or, you may have learned how to trick or manipulate your parents or caregivers into giving you what you wanted by being clever or smart. Unfortunately, you could never be satisfied with what you were given, because you knew, on a deep level, that they didn't want you to have it. Have you ever noticed how you never feel good about what you get, if you have to manipulate someone to give it to you? This is because you know that the gift is not clean or given from a place of unconditional love.

As an adult, you now have the option of asking to have your needs met in healthy ways – ways that satisfy you and make you feel loved and supported. Whenever you are asking your loved ones for anything, it might be helpful to ask yourself whether or not you are doing or saying anything that is manipulative. Are you trying to coerce them with "clever" tricks or are you asking for something that you believe they will enjoy giving to you?

The difference between "clever" and "smart" is that clever is usually a "trick" that you learned from others. Clever is usually a manipulative pattern of relating to a given stimulus.

Smart is a moment-by-moment ability to consciously choose what is right for you. When you make a smart choice, you are using your intelligence to carefully observe your list of options and consider your possible choices. Are your choices clever or smart?

Other Self-Limiting Beliefs and Scripts

The following list of self-limiting core beliefs and scripts may help you become more aware of your unconscious beliefs and allow you to intervene in your automatic reactions. It is by no means a complete list; however, the beliefs that are represented here may expose some self-limiting core beliefs and scripts to your conscious awareness.

As you go through the list, watch for triggers – emotional reactions. If the words aren't exactly the ones that play in your head, take time to change the words to reflect the precise wording of your scripts. When you find a trigger, take the time to write about it and understand that even though it is something that you have believed in the past, you now have the power to consciously rethink it and revise it to express your integrity. Don't waste your time wallowing in blame or anger toward yourself or the others who were involved in the experience that caused you to internalize a self-limiting core belief.

It may be helpful, however, to understand that many of your scripts were learned by listening to the people in your environment. So, whenever you find statements that you can specifically attribute to someone in your past, make a note of it and put their name beside it. Just by observing that you have internalized a script from that person may help you understand that it was actually owned by another person. It may also be helpful to see that script as contained in a cloud of energy that was floating around in that other person's life and you just borrowed it, because you didn't know any better. Or, it may have been handed down to you like a legacy that is no longer beneficial to you. In either case, you don't have to own it anymore.

You may have been simply the next person in a long line of people who practiced those disempowering, dysfunctional habit patterns, which were based on unhealthy scripts and beliefs and they gradually became rules of conduct in your life. You may also find comfort by making a list of any positive beliefs that these statements bring to mind, but make sure that you don't automatically deny the presence of a self-limiting belief by covering it up with denial. Also, if you are truly working on yourself, your soul will gather opportunities to work on any beliefs that have been blocking the light of truth from your Spiritual-Body.

The following list represents many of the most self-limiting beliefs. Go through the list slowly, carefully, and at your own pace. It may be helpful to assess an appropriate number to each item to determine whether or not you have each script unconsciously operating. The number 0 implies that you never have that thought come to mind and the number 10 implies that it is very common in your thought processes.

Never	Seldom	Sometimes	Often	Usually	Always
0-1	2-3	4-5	6-7	8-9	10

About Me:

1. I don't deserve love. I have to earn it.
2. There is something very wrong with me.
3. I'm not lovable.
4. To be lovable, I have to always be "nice."
5. To be loved, I have to agree with others and let them do whatever they want to me.
6. I'm not important.
7. I'm not creative.
8. I have to please others to be worthy of their love.
9. I don't fit in.
10. I'm not capable.
11. I'm not worthwhile (don't have any value).
12. My opinions aren't valuable or wanted by others.
13. My thoughts are dumb.
14. I'm a bad person.
15. The bad things I've done are unforgivable.
16. I can't do it, because I'm helpless, hopeless, or inadequate.
17. I'm stupid (incompetent, incapable).

18. I'm not as smart as others are; so I'm no good.
19. I'm clumsy.
20. I'm ugly.
21. I always fail, no matter how hard I try.
22. I don't deserve pleasure.
23. I have to yell to get anyone to listen to me; (because they don't love me, or they are clueless and I am smarter than them, or .....) .
24. Other people don't want to listen to me (because I don't have anything smart to say).
25. I'm boring.
26. I'm not supposed to have fun.
27. It's bad to grow up.
28. It's bad to grow old.
29. I'm not respected / don't deserve respect.
30. I can't have what I want.
31. It's not okay to feel good or happy. I'm supposed to suffer.
32. I don't deserve happiness.
33. I'm not a loving person. I'm really a bad/selfish/nasty/inconsiderate person.
34. I have to hide my true emotions.
35. I have to sacrifice myself to receive love.
36. I'll never live up to my family or friend's (or my own) expectations.
37. I can't live up to my self-image.
38. I can't say no. I have to always comply.
39. I don't have the right to have any boundaries.
40. I must be agreeable and never fight with others.

About Living on This Planet:

41. The world isn't a safe place.

42. The world is actually an unhappy place, so I have to suffer.
43. Life is unfair.
44. Life is hard.
45. Life is full of stress and worries.
46. The world owes me a living.
47. I should get whatever I want.
48. I just have to ask for what I want and people should give it to me.
49. I deserve the best and others don't.
50. The government always lies to us, so it doesn't matter if I obey the laws, pay my taxes, or support the system in any way.
51. Most people don't care about anyone else but themselves.
52. Most people are out to get me.
53. It's a "dog-eat-dog world."
54. I have to fight to climb the ladder to success.
55. I have to compete with everyone.
56. There isn't enough to go around, so I have to struggle.
57. People of other races don't like me (so I don't like them).
58. I don't like people who are different than me and my family.
59. People are trying to find ways to take what I have accumulated.
60. The world won't survive and neither will I.

About Relationships:

61. Men (or women) are tough, scary, angry, selfish, bad, helpless, hopeless, hateful, etc., (any stereotype).

62. Men/women don't like me, because I'm different from them.
63. To be in a relationship, I have to put up with whatever the other person gives me.
64. I don't have what it takes to make a relationship work.
65. A relationship will only work with the right person.
66. If I love someone, I will be hurt, because that person has the right to hurt me.
67. I'll never find the right person.
68. I'll get hurt if I get too close in a relationship.
69. All the good people are already in relationships.
70. I can't attract or keep a good person with my body looking like this, or, with my education, social standing, family background, etc. (any self-limiting belief).
71. I have to have a beautiful/handsome body to be desirable to my partner.
72. I'm a loser in relationships.
73. I need my partner to survive in this scary world.
74. My partner can't get by without me.
75. He (or she) is just after my money.
76. Men (or women) want only one thing.
77. Women (or men) can't be trusted.
78. To be compatible, my partner and I should enjoy doing all of the same things together.
79. I'm supposed to take care of my partner.
80. She (or he) is supposed to take care of me.
81. It is my job to change/improve my partner.
82. I have to protect/defend my partner.
83. She (or he) doesn't understand me.
84. She (or he) doesn't accept me.

85. Relationships are hard.
86. Relationships don't last. She (or he) will leave me.
87. The people that I depend on always let me down.
88. The one I love will abandon me.
89. Divorce is a sin (failure).
90. Marriage/relationships/partnerships are a trap.
91. Once I commit to someone, I am in prison. I have to give up my freedom.
92. If he (or she) really knew me, he (or she) wouldn't be interested in me.
93. Romance is only for the young.
94. The ones I love always hurt me.
95. When I'm in a relationship, I can't have any privacy/secrets/boundaries.
96. She (or he) should support me by giving me what I want.
97. I drain energy from others. I'm too much work, so they don't want to be around me.
98. If my relationship doesn't work out, it's my fault because I'm bad, ugly, inadequate, etc.
99. I'm not meant to have a relationship, because I don't deserve it.
100. I can't win, so I might as well give up (or get even).
101. What my partner says or does reflects on me.
102. My family must approve of my relationship.
103. Even if I try to explain, I won't be heard or understood.
104. I'll never get it right, so I might as well not try.
105. I have to control (or obey) my partner or s/he will, or won't ……….
106. I'm supposed to make the world a safe place for my partner.

About the God Force:

107. The God Force is "out there" somewhere.
108. I am separate from the God Force and it is inaccessible to me.
109. The God Force is angry with me, because I was bad.
110. The God Force only likes people who go to church, obey the rules of my religion, and are nice and polite/good children.
111. I have to sacrifice my wants and needs and only live to help others, so the God Force will love me.
112. The God Force will always punish me if I make mistakes.
113. There is no way the God Force will listen to me or give me what I need or want.
114. I have to beg, if I want the God Force to listen to me.
115. I have to save the world (to please the God Force, or, because the God Force doesn't care enough to save the world.)
116. The God Force wants me to be the same as the other people in my religion.
117. The God Force doesn't like me, personally. (Has singled me out for some reason and is out to hurt me.)
118. The human race has made so many mistakes that the God Force is angry with me (and all humans).
119. The God Force only loves people who call him/her/it by the right name.
120. The God Force will only love me, if I sacrifice myself to a cause. (Because that's the only way to heaven.)

121. The God Force will only love me when I'm perfect. (Wants me to live in a specific way, or in a specific life-style, or be a model citizen.)

About Mother Earth:

122. The Earth is an inanimate object with no intelligence or destiny.
123. The Earth is a piece of rock floating in space and happened by accident.
124. The laws of nature are meant to be broken.
125. The elements of the Earth are here to be used for our advancement (such as oil, coal, minerals, and water.) So, we can do with them whatever we wish.
126. Man has dominion over the Earth.
127. It is unsafe to be in nature.
128. There is no order in nature. It happened by chance and is destined to be chaotic.
129. It is my fault (or the fault of human beings) when natural disasters happen on the earth.
130. The Earth is dirty and full of germs that are "out to get me."

Now, go back through your notations in the above list and make a list of the ones that you have marked with the highest numbers. For example: If you have three statements to which you have assigned the number 10, put those together in a group. See if they fit together in any way or if those beliefs create an energy package.

Each of the scripts listed above has the power to have a separative, disempowering result in your life. Many of them also have corresponding, dysfunctional rules that are automatically triggered, whenever you run those scripts. If you live by those rules, you are not making conscious choices: those unconscious rules make your choices automatically. If you continue to believe that those rules are the best ways to live, you are powerless to change. If, however, you are willing to examine them and carefully determine whether or not those rules are working for you, you can decide, if you want to love yourself enough to try something new.

You have the ability to rethink and revise your beliefs/scripts as soon as you open your mind to the possibility of change. For example: If you believe scripts 1 to 7 above, you may have developed a rule that says, "I have to accept whatever form of love is offered to me, because I don't deserve any better." Then, ask yourself if you want to keep that rule, or rewrite it, perhaps to say, "Everyone deserves to be loved and respected for the beautiful person they are, so, I deserve to be loved and respected for the beautiful person that I am."

Or, if you have belief #11, you might have a rule that says, "I have to keep my opinions to myself, because they are wrong, stupid, or ridiculous." This means that you were taught that you have no value, or that you have to keep silent, so you won't be judged, ridiculed, or rejected. This leads you to think of yourself as powerless and that you always have to ask someone else for advice before making any decisions. By accepting that rule, you have given away major chunks of your Personal Power – the ability to choose what is *right* for you – your connection with your intuition in your Emotional Body and the wisdom in your Spiritual-Body. Do you want to continue to abide by that rule? Or, do you believe that you have something to say? And, are you ready to say it?

Listen carefully to each of your scripts as they come to mind and see how the rules that you have created affirm and reinforce each prominent belief. Then, consider that the people who taught you those ideas about yourself didn't know any better! You didn't know any better either!

If you want to be free of self-limiting beliefs and unhealthy scripts or rules, each of your beliefs has to be examined closely and verified for validity or deemed invalid. (Remember, invalid beliefs make you an invalid.) Your beliefs create your thoughts about, and your emotional reactions to, every situation. Conversely, your thoughts are a product of your beliefs – your own creations – whether they are conscious or unconscious. So, it is a never ending cycle, unless you stop and examine the validity of each thought or belief.

When you make a commitment to change your beliefs, the rules that you live by will naturally change and your life will then automatically change in ways that you never thought possible. Each belief that you change has the potential to shift your entire consciousness, allowing more light into your life.

To successfully walk down your *Path to Wholeness* from dysfunctional thinking and behaviour, you must be willing to believe in your capacity for positive change. That includes letting go of your self-limiting beliefs and the resulting scripts and rules that you have created. It also includes accepting that you are a divine-spark with the power to choose something new.

How to Release Your Dysfunctional Beliefs and Scripts

Each of your dysfunctional beliefs and their accompanying scripts and rules create emotional reactions. For example: If you believe that people, or the God Force, will only love you *IF* you are perfect, you will probably feel very sad, because you know that you are far from flawless. To protect yourself from feeling that sadness, you could create a mask – an illusion of perfection – all the while, you are actually feeling quite inadequate or even "a phony." This may make you feel helpless and hopeless that you could ever achieve perfection. If you want to change these value systems that you have learned about yourself, you may need to rethink the idea that only perfect people can be loved or accepted.

Therefore, the process of releasing your unreasonable or unhealthy scripts may have the effect of diminishing some of your old emotional reactions and invite new emotional clarity into your life. This will happen naturally as you sift and sort through your beliefs and scripts and discard the ones that you have decided are not in your best interest.

When you decide that you are ready to release your unhealthy beliefs and scripts, it is necessary to become *very* honest with yourself about what you are *actually* experiencing. This level of honesty reveals that some of your emotional reactions may actually be ways of diverting your attention away from the sensations of helplessness, vulnerability, incompetence, etc. It may be necessary to become an objective detective and ask yourself, if, what you are sensing is an old pattern/reaction or, if it is a clear expression of what you are actually feeling.

When you get to a deep level of honesty, you can assess whether that emotion is actually an appropriate response, whether it is *true* or *false*. If it is actually *true*, it may lead you to a new realization about yourself. If it is *false,* you have two choices. You can continue to focus on your perception, which will continue to make you feel miserable about yourself or, you can move out of that perception into your Spiritual-Body to ask for guidance about what that old reaction is covering up.

As has been discussed in Chapter Three, many of our emotional reactions can cover up the truth about our inner state. For example: We have discussed how anger can cover up a variety of more painful awarenesses; but self-righteousness can also cover up sensations of uncertainty; and shame can cover up sensations of inadequacy.

Keep in mind that every emotional reaction is the result of a script, a grouping of thoughts or a belief. Because each unhealthy belief is a cloud in your consciousness, it has a detrimental effect on your life. It dims the light of truth from your Spiritual-Body. So, if you want to uncover the underlying beliefs that are stored there, it's important to ask yourself the following questions:

1. What, precisely, am I experiencing? (Put a name on the emotional sensation, using a specific label that defines it as closely as you can. It may be helpful to use the list of emotions in Chapter 3.)

2. What scripts or stories do I tell myself about why I feel the way I do?

3. What do these theories say about my environment? (Stay with the scripts, until you hear all the messages that have been stored deep in your unconscious mind regarding that subject. Journaling about it could also help.)

4. What are the messages in those scripts saying about me, personally?

5. What do I believe to be true about those messages?

6. Are those beliefs actually based on my present understanding or experiences?

Stay with the process, until you have found ideas that you haven't explored before. Cherish the treasure they are – gifts from your Spiritual connection. These ideas are something new that you have learned about yourself. If you aren't satisfied with the outcome, dig deeper. This is a slow, but extremely valuable process that will lead you to understand yourself more deeply and eventually love yourself more fully.

For example: If you do something that you recognize as an unhealthy choice – a mistake – think about what you could have done differently. Ask yourself what choices you have made that created that situation. Initially, you may beat yourself up – saying old scripts like, "I was so stupid" for what you have said or done. You may consider how you could have done things differently; saying, "I should have/could have/would have done… if … had (or hadn't) happened;" "I wish I had done…"; "If only I had done…"

Pay attention to your self-talk (the scripts that typically run through your mind whenever you make a choice that you think is a mistake). What do those ideas say about your opinion of yourself? What do those ideas say about your opinions of others around you? Perhaps, you were embarrassed, because you believe that you were stupid for having made that particular choice. Perhaps, you believe that others will judge you as stupid. Or, perhaps, you are afraid that they won't like you anymore.

It is natural to run your old scripts in the beginning; however, if you are still in the self-flagellating stage, you won't likely understand anything of great value about yourself. In order to move past your old habit of self-flagellation and find ideas that will help you move into your Personal Power, it may be helpful to use the following steps:

1. Pay attention to the scripts that are expressed in your self-talk.

2. Write about them.

3. Ask for guidance from your Spiritual-Body. "Is there anything I have missed?"

4. Write that down.

5. Make a commitment to change your self-talk and use the lessons that you have learned from the present experience to your advantage in the future.

6. Write an affirmation. "The next time something like this happens, I'm going to think/say/do…"

7. Repeat your commitment at least three times to imprint it into your sub-conscious mind.

8. Relax, and trust the process. Give yourself time to examine each lesson fully, until you are comfortable with what you have learned.

To move beyond self-limiting scripts, beliefs, thoughts, feelings, words, and actions, you must be willing to entertain the idea that there is a way out and use your natural curiosity to find it. If you wish to walk your personal Path to Wholeness, it is necessary to watch your self-talk – the old scripts that you have read from on the stage of your life – release the unhealthy beliefs that have held you captive in your old way of being, and make different choices.

When you are ready to release your self-limiting beliefs, it takes a firm commitment to love yourself and your life enough to become consciously aware, every time you start to run a self-limiting script. For example: One of my clients became committed to releasing the self-limiting script that frequently told her that she was "stupid." This is a woman who has accomplished a great deal in her life, but she never thought that she was "good enough." She constantly compared herself with others and came up lacking.

I consistently reminded her that her script was a lie and a waste of her time and energy. We worked together to write a list of her accomplishments and I suggested that she remind herself every day that she had achieved great things. She began to focus on her successes and whenever her old script came to the surface of her mind, she would remind herself that it was a lie. We created an affirmation that reminded her of her intelligence, which she practiced each and every time her old script surfaced. One day, it anchored in. She suddenly got it! She raised her voice in a shout of joy! Her previously constant negative self-talk never haunted her again.

Another client told me a wonderful story about her seven-year-old son. He shocked her one day when she was yelling at him. He spoke up and said, "You can't talk to me that way. I am a child of God." This stopped her in her tracks and she apologized to him and said, "I'm sorry that I spoke to you so disrespectfully. Yes, you are a child of the God Force and I will try to remember that." Each of us needs to remember that we are a child of the God Force and also remind people who may have temporarily forgotten.

The suggestions and exercises in this book are designed to support and encourage you as you rethink and release your old scripts, which have held you prisoner, and encourage you to listen to the truth from your Spiritual-Body. Be gentle with yourself, because you will need time to change your mind-set, your perception of reality and your patterns of relating to your environment. You will begin to reject the messages from your clouds, because you understand that they are no longer useful.

You can then replace your old scripts with new ideas that affirm your value and your truth. Be consciously aware of your new thoughts and emotions and stay open to new ways of changing your thoughts, feelings, words, and actions. Don't be afraid to ask the people in your environment to be patient with you, as you build a new way of being and ask for professional support when you need it.

Chapter Five

Introducing Healthy Habits

Preparing For Take Off

To begin this chapter, let's explore a very interesting concept. This concept invites you to move beyond all attachment to dysfunctional thinking. Read the following statements and consider whether they challenge any of your perceptions of reality that could cloud the way you view the world.

Acceptance

There are no victims, persecutors, or rescuers.
There are only sparks of the God Force who
have opportunities to learn and grow.
Therefore, there are no accidents or mistakes.
You are exactly the way you are supposed to be.
You are the "right and perfect" sex, colour,
size, shape, and personality.
You were born into the "right and perfect"

family, culture, and environment.
You have all the "right and perfect" talents
and abilities to do what you are meant to do.
You have learned all the "right and perfect"
lessons to bring you to this moment in time.
You have attracted the appropriate experiences,
so you can learn what you need to know, right now.
You always attract the appropriate experiences
that you need to know today,
tomorrow, and every day in your future.

When you carefully consider the above perception of reality, you may argue that it can't possibly include those who were born into poverty or those who are physically or mentally challenged. Actually, it does! Until you are ready to explore the possibility that the Universe is perfect in every way, you are stuck in dysfunctional thinking. Now, read it as if you are saying it as true for you and see if any of your old scripts are triggered, or, if you can accept this concept into your thinking.

Acceptance

There are no victims, persecutors, or rescuers.
There are only sparks of the God Force who have
opportunities to learn and grow.
Therefore, there are no accidents or mistakes.
I am exactly the way I am supposed to be.
I am the "right and perfect" sex, colour,
size, shape, and personality.

> I was born into the "right and perfect" family,
> culture, and environment.
> I have all the "right and perfect" talents and
> abilities to do what I am meant to do.
> I have learned all the "right and perfect" lessons
> to bring me to this moment in time.
> I have attracted the appropriate experiences,
> so I can learn what I need to know, right now.
> I always attract the appropriate experiences
> that I need to know today, tomorrow,
> and every day in my future.

Did it make a difference to put this concept in the first person? Sometimes, we can accept new concepts and theories about reality when they are about other people; but, when we apply them to our lives, they have a very different effect on us. Which of the above statements is the easiest to accept? Which is the most difficult? These awarenesses will help you determine where you are and which areas are calling you to expand your thinking.

In recent years, Quantum Physics has proven many theories that scientists had previously thought to be true that were actually illogical. New techniques have been developed to measure energy and prove the fact that energy follows thought. Your thoughts create patterns in your brain called neural pathways. Those thought patterns become pathways of behaviours – actions – that create your reality.

Therefore, everything in your life is there, because you thought it into being – either consciously or unconsciously. If you don't like what you have created in the past, you must change your thoughts, feelings, words, and actions. To change those patterns, it is necessary to rethink your habits and reprogram your mind by creating new pathways. That's why it is so important to carefully consider your scripts – what you are thinking and saying to yourself – your self-talk – as well what you say to others.

If you move into a belief system that affirms that there is a reason and a logical explanation for every aspect of the Universe, you will no longer believe in accidents or mistakes – your logic will be based upon the Law of Cause and Effect. This acceptance of the nature of this reality will open up new vistas in your perception of your world. "You are what you eat," takes on new meaning. "You are what you are experiencing" comes next to mind. "You are what you think," is the next logical step; then, "You are what you believe to be true about your world, Mother Earth, and the God Force." Wow! You have created your world with your thoughts, feelings, words, and actions! You have the ability to rethink the conclusions that you have come to and change your thoughts, feelings, words, and actions; therefore it is now within your power to think, speak, and act differently to create a different reality. You will also realize that you have the right to determine your own unique identity.

Embracing Your Ego

The word "ego" was first introduced into our vocabulary by Sigmund Freud in his attempt to define human consciousness. He originally defined the word "ego" as "one of three parts of the psychic apparatus – the organized realistic part of the psyche that is expressed outwardly into the world." When you wrap modern terminology around what Freud originally said, the main function of the ego is to define our personal boundaries and identify our individual personalities as separate from other people and forms. Therefore, Freud's meaning of the word "ego" is very similar to what I call your individual personality.

It is important to discuss this, because over the years, the meaning of the word "ego" has been widely expanded and exploited. In some spiritual and religious teachings, ego has become a dirty word. It is suggested that it is *wrong* to have an ego. This implies that a part of you is *bad* or *evil*; therefore, you are intrinsically flawed. In this section, I would like you to rethink this philosophy and let go of the idea that it is wrong to have a healthy ego.

If the main function of the ego is to define and separate us from others and express our unique, individual selves into the world around us, we must consider the possibility that we are *meant* to be different from each other. When we examine other species in nature, we observe that each zebra has a different pattern of stripes; every monarch butterfly is a different shape and size with slightly different markings;

every leaf on the same kind of tree is slightly different. It then becomes easier to conclude that the God Force (or Nature) not only accepts and appreciates, but actually encourages variety.

Your ego creates the boundaries around your uniqueness. It is the part of you that defines and expresses your purpose for being in a physical body this lifetime. However, it is important to consider that your present boundaries and patterns of relating were set in place during the *domestication process* that you experienced in your family environment and the culture, in which you were raised. If these boundaries or patterns are unhealthy in any way, they may not be the *real* you. You may now need to redefine your scripts and patterns to formulate ones that are healthier or more accurately express your uniqueness.

It may also be helpful to consider that one of the aspects of the God Force is harmony. If we were all the same, we would sing in unison – harmony would be impossible. Perhaps, respect for diversity is the only way that harmony can be achieved! We are all different and yet we are all interconnected with each other in many invisible ways.

Ego problems arise when a person has an unbalanced or wounded self-perception, and therefore, a weakened or unbalanced Total-Self. You are probably very familiar with people who have "inflated egos" or are called "egotistical." To be egotistical, is defined as, "To think too highly of ones' self." However people who "puff up their chests" and "blow their own horns" are often just *pretending* to be important, because they actually have *low* self-esteem. They believe that unless they tell others how important they are, no one will accept the illusion that they are trying to create.

They believe that they must cover up their weaknesses and vulnerabilities and *pretend* to be clever or important. This habit is simply an unsuccessful attempt to *seem* important. They have covered their weaknesses with defensive-mechanisms, but they will never feel real or secure. This pretence is actually a cloud that weakens their Total-Selves, because it prevents them from expressing the truth from their whole being.

On the other hand, people who openly display their lack of self-esteem also *pay too much attention to themselves*. In this case, however, they are thinking of themselves as unimportant, insignificant, incompetent, inadequate, or unworthy. Self-depreciation, unfortunately, is often excused or encouraged by people who say, "It is *good* to be modest." Nevertheless, this excessive focus on themselves (often used to protect them from further injury) also makes their clouds denser and fragments their integrity. This is because they are constantly running untrue scripts about their inadequacies.

Dysfunctional families and cultures suppress individual Personal Power by downplaying the talents and abilities that are the unique ways that we express our Total-Selves.

People seldom are encouraged to say complimentary things about themselves, because others may believe that they have "swelled heads" or "inflated egos." In many unhealthy groups, people aren't even supposed to say complimentary things about other people, because they might get "swelled heads." It is implied that, if we say complimentary things to others, they will become monsters who cannot be controlled, because they will be filled with conceit. The opposite is usually true. If people truly believe *good* things about themselves, it is more likely that they will think and say *good* things to, and about, others. This may be because individuals, who wanted to control you, have previously told you that it was *safer* to pretend to be *small*. Conversely, if you were bullied, you may have concluded that you would be *safer* if you pretend to be *big*.

When your ego is unbalanced, you are likely to be so preoccupied with running your dysfunctional scripts that you won't be able to access the vast store of information that is available from your other aspects, such as your intuition, your mental processes, your previous life-lessons, or the wisdom or calling of your soul. If you ignore your intuition, you limit the range of sensations from your Emotional-Body and dim the truth from your Spiritual-Body, but you also disconnect from the people and things in your environment. When your mental processes are ignored, the information that you have learned during your previous experiences isn't taken into consideration. If your previous life-lessons are ignored, you eliminate the opportunity of changing how you have responded to similar situations in the past. This is perhaps due to the fact that you actually haven't finished the lessons that you were supposed to learn from your mistakes. If, however, you allow every aspect of your being to be involved in your decisions – aligned with your integrity – you can access your divine wisdom and flow in harmony with the Universe. Your ego and your soul will work together to create a balanced expression of your Total-Self.

The best way to heal your ego is to understand that it is an essential part of your Total-Self. When you look at your ego as a *positive* aspect of your being, you can choose to develop it, until you are able to see yourself as a unique expression of the God Force. Then, you can discover where you best fit into your culture and work in harmony with the rest of the Universe.

A person with a balanced ego understands that each person is a unique and precious part of the entire picture. What a dull world it would be, if we were all the same! Our uniqueness is what makes us *real* and *exceptional!* It gives our lives meaning and purpose! It opens up our lives to limitless possibilities! When you have a healthy ego, you know who you are – that you are different and unique in your own special way. Consequently, you can respect the uniqueness of others.

For example: Several years ago while I was delivering a product from my natural food store to an acquaintance, she said something disparaging about herself, as she thanked me profusely "for going out of my way" for her. I said I was glad to do it for her, because she was "special." She dismissed my compliment by saying, "Oh, you say that to everyone!"

My response was, "Yes, I do!" At first she was shocked and confused by what I had said; so I had to explain that I try to see the good or the divine-spark of the God Force in everyone. When we see others as special, we are much more likely to want to share our good with them. This is a very different attitude from the dysfunctional rescuer attitude of, "I want to rescue you, because there is something wrong with you; you are inadequate; or a poor victim of …" When you see others as sparks of the God Force or divine beings, you will treat them with honour and respect.

You honour others by:

1. Listening to their point of view.

2. Knowing that they are on their own special, unique, spiritual journey.

3. Realizing that they are responsible for themselves, i.e., able to respond to their environment in their appropriate way.

4. Acknowledging their right to choose what is appropriate for them – based upon their beliefs at this time.

This doesn't mean that you would pretend to agree with them, if you don't. It just means that you are able to honour and respect their right to their perspective. You may need to tell them that you don't share their perspective, if you believe that it is important, but it is possible to do it in a respectful way.

Whenever you have a clear desire to interact with others in healthy ways, you must accept responsibility for what you contribute to the situations or conversations that you share with them. It may be helpful to take a moment to observe *what* is actually being communicated and *how* it is being communicated. You may want to ask yourself whether unhealthy, unconscious patterns of relating are interfering with what you would like to say to them.

To find this balance, it is necessary to keep in mind that you are no better or worse than any other being. You are a spark of the God Force – a divine being having a human experience. Your personal boundaries are simply preferences that you have created to direct your path in this particular lifetime.

If your "ego pendulum" has swung in either direction, it is helpful to realize that, if your ego is the only aspect of your Total-Self that is in the "driver's seat" of your life, you will perceive your world as disconnected from you, so you will feel alone and unsupported most of the time. When you choose to align all your parts, before you make up your mind to do or say anything, you will see yourself as a total person and you will eventually be more connected with the greater whole.

The following questions may help you bring balance into your life:

1. Am I doing what I want to do, without any regard to how my actions will affect my life or the lives of others?

2. Do I expect others to do exactly what I want them to?

3. Do I expect others to put me up on a pedestal as superior to them?

4. Do I put my needs ahead of other people's needs?

5. Do I feel good when I misuse or mistreat others to get where I want to go?

Or,

1. Do I always put other people's needs ahead of my own?

2. Do I set other people up on pedestals and see myself as inferior to them?

3. Do I wait for other people's approval, before I proceed toward my dreams or goals?

4. Do I believe that I am disconnected from others in my circle?

5. Do I believe that no one appreciates or respects me?

If you have answered *yes* to any of the above questions, it is necessary to rethink your ego position and the role that it plays in your life. If you believe that you are *better than*, or *worse than,* others, you have slipped back into the VPR Cloud and you will always perceive yourself as isolated and alone in an unsafe, "dog-eat-dog world." Ask yourself:

1. What do I really like to do?

2. What am I good at?

3. How can I be of service to others in a way that is my own special gift?

4. How can I express myself in a way that would be caring, loving, accepting, and respectful to me and others?

5. How can I fulfill my purpose on this planet?

Consider the idea that there is an upwardly moving spiral of energy, which invites you to evolve into a greater awareness of your personal divinity and a greater connection with others, Mother Earth and the God Force. Consider the possibility that you may have a unique role to play in the evolution of this Universe and that it is your personal responsibility to achieve your highest potential. If you adopt this attitude and purpose for your life, you will be motivated to stretch and grow into your greater potential. You will expand into a greater awareness of your divine creativity. It will then be easier to share your gifts with others without reservation.

Your potential to be a magnificently powerful person depends upon your ability to develop healthy boundaries and have a healthy ego. When you accept your right and responsibility to become aligned with your integrity, you are truly on your *Path to Wholeness*.

> *Everything that is in my life is there, because I have either consciously invited it, or, I have unconsciously accepted it.*

Making Healthier Choices

The above statement anchors the belief that you are the creator of your life. It may be helpful to say it a few times a day, until you accept that you are responsible for creating everything that is in your present environment.

When you were a very small child, you were curious about everything. This is the natural way that children learn about their environment. However, if your curiosity created stress, rejection, or punishment, you probably stifled it; but when you stifled your curiosity, you also stifled your creativity. When your creativity was diminished, it inhibited your ability to consider your list of options. This may have eventually created a habit of avoiding every challenge that seemed impossible to solve. If this has happened in your life, you are living in the prison of your past. Now is the time to learn how to make healthier choices by remembering your childlike curiosity and accessing your Divine Creativity that is part of your Spiritual-Body.

As a child, many of your choices were made for you. As an adult, you have the power to make your own choices, instead of relying on the choices of others. If you are stuck in dysfunctional patterns of relating or scripts, they will cause you to keep making the same decisions over and over again. Becoming a "grown up" means that you accept the responsibility to change your patterns, and thereby change your life.

It is never a good idea to let others make your decisions for you, because this disempowers you, reinforces your belief in your victim position, and reaffirms your habit of looking for a rescuer. However, it is a good idea to surround yourself with people who inspire you with their ideas; then you can add their ideas to your own list of possibilities and consider your entire list of options, before you make decisions.

Be gentle with yourself. While you are experimenting in new territories, you will likely make a few mistakes. Remember that mistakes are opportunities. It isn't necessary to tackle the big decisions at first. Take the time to play with the small decisions – such as what would be a healthy choice for breakfast. Pick a small challenge area; and work on that one thing, until you are comfortable with your new choices. When you achieve that goal, give yourself credit for having made a different, hopefully healthier, decision and move on to the next.

It is always easier to make big decisions when you have been successful in making smaller ones, which have proven to be right for you. Set your intention to only change one thing at a time. Give yourself achievable goals that you will be able to accomplish in a short period of time and be sure to reinforce any good choice by giving yourself healthy rewards. Adopt the attitude of gratitude for finding the strength and courage to change and take the time to appreciate every small success. Take credit for your own successes and rejoice in the successes of those around you.

> *Chaos and confusion are often the first stages of problem solving.*

When you keep this statement in mind, it is easier to sort through your options, until you find something that works well for you. Sometimes, the most difficult task is to appreciate that every challenge is an invitation to grow into a better person. You may have to search through a lot of trash, until you find the treasure – your truth – but the journey is worth it.

Every new beginning requires that we take risks. Some risks are greater than others. To follow your *Path to Wholeness*, it is essential to consider the risks, but also the potential gain. The following poem may help you consider what you are risking.

Risks

To laugh is to risk appearing the fool.
To weep is to risk appearing sentimental.
To reach out for another is to risk involvement.
To expose your feelings is to risk exposing your true self.
To place your ideas, your dreams, before a crowd
is to risk their loss.
To love is to risk not being loved in return.
To live is to risk dying. To hope is to risk despair.
To try is to risk failure.
But risks must be taken, because the greatest
hazard in life is to risk nothing.
People who risk nothing, have nothing, and are nothing.
They may avoid suffering and sorrow.
But they cannot learn, feel, change, grow, love, or live.
Chained by their certitudes, they are slaves.
They have forfeited their freedom.
Only a person who risks is truly free.
-Author Unknown-

There is a risk in every choice. New choices may seem to be riskier, than following your old habits. However, by making no choice, or repeating the same choice as you made before, you risk perpetuating your misery or living in the same unhealthy environment, which you have previously created. By assessing the risk in every choice, you are able to determine whether or not a risk is worth taking.

Of course, there are *good* choices as well as *bad* choices. How do you tell the difference? A good place to start is by inserting the words "functional" or "healthy," instead of the word *"good,"* and "dysfunctional" or "unhealthy," instead of the word *"bad."* If your choice is functional or healthy, it works; you create what is *right* for you; and you experience a deep sense of peace, connection, and satisfaction. It will open doors for you – allowing you to experience more life, more power, more peace of mind, and more love.

Every thought, feeling, word, and action can be compared to throwing a pebble into a still pond. The pebble penetrates the water and disturbs its natural state, causing ripples. By watching the ripples that radiate out from the point of entry, you can clearly see the *effects* of the pebble's "invasion" into the water. Your thoughts, feelings, words, and actions have a ripple effect, because they cause "invasions" into your environment. They *affect* your environment – sometimes in small ways, and, at other times, in huge ways. This is a good analogy, but it is important to keep in mind that ripples actually move slower than your thoughts and the effects or results of your choices. The actual speed is actually more like flashes of light, the speed of a lightning bolt.

If the choice is unhealthy, your energy runs away from you – making it inaccessible to you – and making you feel more powerless. It is your personal responsibility to adjust your habits, until you are able to reclaim and reroute that type of energy in the future by making choices that are in harmony with your integrity – your Personal Power. This is an act of self-love.

Unfortunately, people who have lived in dysfunctional or confusing environments usually haven't learned how to be loving and honest with themselves or others, because these attributes have not been adequately modeled for them. It is much more common for them to project blame and shame onto themselves or others, rather than honestly taking responsibility for their own decisions and needs; or holding other people accountable for their thoughts, feelings, words, or actions. Therefore, their methods of saying no are usually fraught with ineffective communication skills.

The common habit of avoiding responsibility is to find fault with others, which often creates a distance or blockage of energy between the two parties. This creates even greater separation and loneliness on both sides. It is important to become creative and find a new and more connective way of communicating your desires to others. By being genuinely honest with them and speaking from your integrity, you may also call forth an opportunity for them to become more responsible for their choices.

Whenever you treat others as if they are *evil/bad/wrong*, you create a separation between you and them. When you treat others with respect – honouring their divinity – you connect with them on a deep level. This doesn't mean that you have to spend time with them if it isn't *right* for you to do so. It means that you can be open to learning from your experience with them and you can acknowledge them as unique, divine-sparks who are making the choices that are *right for them* at this present time.

There is an old saying, "Whatever you see in others is what you see in yourself." This means that there is a mirror image of yourself in the people that you like, but also in those that you condemn. We project our own judgments onto others. Therefore, what we judge in others is also what we judge in ourselves.

Therefore, if someone causes you to believe that you are inadequate, unworthy, hopeless, etc., it is always a projection of their own self-images; but, if you accept their opinion, it may also be an old script that has been triggered in you. Thoughts can only impact you *IF* those ideas have an anchor. There must be some of that energy buried deep inside you, to allow that idea to "hook" into your awareness. (It may be helpful to reread *How Your Clouds are Triggered* in Chapter 1.)

Whenever you are triggered, the resulting emotional reaction is an opportunity to examine the messages that are coming from deep within you. Your soul is calling you to heal these clouds, so you can live life freely and reach your highest potential. Recognize the gifts that they truly are and be grateful for the opportunities that are being presented to you. Your triggers have no real power over you once they are brought into your conscious awareness. You can release the recurring pain and reprogram your old, emotional reactions once you consider that those painful moments are actually *gifts* to assist in your healing.

Another gift may be revealed, if you observe how you choose to react to appreciation, when others see beauty in you or compliment you on a talent or ability. If you reject their appreciation, you haven't yet connected with your inner beauty or accepted your unique abilities. When you recognize the truth in their appreciation of your inner beauty or ability, this means that you have already connected with that aspect of your unique Total-Self.

Recognizing these truths about yourself, can help you understand why you react in certain ways to certain people. When you take time to carefully think through your list of options about how you would like to respond to others, you will create different experiences with people. This will prevent you from making choices by default or letting your habits make your choices.

Remorse as a Healing Force

There are two types of remorse: healthy and unhealthy. Unhealthy remorse is the result of a combination of factors, making it somewhat confusing to unravel; so let's take it apart to simplify it. It usually begins when we have made an inappropriate choice – a "missed-take" – and we start to criticize ourselves with abusive self-talk about how "stupid" we are. (It may be helpful to review the topic of Mistakes in Chapter 2.)

Unhealthy remorse is usually self-flagellation about making mistakes. It is usually expressed by the words "should have," "could have," or "if I were ..., I would have." These are often shortened to what I jokingly call "shoulda, coulda, woulda scripts." These scripts are a terrible waste of time. Unhealthy remorse about what happened, or didn't happen, wastes time, because you are focused on thinking about the past, and therefore, you are not exploring any opportunity for change in the present or future.

When we become totally honest with ourselves, we can become aware of *how* or *why* we have made our unsatisfactory choices. Our choices may be the result of an unconscious script that has repeatedly clouded our thinking, so we may have to thoroughly examine them.

Then we are in a position of power, where we can say, "I'm sorry that I made that choice." If we examine each choice fully, we can come to the conclusion that it was lacking in some way, such as: insight, intuition, information, intelligence, or careful planning. Now that we have additional insight and information, we can say, "I don't want to make that choice again." This new awareness helps us expand our creativity to imagine a different choice the next time we are in a similar situation. We can ask ourselves, "What would I like to change to create a different effect in the future?"

If you experience remorse in this way and don't get sidetracked by old habits, such as making excuses, finding a scapegoat, or wallowing in blame, shame, or guilt, you have the opportunity to imprint your Total-Self with a commitment to make a better choice in the future.

Whenever you take full responsibility for having made inappropriate choices, it is a huge opportunity for growth. By assuming responsibility for your choices, you push out the belief that you are a helpless victim of circumstances. You will then be able to think more clearly and make healthier choices. By making sure that your choices are in harmony with your integrity, you will avoid similar situations in the future.

You may also use that power to reach a state of self-forgiveness where you can fully understand that you made that choice because you didn't know any better at the time, or that you didn't trust your inner voice. This awareness allows you to embrace the wisdom attained during your assessment of your previous choices. You can fully accept your ability to make different choices in the present and future.

True forgiveness is a powerful healer. To forgive yourself, you must reach a deep understanding of yourself. Then, you will be able to accept that you just didn't know any better – you simply had a pattern of relating that caused you to act in an inefficient or hurtful way. If you have caused pain to others, it may be necessary to ask for their forgiveness. You may need to apologize or make restitution for your actions as a part of taking responsibility, but the end result must be to come to a place of peace within yourself.

You must love yourself enough to listen to your Spiritual-Body and reach a level of clarity in your mind that reveals the truth about why you spoke or acted in that manner. Then you can expand into understanding the pain that you have caused in others. Only then can you reach true remorse, because you can see how your choice has affected those around you. Next, you must do a "reality check" and admit that, because you didn't know better at the time, it is now your responsibility to create a different reality in the present and future. Then, you must love yourself enough to make a commitment to not follow that self-limiting pathway, ever again.

Many religions give the message that the God Force is a critical being who is keeping track of our mistakes and harshly judging us for them. Whenever I open myself to the God Force, however, I find a very different energy available to me – a forgiving, understanding energy that I call the unconditional love of the God Force. When I ask for forgiveness, I receive the message, "There is nothing to forgive! There are, however, lessons to be learned from the experience." Consequently, I have the belief that I am an integral part of that Love Force, the Creative Force of the Universe – a child, or component, of that Creative Force – a dynamic power – a being with the ability to make my own choices – an "agent of cause." Then, I acknowledge that it is within my ability to make better choices in the future.

When you take back your divine connection, you will again have access to your creativity and the Personal Power to choose what is right for you – every moment of every day. You can say to yourself, "I made a mistake! Now, I see that it didn't work; it didn't feel good/right/loving. So, the next time I have the opportunity to experience a similar scenario, I will choose differently." By affirming that you are an integral part of the Source of Creativity – the God Force – you are able to take personal responsibility for your thoughts, feelings, words, and actions. You will then realize that you can choose the realities that you would like to experience. You will accept that your choices today create your future.

The commitment to consciously learn from your mistakes is one of the most essential steps along your *Path to Wholeness*. Whenever you are tempted to sink into unhealthy remorse when you make a mistake, it may be helpful to ask yourself whether you have learned anything from the experience. If you focus your attention on what you have learned, you will move into a better frame of mind. Remember, the only *bad* mistakes are when you haven't learned anything from your choices. You caused pain with those choices – pain that created "hell" in your life. You can then make better choices and create your own brand of "heaven" in the future.

Letting Go of the Need for Approval

Children who have lived in confusing environments often develop an addiction to approval, (mostly because they never received enough) so they came to the conclusion that by complying with the wishes of others, life will be less confusing. You may have learned to conform and comply to get love or attention. You may have learned the rules of conduct in your environment and adapted your identity to fit in. You may have altered your true nature to accommodate the people in your environment. You may believe that you will not be loved or even accepted, unless you conform to the wishes of the people in your environment.

As an adult, you may have continued these childlike habits. You may have been trapped in the habit of giving away parts of your Total-Self to the values of other people. Now, you may wish to rethink your earlier choices. Following are some examples of the ways that you may still be giving away your power to gain approval from others.

The Way You Look

If you are lacking in a strong commitment to consistently express your true self, you may try to fit into your circle of influence by wearing the type of fashions of which the others in your environment approve. You may spend most of your pay-check on external trappings, such as: clothes, make up, the latest hairstyle, a better car, a bigger house, or a new toy of some sort – with the hope of fitting in. You may believe that you *have to* comply with the latest fad to be liked or accepted by others.

Young people often believe that they are being *different* when they rebel against the expectations of their parents and they think, speak, and act the same as their peers. They don't realize that they are still *complying* with the wishes of others, losing their personal identity, and sacrificing their individuality. They may be actually weakening their boundaries and leaving themselves vulnerable to abuse. They are also diminishing their connection to their Spiritual-Body, making it less possible to reach their greatest potential.

Whenever you make decisions simply because you believe that others will like you better, you diminish your connection with your real, authentic-self, your integrity, and the Source of your being. Until you can express your uniqueness in healthy ways, you are still a victim to the whims of others – or more precisely, you may have adopted the habits and behaviours that you *believe* will bring approval from others.

Sometimes, when I start a new development group, I pair people off and tell them to ask the other person questions about him or herself, until they are comfortable enough to introduce the other person to the group. After I give each person time to do this, I ask everyone to come back into the circle and face the center. I then ask them to close their eyes and describe the person that they have been looking at. Usually, less than half of the people can tell me one specific thing about what the person was wearing, whether or not they had makeup on, whether or not they were wearing jewellery, or even, in some cases, whether or not they were wearing shoes.

I then ask them to remember their thoughts before they came to the group. Most people admit that they had taken special pains to make themselves "look good" to impress the others in the group. One woman confessed that she almost didn't come to the group, because she "didn't have anything new to wear." She eventually laughed at herself, when her partner pointed out that he wouldn't have known whether or not her clothes were new, because he had never seen her other clothes.

If you are dressing to please others, you are expressing yourself to the world in a way that is at least partially untrue – whether it is trying to dress in accordance with the dictates of current fashion; an attempt to mask your feelings of inadequacy; or create an illusion of confidence. Ideally, the way you look will be a clear expression of your unique personality and your purpose in life. When you consciously choose the way you look, you are expressing your true identity to the physical world in a healthy way.

What You Think

Original thought is seldom appreciated in dysfunctional environments. It is too threatening to the established philosophy of the group. Sir Isaac Newton was scoffed at by the scholars of his day, when he introduced his Laws of Motion. Louis Pasteur was called a "quack," when he said that germs had the potential to carry sickness. Madam Marie Curie was said to be "insane" to think that there were harmful rays, such as radioactivity, that could not be seen. All of these people were brave enough to use their creativity to explore the unknown and speak their truth – even though they ran the risk of being ridiculed. Because of their bravery, each of these people made a huge contribution to humanity.

Many people are afraid to express their thoughts, because they are terrified of ridicule. You will never be able to share your unique gifts, if you limit your thoughts to the ideas that you *believe* will achieve approval from others. When you are willing to go beyond the limits that have restricted your thinking, you can then explore greater and greater spheres of thought. The habit of consistently expanding your thinking may lead you to a plane of perception where you can find *original* thought. You then have the potential to explore unknown and exciting territories. Then, if you are brave enough, you may contribute something of great value to the world.

You have that potential within you. Your original thoughts have value. Your thoughts have the potential to change your worldview, and, eventually, your world. Whenever you share your thoughts and ideas with others, their opinions may change and *their* world could possibly change. Your "original" ideas are potentially your greatest gift to the world.

What You Say and How You Say It

Many people who were raised in confusing environments learn to communicate in a manner that will cause the least resistance. It is natural, and often very considerate, to adjust your words to the scope and interests of your audience; however, if you speak in a way that is out of harmony with your integrity, you are not honestly expressing your unique, Total-Self, and, therefore, you are diminishing your true gifts to the world.

One of the greatest fears that people have is public speaking – especially into a microphone. If you are afraid of expressing yourself publicly, it is very difficult to make a difference in your environment. If your fear of ridicule keeps you from expressing who you are and what you believe to be true, you are hiding your light from the world. Each of us has a unique and special gift to share. You become a true hero whenever you are brave enough to express your light to the world.

For example: I once knew a man who complained about how dysfunctional his family was. However, even though he had moved away from that kind of behaviour in most cases, he still condoned it in his family's sense of humour and often lapsed into their type of humour when he was with them. I seldom found their humour amusing, because it was often demeaning and abusive.

Eventually, his sister took me out to lunch to tell me that I just had to learn to enjoy their humour. She shared a story about how she had once fallen backward off a porch and had broken her wrist. Her family had thought it was so funny that they were unable to help her. She informed me that I would just have to learn to join in with the fun and not be so offended by it. I was shocked!

Instead of agreeing with her acceptance of such abuse, I leaned across the table, put my hand upon hers, looked into her eyes, and said, "I will never be like your family, if it includes finding your pain humorous." She burst into tears. I was the first person who had peeled away the layers of her defensive-mechanisms and had actually *heard* her pain. By staying in harmony with my integrity, I had spoken words that had touched her heart and a deep intimacy was established between us. She saw that she had been repressing her pain and making excuses for the unhealthy habits of her birth family.

Finding humour in another's pain reveals separation, apathy, insensitivity toward others, and a lack of empathy. Words are powerful! They have the power to connect or separate us from our truth. They have the power to open or close communication. They have the power to hurt or heal. It is essential to choose them wisely, because once words are out of our mouths, they can't be swallowed again.

Some people say things that are mean-spirited, and then say, "Just kidding;" but the hurtful energy is already out! Those ideas cannot be retrieved. Our words are a permanent record of what we believe to be true in that moment. They expose our truth to the light of day. Even other words, such as those in the form of an apology, seldom have the power to undo the effect of thoughtless words.

If you are fully aware of what you are thinking, you have the capacity to observe your thoughts objectively and perhaps intervene before they are expressed verbally. Words expose your thoughts and beliefs to the people in your environment. Your willingness to be responsible for your words reflects your level of integrity.

What You Believe

As has been addressed in Chapter Four, from early childhood, people in your surrounding environment have inundated you with suggestions – *shoulds* and *shouldn'ts* and ideas that implied *good* or *bad, right* or *wrong*. Most of these pieces of advice were given with good intentions; however, there comes a time when you may need to ask yourself who you really are – what *you* want to think, feel, say, and do. You express your beliefs whenever you open your mouth to speak. Pay attention to what comes out of your mouth.

Remember, beliefs are simply energy packages that are stored between your Emotional and Mental Bodies. If you are willing to carefully observe what you think, feel, say, and do, you will find the truth about what you believe. You will find out whether you believe that you must give up your true, authentic-self in order to receive the approval of others. The truth will be shown to you in your thoughts, in the words and tone of your message, and how you act toward others. You may find the following questions helpful to access your unconscious beliefs about the approval of others:

1. What is it that I stand for?

2. What is important to me?

3. What kind of person do I want to be?

4. What kind of message do I want to share with others?

5. What are my goals in life?

6. What is my purpose?

7. How do I want others to see me?

8. How do I want to be remembered when I'm gone?

Only by giving up your addiction to approval from others can you answer the above questions from a place of honesty, integrity, and clarity. Whenever you examine the intent and attitude of your thoughts, feelings, words, and actions, you have the opportunity to fully understand the beliefs that automatically produce your words and habits. This will allow you to see how your unconscious beliefs have been controlling your thoughts, feelings, words, and actions. By seeing how they create a spiral of energy that not only affects others, they return to affect each of us through the Law of Cause and Effect.

You have the power to interrupt the cycle. (See Cycle of Beliefs on page 211 It doesn't matter where you intervene in the cycle, as long as you are creative enough to interject a new idea – one that is more effective, more efficient, or more functional.

If you find the source of an underlying belief that you have to comply with others, you then have the option to become more in alignment with your present perception of reality. You may also see how many options you actually have in the present. When you adjust your perception, a miracle will happen – you will create an exciting new reality! Instead of thinking like a helpless robot that automatically acts out your unconscious beliefs, you realize that you are the creator of your life. You then have the power to be whom you were meant to be – a unique spark of the God Force.

Letting Go Of Control Dramas

There are two types of control – internal and external. Internal control is Personal Power. The belief that we can control others is a delusion or cloud. The only person we can completely control is ourselves – our thoughts, feelings, words, and actions. We can't control others, unless they are willing to let us. So, we aren't really controlling them, they are choosing to comply with our wishes. This is how and why control dramas are formed. Instead of being open and honest in our desire to control others, we design control dramas to *trick* people into complying with our wishes – covertly – without overtly expressing what we want them to do. Consequently, every control drama creates a cloud of confusion.

External control seems very important whenever we are afraid that others will do or say something that we don't want them to. We may have a variety of reasons for wanting to restrain or regulate their behaviour: we may be afraid that they will say or do something to hurt us or others; we may want the outcome to be exactly the way we want it to be; we may believe that they are incapable of *correctly* controlling themselves; or, we may simply believe that we can do a better job of managing the situation than they can. Therefore, every attempt to control others is always an attempt to create a safety zone within our circle of influence.

All conflict, whether on a personal or global level, is the result of the struggle for control over boundaries, whether those boundaries are physical, mental, emotional, or spiritual.

Everyone has their personal set of boundaries. Boundaries are the restrictions and limits that you place on yourself and others – what you will accept or put up with. It is your right and responsibility to set and maintain your personal boundaries; however, you may have come to believe that you have to control your entire environment *plus* defend your personal boundaries at all times – that you are never safe, unless you are constantly on guard against invasion.

When children are shown healthy boundaries by their parents and caregivers, they will automatically develop their own healthy boundaries. If others constantly disrespect or invade their boundaries, children learn that they are never *safe* in their environment and believe in the necessity of external control. Therefore, it is very important to examine your *intent* and evaluate the hidden reasons for your desire to control others. This is especially true when you are caring for very small children and you assume that they *need* to be controlled. When you control out of fear, you teach children to fear. Granted, you may believe that it is necessary to keep children from hurting themselves and others; however, there is a fine line between the necessity to control and the projection of our own fears.

Manners and etiquette are more universal control tactics that are firmly established in our culture. Society's rules are designed to keep people in line and, for the most part, these rules have merit. All too often, however, we may judge other people by the set of rules that we internalized from our family and community values – sometimes without any thought for individual expression. It is important to guard against the habit of judging others for the differences between us. People who *believe* that they have the right to dictate the behaviour of others are often extremely afraid of the other person's potential power.

The desire to control is often so deeply embedded in control addicts that they even try to control others who are assisting them in getting what they believe they want. Surprising as it is, these people are so addicted to control that they often sabotage any attempts to help them. They will do anything to prove that they are *right,* even at the expense of losing their individuality. These people have carried the fear of being controlled to the extreme. They are unwilling to let anything stay the same long enough to create safety and comfort. It creates a constant state of chaos, because they are continually changing the rules of the game. There is then no room for peace of mind or the possibility of experiencing safety or security, even for a moment.

Some control addicts believe that, if they were to stop controlling their environment, it would automatically fall apart. This goes beyond normal fear of the unknown to terror. They become addicted to work, stress, or perfection. It can cause scripts, such as, "No one can do the job as well as I can;" or, "Everyone is out to get me;" or, "*They* only want to compete with me – or *win* the situation." Their fear of losing control immobilizes them into a form of rigidity. Their minds are so full of the fear of losing control that they don't consider the disconnection from their Personal Power that is at the root of the problem.

Denial of our Personal Power usually manifests as scripts of powerlessness and defensive-mechanisms. For example: When we are afraid, and we deny our fear, we usually act out our fear with aggression – like a bully. When we believe that we are *stupid,* we pretend that we are *smart* and become *arrogant.* When we fear rejection, we often display a "chip on our shoulder" and pretend that we don't need anyone. When we deny our awareness of disconnection from the God Force, we may pretend to be the "missing god" and express qualities that we have incorrectly assumed to be godlike and become distant, judgmental, or superior.

Some control addicts assume that everyone is beneath them – less intelligent, less important, or less capable in some way – denying other people the right to express *their* divinity. They often have arguments with people who don't bend to their superiority, and ultimately, they eliminate those people from their circle. Of course, control addicts have *good reasons* for eliminating certain people from their list of associates. These *good reasons* are based upon the belief that their logic is *infallible,* their opinions are *right,* their values are *superior,* and their separation is *necessary* for their survival.

To change these beliefs, it may be necessary to consider the possibility that you are being closed-minded, or that you are protecting your territory, because you are afraid of other possibilities. This self-honesty is a very scary thing to do at first, because it requires that you examine your beliefs and determine the *real* value of the defensive-mechanisms that you have erected to prevent you from experiencing painful sensations. This honest self-examination is essential, however, if you wish to release your self-limiting beliefs and access your potential.

People who are addicted to control have many opportunities to observe feedback from their environment. They are usually "accident-prone" – constantly the "victims of circumstance;" because they attract to them that which they fear the most. We hear them say that they are "always frustrated," because they are "always behind," and they can "never catch up." They are constantly affirming, "Nothing ever goes my way." These are warning signs, revealing that they are trying to force their environment to be the way they believe it *should* be – instead of taking responsibility for having created their environment with their previous choices.

If we objectively observe the nature of this planet, we see that the more we try to control it, the more out of control it becomes. Whenever human beings try to change the nature of matter on this planet to make so-called "progress," major problems result – pollution, global warming, and other ecological imbalances, to name a few.

The same rule of cause and effect is true for every person who lives on this planet. We can swim with, or against, the flow of the *river of life*. The idea that we are able to control the *river of life* is an arrogant, self-righteous illusion, or more accurately a delusion. The only way to find peace of mind is to let go of that delusion and learn how to live in harmony with our environments. Letting go of the delusion of, or addiction to, control is very scary when we have the belief that we will perish, unless we are the ones who are in charge.

Keep in mind that whenever you are uncomfortable in a situation, or you believe that your integrity is in jeopardy, it is your right to express your discomfort by stating specifically what you are experiencing; however, ultimately the only *real* control that you have over any situation is whether you choose to stay in a situation or relationship, or move away from that situation or person.

People who were raised in unsafe or confusing environments usually build up a vast number of control-strategies that become unhealthy habits. These habits may be seen as "small" and even "petty" to others. They may be attitudes about the way that you wash your hands, or comb your hair, or squeeze your tube of toothpaste. Comedians act out scenes in which spouses argue over the *right* way to do such mundane tasks. While these examples seem funny, because we can relate to the absurdity of arguing over something so trivial, in real life, they often reflect the level of addiction present in our lives. They may even reflect a defensive-mechanism that we have created to hide our control dramas.

Many couples argue over these trivial issues to cover up the dissatisfaction that is present in other areas of their relationship. For example: I once counselled a couple who had an ongoing struggle over a particular hook in their bathroom. The woman wanted the hook for her hairdryer and the man repeatedly "put his dirty pants on it." The resulting discussion eventually uncovered the fact that the woman saw the house as *her* territory, because she had so little control over many other areas in their relationship. She thought that, because she had to clean their home, she should be able to organize it to her liking. Her control drama was covering up the fact that she wanted to be a successful business woman – not a homemaker. The man, on the other hand, diminished her job as a homemaker, because he wanted his job to be "the important one."

If you are addicted to controlling the *small* things in your life, you may be filling your mind with detail, because you don't want to look at more significant things that are bothering you. This preoccupation with the small things (your addiction to control) keeps the chaos, which is just below the surface, from *oozing up* and creating a helpless or insecure state of mind. Preoccupation with maintaining unhealthy habits can prevent awareness, understanding, and expansion into new opportunities. It can keep you preoccupied with the past and prevent you from reaching your potential.

If you try to fill every second of your day with meaningless activities, it may be because you believe that, if you allow your pain to surface, it will overwhelm you and you will be "out of control." You may also be afraid that someone will try to control you, unless you are the one who is in control in every moment. The best way to eliminate the fear that anyone has the power to control you is to seize your Personal Power and be responsible for every aspect of your life. Then, your personal integrity will be intact and you will allow no one, other than yourself, to make your choices. It is essential to set your intention to be responsible for what you allow or invite into your life; what you give to other people; what energy you wish to share with others; and what energy to reject or walk away from.

It is important, however, to consider the difference between the energy of walking away from a situation in strength and the act of running away from your problems. If you run away from something or someone, instead of resolving the issues causing your problem, the pattern that originally caused you to be involved with that energy will surface again in a different form. For example: If you were to run away from a partner who is an alcoholic, you may then be attracted to a person who is a sports addict or workaholic. Lack of accountability and personal responsibility may be dominant in each of these individuals. They just look different on the outside and have different addictions that are designed to avoid their personal responsibilities. When you are fully connected with your authentic-voice from your Spiritual-Body you will know what is in your best interest.

This final step out of the VPR Cloud, into a balanced Total-Self, will mean that others no longer have the power to control, misuse, or abuse you. You will become unwilling to accept unhealthy attitudes and behaviours within your sacred space. You will no longer need to keep abuse a secret (even from the abusive person). Once you take full responsibility (your ability to respond differently to your environment), your divine creativity has the opportunity to explore other choices – ones that will lead you to live in harmony with your environment and the God Force. You will then be free to play in the field of possibilities and fully express your Total-Self. You may become like the little child who says, "You can't speak to me that way, I'm a divine-spark of the God Force."

Because you are a spark of the God Force, you have the right to express yourself in your own, unique way. You have the power to choose whether or not you wish to play the way others want you to play. You don't have to play by their rules; nor do you have the right to impose the rules that define your boundaries upon others.

Chapter Six

Reinventing Your Life

In this chapter, we will discuss some other ways that you may need to adjust your thinking, if you wish to bring your life into greater alignment with your integrity and balance your Total-Self. Some of the suggestions may be easy to follow and others may take some getting used to. Consider that it may take time to process the necessary information to release your old theories and scripts about how to live in this world – the stories that are held in your clouds.

Reconnecting With Your Body

Many people who were raised in unhealthy family environments have learned unhealthy ways of caring for their bodies. If you wish to have a healthy body, it may be necessary to carefully think about your attitudes regarding your body and how you first began to create those attitudes and habits.

When children grow up in an environment where less than nutritious food is offered, they soon develop the belief that eating junk food is "normal." Health proponents claim,

"Unless you are hungry for the simplest of foods, you aren't hungry – you just think you are. Unless you are thirsty for water, you aren't thirsty – you just think you are."

If you usually choose processed food, instead of whole food, you may be trying to compensate for some *lack* in your life. Most fast food or junk food facilities would go bankrupt, if people stopped eating to compensate for the *lacks* in their lives. When you eat denatured food, it fills up your stomach – so you don't have room for natural, healthy food. Many children become so addicted to junk food that they are unwilling to eat anything else. This leads to obesity and poor health.

Much of our food supply is grown in artificially fertilized soil, instead of organically grown – the way nature intended for us to get the nutrients to feed our bodies. The huge problem of obesity in our society may be directly linked to the inferior quality of the food in the mainstream diet. This begs the question, are obese people craving food, because they are lacking certain nutrients from the food they have eaten, so they think that they need more? Is this because in reality, they are actually starving, because they are only eating denatured foods?

Another type of addiction to food is the fad diet. We are besieged with new "miracle" diets almost daily. The Macrobiotic Diet was the first major "miracle diet" in the 1980s. It was a very restrictive diet that claimed to cure a number of health problems. It actually helped a great many people; however, some people who continued to use it, after they were over their health crisis, found that it created other health problems.

Vegetarianism became popular next. It has been more widely accepted as a healthy way of life in recent years. Surveys showed that those practicing a healthy, vegetarian diet were less likely to suffer from high cholesterol and heart disease. This increased the awareness of the benefits of avoiding animal products; however, many vegetarians also run the risk of certain dietary deficiencies, because they eat too many denatured, processed foods. The only way to become a healthy vegetarian is slowly and carefully, and by making sure all your nutritional needs are fulfilled.

The saying was introduced, "You are what you eat!" This greater awareness shocked a great many people who had previously not even considered what they were putting into their mouths. They had unconsciously repeated the diet that their parents had supplied when they were young. The habit of compensating with food to fill their psychological and emotional needs was a deeply imbedded, socially accepted pattern of relating. If you wish to change your patterns of relating to your body, it may be necessary to examine your basic, primitive reason or motivation for your desire to eat or drink. Making healthy choices requires expansive thinking; you can no longer be limited by your old patterns. Before choosing the food or drink that you *think* you want, you may wish to ask yourself the following questions:

Do I really need something to eat or drink at this moment? Or, am I eating or drinking out of habit or to compensate for a lack in my life?

Am I hungry for the simplest of foods or beverages? For example: Does my body need this pizza, or would I be healthier if I ate an apple?

Practice making healthier choices by tuning into your body and choosing the appropriate food or drink that will bring true satisfaction – both immediate and long lasting. To make appropriate decisions that are loving and supportive to your body, start by asking yourself the following questions:

1. Am I making this choice automatically?
2. Am I blindly following a habit, or an unconscious pattern?
3. Is the food that I am considering going to serve my highest good?

Proponents of natural eating have created a simple way to remember which food substances are the most stressful to our bodies. They have labelled them the "White Devils" and the "Black Devils."

The "White Devils"

1. White sugar (instead of unrefined, natural sugars);

2. White flour (instead of whole grain flours);

3. White salt (instead of natural sea salt);

4. Milk and dairy products (which have been produced by unhealthy farming practices, and pasteurized, homogenized, and chemically preserved);

5. White powders (additives and preservatives that aren't food, but are the chemical flavour enhancers that are used to make inferior food more palatable- such as MSG/monosodium glutamate.) This category also includes substances such as saccharine, aspartame, etc. used to artificially sweeten foods and drinks. These chemicals cause many harmful side effects and allergic reactions. Diabetics and dieters have been misled to believe that chemically produced sugar substitutes are harmless; however, recent studies have confirmed that they actually create obesity. The use of the natural substances such as honey or maple syrup or an herb called "stevia" are safer, sugar-free, and much healthier substitutes.

"The Black Devils"

1. Coffee (which contains caffeine – a drug and is very acidic);

2. Tea (which contains caffeine and tannic acid – both drugs and very acidic);

3. Alcoholic beverages and drugs – legal and illegal (which are mood altering and cause cellular damage);

4. Chocolate (which contains caffeine, and usually white sugar and dairy products to make it palatable);

5. Black pepper (which is an irritant to the digestive tract).

Many health proponents also add barbequed foods to the list of Black Devils, because when fats are heated or seared (blackened), they become harmful.

Each of the above substances creates an acidic state in the human body that prevents normal digestion. If you think about the "White Devils," you will realize that they are so denatured there isn't any *real* food left. For example: They throw away the best part of the wheat berry when they make white flour and then add bleaching agents to make it look *more white.*

If you think about the "Black Devils," you will see that none of them is actually whole food in its natural state. The body knows what to do with something that is in its natural form. For example: If you were to go into an orchard and pick an apple, you could eat it immediately and your body would know how to process the nutrients it offers. However, if you were to go into a farm where they grow coffee beans, you couldn't just pick and eat them. Many things must be done to coffee to make it palatable. This is a clue to understanding why it is so stressful to the body. On an energetic level, both the black and white devils blow holes in the human aura that "bleed" away energy and may even allow harmful energies to enter and lead to sickness or emotional distress.

It may be helpful to keep the above list in mind when you are asking yourself whether or not you are using foods and drinks to try to fill the "hungers" in your life. A simple way to make healthy, nutritional choices is to decide whether you are interested in the food or drink, because you are *truly* hungry or thirsty, or just because you have an empty sensation that you hope will be filled by the substance. Keep in mind that when you are making unhealthy choices in an attempt to avoid the pain or emptiness in your life, you will *usually* choose unhealthy foods.

It may also be helpful to observe your reactions when it is suggested that you may be hurting your body when you drink coffee, soda pop, black tea, or alcoholic beverages. Are you thinking, "I can't wake up in the morning without my coffee!" or, "What will I drink with my lunch if I can't have my soda or black tea?" or "How can I get through the dinner hour without my martini?" Each of these panic thoughts is an expression of an addictive pattern of relating to your body. Take a moment to consider your reactions while those ideas are still in your thinking process and you will have the chance to choose differently.

If it is true that you are in need of a stimulant to get out of bed in the morning, you may need more rest, better nutrition, or alternative health or medical advice. Coffee isn't the solution to your problem of fatigue; and your addiction to coffee may actually be covering up a symptom of an underlying problem. A decision to use coffee to cover up the symptom of tiredness is typical of the addictive choices that people make when they try to substitute an *artificial* solution for a *real* one! Remember, every addictive thought includes the idea that if you have …., you will feel better.

If it is true that you are afraid that you will have nothing to drink at lunchtime, you may need to expand your thinking to include water, herbal teas, or natural juices. Or better yet, you could try to avoid drinking any beverages with your meals, so your digestive juices will have a better chance of doing their job.

If it is true that you have trouble getting through the dinner hour without some alcoholic beverage to help you forget your worries, you may need to reduce the stress in your life and make better choices about how you are relating to the people who share your life.

Do you ignore your body's reaction to different foods? Are you aware that different body types need different types of food to be healthy? People who are allergic to substances or are unable to digest certain foods often ignore their body's warning signals and carelessly eat or drink the offending substances. This is a blatant lack of respect for their physical needs. They are demonstrating to their body that they don't care whether it is healthy and they are ignoring their responsibility for creating a healthy body.

If you have the attitude that your body will survive no matter what you eat, you may need to consider your diet carefully. It may be possible that you have absorbed your neglectful attitudes from your early environment. If your caregivers treated your body (or their bodies) carelessly, you may have developed a similar attitude. Now, you think that you can put anything you want into your body and it will "just have to put up with it." These attitudes reveal a lack of personal integrity and a lack of willingness to accept and respect the needs of your body.

Making healthy choices about what to eat and drink is often the best place to start disciplining your mind, and consequently, healing your body. It may be helpful to consider that your body naturally wants to live – it has its own life force – so, if you give it what it needs, it will be happy and you will be healthy. Additionally, eating whole foods and having proper nutrition actually helps you deal with stress more efficiently, meaning that your mind will be clearer and you will be able to solve your problems more effectively.

Eating and drinking are such common occurrences. You usually eat at least three times a day and drink more frequently. Therefore, if you make a conscious decision about what is the *right* food for your needs, each time you choose something to eat or drink, you will find that your body responds very quickly to your tender, loving care. You may also, eventually, transfer that good habit over to thinking about what is *right* to think, feel, say, and do.

Each time that you make a healthy decision, pay attention to what you are experiencing – deep inside you. Notice the different sensations that you experience when you make appropriate and inappropriate decisions. You may learn how to choose wisely and you will be able to take credit for making the decisions that are best for you. Appreciate your ability to make healthier choices, and feel *good* about yourself, because you are creating healthier patterns and setting healthier goals. It may be helpful to answer the following questions:

1. Do you consider the quality of the air you breathe? Is your daily environment polluted with chemical toxins or exhaust fumes? Do you pollute it with tobacco smoke or do you live, work, or play in a space where others smoke? (Studies have shown that tobacco is more addictive than heroin and that second-hand smoke is extremely harmful.)

2. Do you consider the quality of the water that you drink? It is recommended that we drink eight 8-ounce glasses of pure water each day. In most urban areas, it is necessary to buy or make purified water, as effluents from sewage systems and factories have polluted our public water supplies. (It is particularly important to drink extra water, if you are on any type of medication, as the body needs more water to flush medications out of your system.)

3. Do you use artificial perfumes or antiperspirants? Keep in mind that everything you put on your skin is absorbed into your body.

Perfumes are usually made from synthetic combinations of chemicals that have never been tested for their affect on human health. Antiperspirants prevent the natural release of perspiration by clogging or closing the pores. There are more sweat glands in your armpits and groin than in other parts of the body, because these two areas contain a great number of lymph nodes. The extra sweat glands are designed to release the toxins from your lymphatic system. When you produce an odour in these areas, it is because your lymphatic system has released harmful toxins. When you use an antiperspirant, you prevent the release of natural waste; and the toxins are forced back into your body. (This is more harmful when the person is ingesting allopathic drugs, because most medications are very harmful when they build up in the body.)

There are other influences that impact on our ability to connect with our bodies. Repeated messages and depictions of violence in our environment, on television, in movies, or on the internet can numb us into a state of lethargy or apathy, because we simply can't allow any more stress to influence our minds. Do you ignore or suppress the disgust or repulsion that occurs whenever abnormal or disrespectful sounds or pictures are presented to you? The suppression of these emotions builds up stress in the body.

Heavy metal and rap music invade our airways and subliminally suggest disrespectful, antisocial, or violent actions. Casual sex is presented in the media as a "normal" way of life. People who produce pornography or movies that exhibit degrading sex acts disrespect and degrade the human spirit, as well as the human body.

People live in fear of rejection when their bodies don't conform to the *norm* that is portrayed in the media. They think that they have to "look good" to find or keep a mate. Advertisements for fitness equipment promise sure-fire ways to "look good" for the opposite sex. Some women endanger their health even further by having plastic surgery, liposuction, and unnatural body "enhancements," such as breast implants and "butt shapers," or Botox, and permanent mascara tattoos, or even what they consider "decorative" tattoos.

It used to be that women were the only ones who were concerned about their body image; but that is no longer true. Men work out to develop their "six pack," because they think that women will be more attracted to them if they are "buff." They decorate their body with body art and some even wear penis "enhancements" in their tight fitting jeans.

The attitudes that you have toward the health of your body are revealed in the choices that you make. Every time you make a choice that isn't healthy for your body, you create a disconnection in your integrity – a disconnection between your body and the part of you that chooses the unhealthy substance or activity. It isn't logical to expect a living, physical being to be healthy, when you don't provide the elements that it needs to survive. In other words, you can't expect your body to function well, if you treat it badly.

It may be helpful to think of your body as *separate* from your spirit, because you are a spirit having a human experience. Consider that your spirit has "borrowed" molecules from Mother Earth to form your physical body. It may be helpful to think about the kind of emotional state that you would be in, if you were in a relationship with another person who treated you the same way as you have been treating your body – if every time you wanted a glass of water, that person gave you something harmful – like soda pop; if every time you wanted a raw, vegetable salad, that person gave you something that has no nutrition – like a piece of white bread; if every time you wanted a breath of fresh air, that person gave you something harmful – like a polluted atmosphere. Soon, you would feel unloved and want to get away from that person. Perhaps, illness is the body's way of trying to get away from the entity who is harming it.

Sickness and disease are the body's way of getting your attention. Your body was not designed as an opportunity to get to know your doctor. Ill health is the natural result of unhealthy choices, offering you opportunities to pay attention to your body's needs. If you repeatedly hurt your relationship with your body, you can't expect it to forgive you – time and time again.

It may be helpful to calculate the monetary value of your body. Start by thinking about how much money you spend on the things that you put on or in your body in a week. Now, multiply that number by 52, (for the number of weeks in a year), then by the number of years in your age. You will now have the approximate dollar value of your physical body. Now, imagine how you would cherish, care for, and appreciate an object, if you had paid that much money for it. If you had purchased a vase of that value, would you put coffee or soda pop in it?

If you have been influenced by the people in your environment to think that it is "acceptable" to mistreat your body, it is necessary to rethink your beliefs about your connection with, and your responsibility for, your physical form. Think about the possibility that your Total-Self has created your body in the most efficient way to maximize your evolution in this life. If you have been ignoring your responsibility for your body and making unhealthy choices, the present state of your body is the result of those choices. If you have produced an unhealthy product (body) with your choices, you are now responsible for making different choices, *IF* you wish to create a different body. Your present and future choices will allow your body to evolve differently, depending on your choices.

It may take time to observe significant changes in your health; however, in most cases, there is the potential to heal your body with your choices. This healing process is your individual responsibility. It is your responsibility to align every part of your being with your integrity. When you listen carefully to the needs of your body, it will soon become natural to choose substances that will facilitate the production of a healthier body. Your connection with your Spiritual-Body will also create an inner beauty that will be reflected outwardly.

Appreciation of your body is a good way to begin each day. An attitude of gratitude opens your conscious awareness to the value of your physical form. When you first wake up in the morning, take a few moments to wiggle your fingers and toes, and be fully conscious of them. Think about how they have a multitude of tiny muscles and bones working together to move them efficiently. Stretch your long muscles and luxuriate in the realization that you can move your body. Be grateful, if you have the ability to get out of bed by yourself.

When you get to the bathroom, look into the mirror and give thanks for what you see there. Try not to complain about what you see or criticize it for its inadequacies; however, if you see the results of poor choices, promise your body that you will make healthier choices – today! Every choice that you make either brings you closer to, or takes you further away from, living in harmony with your integrity and the fullest expression of your Total-Self.

Rethinking Selfishness

There are two kinds of selfishness – healthy and unhealthy. We are most familiar with the unhealthy type, so let's discuss that first. The word "selfish" is usually defined as caring mainly for ourselves or acting in a way to manipulate others into fulfilling our needs. This type of selfishness disconnects us from others, making us feel lonely, because we aren't including anyone else in our thinking. So, the normal usage of the word "selfish" actually denotes unhealthy selfishness.

Every addiction can be called unhealthy selfishness. When people are addicted to work, sports, sex, drugs, or alcohol, for example, they seldom think about the friends or family that they are neglecting and how they are hurting those relationships. When people are addicted to excusing their bad habits with activity or productivity, for example, their addictions may be the only things to which they are willing to give their full attention. Their selfishness blinds them from seeing the results of their actions. Therefore, addicts are usually seen as unhealthily selfish and self-centered by the people around them.

Some romantic relationships are built on unhealthy selfishness. Some people live their entire lives in denial of their needs, because they agree with their partner who thinks that his or her needs are the only important ones. There are many selfish relationship archetypes. For example: A man may be addicted to sex and his female partner may not be interested because she is tired or not well. If he has convinced her that his needs are more important than hers, she will comply with his sexual demands. Or, if a woman is addicted to clothes or shopping, she may spend more than her share of the family income on her needs and her partner will comply. In both of these cases, the relationship will suffer.

We are familiar with these stereotypes; however, the roles could very easily be reversed. In relationships, if clearly defined roles develop, both parties may find it necessary to learn covert, manipulative skills, so they can have *any* of their needs met. These are all forms of unhealthily selfish, manipulative patterns of relating.

Some people learn how to cover up their unhealthy selfishness by acting in a scornful, disrespectful, or superior way toward others. Unhealthily selfish people or groups often formulate beliefs that exclude or disrespect people of other nationalities, colours, beliefs, values, interests, or persons of the opposite sex. This leads to "clique mentality" that supports their separative attitudes. They may join a club that may be closed to anyone who isn't of a certain income bracket or ethnic group. They may surround themselves with people who have the same unhealthily selfish patterns of relating – the same extravagant hobby or expensive sport activity.

We frequently see people who are so involved in their own little circle of interests that they are totally unconcerned with how their present lifestyle will affect others or Mother Earth in the future. They may live in massive houses – built with far more than their share of natural resources; properties with perfect landscapes – the result of pesticide and herbicide use; drive monster vehicles – that recklessly pollute the environment; or carelessly pollute by buying unrecyclable gadgets, toys, plastics; or refusing to recycle the things that could be reused or recycled.

The level of our blindness to the welfare of others reveals our level of unhealthy selfishness. Therefore, it can be concluded that unhealthy selfishness leads to self-righteousness that can prevent us from taking responsibility for our thoughts, feelings, words, or actions and doing the real work of becoming balanced in our Total-Selves.

Healthy Selfishness

How can selfishness be healthy, you may ask? Healthy selfishness is the act of being fully responsible and accountable for oneself. Healthy selfishness is the concept, "I am responsible for everything I think, feel, say, and do. I am the creator of my environment and responsible for *inviting* everyone and *everything*, into my life – that is in my life. I am responsible for every choice I make: Therefore, I have the right and responsibility to say *yes* or *no* to others – to maintain healthy boundaries in my environment. I am responsible for expressing my Total-Self in my own unique way and living up to my greatest potential."

When we believe the above statements, we realize that we are the creators of our lives – responsible for everything occurring in our environments – either directly or indirectly. It also implies that we are responsible for how we have created our external environment in the past. This is a firm step out of the VPR Cloud.

The concept of healthy selfishness may be new to you. You may not have been encouraged to be responsible for fulfilling your own needs in healthy ways. You may have been told repeatedly that you must do what is expected of you and conform to the rules of the VPR Triangle, *IF* you wish to have *any* of your needs met. The act of conforming to these rules seldom has anything to do with true, personal responsibility. The rules of how to conform are, for the most part, the control tactics of unhealthy people.

You may also see that it is possible to meet your own needs – by yourself – or by asking others to assist you by trading the appropriate amount of time, energy, or money with them to create a balanced exchange. If you have made sufficient deposits into the "emotional joint bank accounts" that you hold with those other people, they may be happy to do something for you in return; or, you may need to negotiate with them to arrive at terms for a fair exchange. This is healthy interdependency.

It is also important to note here that, when you first step out of dysfunctional thinking and behaviour, people may tell you that *you* are being *selfish*, because you are making choices that may inconvenience them, challenging their right to control you; or, because you are choosing to do something that they don't want you to do. They may try to shame you, so you will comply with their wishes by implying it is *wrong* to be healthily selfish.

Many families, religious leaders, and educators teach that it is a *virtue* to be unselfish – being selfish is *bad*. However, there is a fine line between being unselfish in the positive, healthy sense, and being overly self-sacrificing – a martyr to the cause of another person or to unhealthy beliefs.

Many slogans or sayings are used to perpetuate the belief that you must always put others ahead of yourself. "Turn the other cheek;" or, "Give until it hurts;" or, "Love is sacrifice;" or, "God loves a cheerful giver." Unfortunately, people who live in the VPR Cloud often use these slogans to keep others in dysfunctional roles.

If you want to be a mature, functional adult, it is necessary to learn healthy techniques to recognize your *real* needs and fill those first. Other human beings seldom satisfy your *real* needs. Granted, there are material needs or social needs that can be filled by others – for a price – however, those needs are usually secondary. Functional communication and energy exchange create a healthy balance and make it possible to be satisfied by your interactions with others.

It is also necessary to understand that, if you don't take care of yourself first, you will resent any gifts that you give to others, because they are not willingly offered. You will be depleting yourself and soon your cup will be empty. This builds up resentment. If you take care of yourself first, your own cup will be full to overflowing and you will be more willing and able to share with others.

Healthy, responsible selfishness eliminates your addiction to approval from others. Healthy selfishness opens the door to true responsibility – the kind that truly expresses a balanced Total-Self and empowers you to live in harmony with your integrity. You can't follow along like a sheep when you are committed to self-expression in your own unique way. Free will is your God-given right. It is your birthright to learn from your mistakes and use your creativity to make more appropriate choices in the future.

If you wish to be free from unhealthy thoughts and behaviours, it is also essential that you are healthily selfish enough to think about your choices and decide which choice will bring about the best results for you first, then others. As you become more conscious, you will gradually change your environment with your current choices. You can't alter the choices that you have made in the past; however, you can change your perception of those choices. You now have the power to make different choices in the present – in the now. By living in the now, you will live outside the VPR Cloud, in alignment with your integrity – in healthy selfishness.

Real Lasting Pleasure

Real Lasting Pleasure is the pleasure that comes from making choices that are good for you today, and will continue to feel good in all your tomorrows. Real Lasting Pleasure is always the product of a healthy choice. Healthy choices create healthy bodies, healthy emotional responses, healthy mental processes, and healthy spiritual connections. All this adds up to integrity and a sense of peace.

Living for Real Lasting Pleasure may seem, at first glance, to be hedonistic; however, it is often the exact opposite. Hedonism is defined as: "The desire for immediate gratification through pleasurable sensations and the avoidance of painful ones." Real Lasting Pleasure, however, may lead you through the pain of re-evaluating and replacing your old patterns of relating, into the struggle of self-examination, personal responsibility, and even into experiencing sadness or remorse for your previous choices. All of this struggle may need to happen before you reach a place where there is less stress, the pleasure of self-love, and the joy of healthy living.

An analogy of the process of Real Lasting Pleasure in your daily life might be, when you have a backache and you want to decide how to alleviate the pain. You could take a painkiller – a "quick fix" that could temporarily alleviate your pain. Or, you could take a more productive and personally responsible path by seeking assistance from a holistic practitioner, such as a massage therapist or chiropractor. The holistic practitioner may actually create more discomfort in the beginning stages of the healing process, but it is a good pain, which may eventually promote true healing and permanently correct the original cause of the pain.

The holistic approach is often longer and more uncomfortable than the allopathic approach, because it is often necessary to work with the entire body to eliminate the cause of the disorder. For example: If you perceive your backache as an isolated symptom, you may not be taking into consideration that the pain could be connected to other areas in your body. True healing may have far-reaching effects. If your back pain is coming from a slipped disc in your spine, the real cause could be a spastic muscle on one side, pulling the disc out of place. It could also be pinching the nerves to your stomach, making it difficult to digest food. By correcting the imbalance in your spinal column, it may also improve your digestive system, which will also improve your over-all health. Or, by improving your dietary choices, you could reverse the process and eventually release the spastic muscle in your back.

The example above illustrates the power of Real Lasting Pleasure, because, in that case, you would be going into the depths of the issue. This level of consciousness is very different from the attitude of expecting instant gratification, which is common in our society. The belief that there is someone who, or something that, is able to immediately fix your pain usually causes a whirlwind of stress-producing ideas and actions. The "quick fix" pattern usually creates a temporary solution to a problem, causing more stress in the long run, by creating other issues that must be addressed at a later date. It also creates an internal imbalance, because you are looking for an external solution, or rescuer, thus giving away your Personal Power to external agents. The following are some examples of this unhealthy habit:

When you are lonely, if you choose the "quick fix" route, you might go to a bar or social gathering where you "pick up" a partner. You will usually find that the people you "pick" are very similar to the people you have "picked" in the past, so it is very unlikely that your real need for true intimacy will be satisfied. The person that you choose may be in more emotional turmoil than you are and you could start down another whirlwind path, which will eventually bring more loneliness.

When you are hungry, if you stuff yourself with junk food, which is denatured or loaded with sugar or fat that you can't digest, you could end up with indigestion or more long-term health issues, or at least some extra pounds.

When you use alcoholic beverages or drugs to avoid your problems, you always have to face those issues when you come down. Also, you will usually find yourself further down, than you were before you took the so-called "fix."

Or, when you use control tactics to "fix" conflicts with others, you may begin a chain of events that will adversely affect your relationship with that person in the future.

It is important to recognize the pattern of looking for a "quick fix" as dysfunctional thinking and stop it! Before following an idea that you hope will solve a problem, you may want to ask yourself the following questions:

1. Is this idea a "quick fix" pattern, or is it an idea that will produce Real Lasting Pleasure?

2. Is this idea or action going to actually resolve the situation, or is it going to prolong it, or make more trouble? (Keep in mind that, when we are going against the wishes of others, they may perceive it as making trouble – even though it may actually be an appropriate resolution.)

3. Will I feel really good about myself tomorrow or next week if I were to do this?

It is by honest self-examination that you will come to fully embrace your own integrity. How can you be true to yourself, if you live in a cloud of dysfunctional thoughts and behaviours? How do you know, if a substance or a solution will satisfy you, unless you examine your list of options? It may be necessary to explore the idea in an intuitive and contemplative manner. It may also be necessary to struggle with your list of options, until you find one that will bring you Real Lasting Pleasure.

When you are making a decision, if you take into consideration the way your thoughts, feelings, words, and actions affect those around you, you will automatically be more connected with the people in your environment. This doesn't mean that you will choose to live for their approval, or by their standards and value systems. It means, however that you will think carefully about how you treat others and make your decisions based on whether you will feel good about yourself later. Eventually, you may even become a role model of healthier thinking and behaviour.

As you practice the habit of choosing Real Lasting Pleasure over immediate gratification, you may find that you are so pleased with the results that, eventually, you will automatically take time to think through each decision. Living for Real Lasting Pleasure means that you are living consciously, within your integrity, in a way that will lead you to inner and outer harmony and joy.

Instant Replay

This technique has been a constant commitment in my life for many years. It was first suggested to me to help accelerate my spiritual growth by one of my most memorable spiritual teachers, Heidi Cross. I recommend it highly to those who wish to take responsibility for their emotional and mental health, accelerate their spiritual growth, and progress more quickly along their Path to Wholeness.

It is a powerful commitment to peel away any resistance or blockage that has prevented you from receiving the abundance of the Universe.

Before you begin to use it however, you need to decide what name you wish to use for the God Force. You can use whatever name you find suitable – one you are comfortable with. Select a name that is totally comfortable to you, one that doesn't have any old garbage attached to it. Use a word that is special to you – one that creates a special connection between you and the God Force.

It is very important to think carefully about the word you use to connect with the God Force, because words represent concepts and beliefs that you hold to be true for you. For many years, I used the terms "Great Spirit" or "Creator," because those words eliminated the power-over, patriarchal associations that had been previously triggered in my mind by the word "God." Unless you find a word that is free of limiting beliefs, you will automatically limit, not only your connection with the God Force, but you will also limit the amount of power you receive from that Source. When you are ready to make your commitment, begin the following steps:

Step 1 – Connection

Start your day by saying "Good Morning" to the God Force (whatever name you have chosen). Meditate on the purest form of that Power, until you align yourself with a greater awareness of yourself and your place in the Universe.

Step 2 – Commitment

When you are ready to trust your connection with the God Force and you are absolutely certain that you are willing to expand your consciousness, speak the following words.

> *"I am willing to experience whatever is necessary, that I may become a clearer channel of love and light."*

Be sure to think about what you are saying. Don't underestimate the power of these words. When you say them, you are making a commitment to be totally responsible for your personal growth, as well as welcoming guidance from the God Force. Very beautiful confirmations of your connection with the God Force may manifest. Don't be surprised, however, if very challenging situations also arise, that show you what erroneous beliefs have been controlling or blocking your energy.

Step 3 – Replay

In the evening, take time to consciously review the experiences of your day. (I like to pretend that my day has been documented as a video. I have heard others say that they review their daily schedule as an itemized list, and pick apart each encounter, as if they were grading each situation as a nonbiased observer.) Start at the beginning of your day and remember each encounter and experience, until you come to a scene in which you felt uncomfortable.

It is very important, at this point, to stay centered and not become caught up in any emotional "stuff" that arises. You must accept that the experience happened in the past. There is nothing that can be done to change it; so there's no point in becoming caught up in it emotionally. (If you find that you can't release the emotional charge, it may be helpful to pretend that the situation happened in a movie or to a stranger.) From this vantage point, it may be easier to change how you perceive the situation. It is much more likely that you will be able to understand what caused it, when you take the time to detach from the situation. Then you can become more honest about what you did to create it.

The object of this exercise is to sort out what happened internally to trigger your emotional reactions. Be careful not to become caught up in shame for your emotional reactions, or in projecting blame toward the other people in the "scenes" in your movies. Try to name all the emotions that you felt. (If you can't find the correct label for your specific emotion, see the list of emotional reactions in Chapter 3.) Keep going until you have explored the depths of your emotions. It may be helpful to journal about them, paying very careful attention to any old scripts that arise.

Also keep in mind that it was natural to have those emotional reactions. You are not a *bad* person to have had those uncomfortable reactions. Everyone has them, but, if you allow them to control you, you continue to hurt yourself for as long as you experience those emotions.

Step 4 – Assessment

Try to remember whether you have ever experienced similar emotions before. If you can think about other scenes, let them slide through your mind's eye like scenes from a movie. Stay in the observer position and try not to become hooked into your previous emotional reactions and their accompanying scripts. Just observe them, let them teach you, and make a note of them.

For example: I had three very difficult encounters with overweight men in one day. If I had not been practicing this exercise, I might have continued in an unconscious belief that I had held since I was a small child. My unhealthy script said, "All overweight men are bullies, inconsiderate, bad, selfish, etc." By using this technique, I was able to catch myself as I thought these horrid thoughts. I consciously looked back through my life, until I found the source of my emotional reactions and those separative, judgmental scripts.

I remembered the time when my older sister had eloped with my brother-in-law, who was a very overweight man. As I became fully aware of this memory, I consciously observed the pain that had ensued in our family. I remembered the personal loss that I felt, when my sister chose to live in a different house with her new husband and how abandoned I had felt. I also remembered how confused I was when I saw our mother sobbing on her bed.

I was then able to understand the reason for the core belief that had created an emotional wall between me and all overweight men. I was able to understand the painful experience I had gone through as a child and how I had created my core belief that continued to influence my thinking as an adult. From my adult perspective, I realized that it is customary in our society for a woman to leave her birth family to live with her husband. It was only painful to our family structure, because our parents hadn't respected my sister's choice of husband, so she had chosen to elope.

I began to realize that, if my sister had been able to communicate more clearly, or if my parents had been able to listen more fully, they could have come to a mutual understanding. Unfortunately, that didn't happen. There were hurt feelings on both sides and it had left me with an erroneous belief that had affected my relationship with all overweight men.

As I released my childlike beliefs, I released the beliefs and scripts that I had invented as the result of that pain. As I viewed the situation from my adult perspective, my perception shifted away from the size of my brother-in-law's body to the man himself. I began to remember all the good things that he had done during the time I had known him. I began to expand my awareness of appreciation and love toward him.

He must have sensed this change in me, because the very next time I saw him, he shared some very intimate and beautiful insights with me. I was extremely grateful that I had done the work on my old belief, as this had opened the door to the depth of intimacy that we had shared. Ultimately, I was able to expand my capacity of love and expand my ability to more fully embrace all beings – heavy or thin, big or small.

As you use this technique, pay attention to any similarities in the situations that you recall from your past. You will soon be able to rethink your old patterns and you will automatically respond differently to your triggers and patterns of relating when you are faced with a similar situation in the present or future. By taking the position of responsibility, you have claimed the power to restructure the pattern and it will no longer be an automatic reaction.

Your point of Personal Power happens when you become aware that you have the ability to choose your responses now and in the future. While you were experiencing life through the filter of your old perceptions of reality, you were living in a reactionary way, instead of making healthy choices. Now, you can choose healthy responses to your daily situations.

Step 5 – Self-Acknowledgement

Take time to give yourself credit for taking responsibility for your choices. You may wish to acknowledge your new ability to think more independently or acknowledge how courageous you are for choosing to walk in new territories. Make your acknowledgement personal, but celebrate! Make a joyful noise and be grateful!

This is a very important step, as it requires that you give yourself credit for working through your internal processes. In so doing, you acknowledge your ability to engage the wisdom from your Spiritual-Body to make healthier choices. As you heal your self-limiting beliefs, you will soon begin to respect your courage to try new things – allowing you to venture out into new and exciting possibilities. The next step is to put that connection to work.

Step 6 – Your New Plan

Ask yourself, how you would like to handle a similar kind of scenario, when, or if, it happens again? What could you do differently? What could you say? What emotional responses would you like to experience? Be creative, and let your ideas flow freely. Give yourself some time to let all the possibilities flow into your mind.

Create a list of options, write about them, or speak your ideas into a recording device. The main focus of this exercise is to bring you fully into your Personal Power, until you connect with your right and desire to be in control of your life. When you have completed your list of options, edit it, until you arrive at your best choice. Then create a positive affirmation, such as, "The next time that I am in a similar situation, I am going to do ... or say ..."

Make sure to create your affirmation with positive words and in such a way that you can agree completely with the words. It is unproductive to word an affirmation in a manner that a part of you rejects. For example: If you believe that you are ugly, it is pointless to say a positive affirmation such as, "I am beautiful," because a huge part of you will argue with that statement. Your subconscious mind will see it as a lie. It is important to word your affirmation in a way that you can believe your own words. In this example, you might choose to say, "I want to see myself as beautiful," or, "I am willing to stretch into the idea that I am beautiful."

Whenever you create an affirmation, it is important to create plausible and believable statements that will make firm commitments to bring about change in your life. If you focus your intention on attaining love and peace in your communications with yourself and others, you will think of different words than you have previously used – words that will open doors for you. After you have chosen a way of communicating differently, think of the probable outcome of this kind of communication, if you were to use it with several different types of people. See how you may have to adjust your format, content, tone of voice, etc., with each person.

Objectively observe your ideas, and honestly decide whether or not you are repeating any self-defeating patterns of relating. Take a moment to consider the type of people you have manifested into your life. You may be saying, "I have to accept whatever people 'dish out,' because if I don't, I am not going to have any friends;" or, "Nobody cares about me as a person;" or, "They are going to hurt me, no matter what I do or say!"

Those scripts reveal victim consciousness, which claims that everyone else has power and you have none. That belief doesn't make sense. If others have power, so do you! If you have surrounded yourself with people who reinforce a dysfunctional self-image, however, it is important to take responsibility for having chosen those friendships. Begin by thinking about your usual reactions to those people. Then, try something new; and observe whether or not your words and actions have a beneficial effect on them. If they refuse to treat you more respectfully, you may have to choose other friends, if you wish to be happy and healthy.

Step 7 – Letting Go and Letting God

Once you have examined your list, and you have chosen the best idea that you can think of at this time, write it down three times. This imprints the affirmation in your "personal computer" – your subconscious mind. Then let it go – forget it! Each time you more fully trust your alignment with your Spiritual-Body, which is in turn aligned with the God Force, the "letting go" will become more natural to you.

The next time that you are faced with a scenario that is similar to the one you previously experienced, you will be able to create a different response, hopefully one with a more pleasant result. If not, try again. Give yourself credit for having eliminated one possibility that doesn't work, or consider that it might need a slight overhaul to make it work better. Life will give you plenty of opportunities to try again.

After all, it is your life! You have created it – so you can change it to be any way you want it to be! If your intent is to find love, peace, and joy, it is necessary to first move aside your separative beliefs. It is your responsibility and right to make your choices. If you are diligent in your attempts to choose love, peace, and joy, soon your life will be filled with love, peace, and joy!

Reconnecting With Your Parents & Siblings

When you commit to healing the dysfunctional patterns that developed in your life, it is often necessary to begin by releasing the clouds between you and your birth family, or your adopted family. Because many of your clouds were formed in your early life, due to the unhealthy patterns that were modeled and expressed by the people in your early environment, it may be necessary to go back to the beginning and observe your family environment from a different perspective.

Keep in mind that all of your wounds were caused by external forces that hurt you in some way. Your perceptions of those experiences had an ongoing affect on you – conclusions that you formed regarding those experiences. Therefore, to release your clouds, it may be necessary to change your perception of what happened, by considering the possibility that you had previously come to incorrect conclusions or conclusions that were missing some element of truth.

Now, also consider the probability that you only know a small portion of the story about what happened. You obviously have your perceptions about what happened, but others probably have made different conclusions. You may have projected blame or made incorrect judgments about what motivated the actions of the people in your past experiences. Or, you may have taken on blame for instigating those situations when you were not the cause of the problem.

If you look at your past experiences from the perspective of the Blame, Shame, and Guilt Triangle or view the experiences from the very limited worldview of the VPR Cloud, you will feel more isolated and separate from others. It may be necessary to broaden your perspective, encompass a wider worldview, and expand your opinions, for complete understanding to take place.

You can't change the past, but you can change your perception of it and release any emotional energy packages that are still attached to it. Also, it is essential to understand that the other people in those experiences acted the way they did, because that is who they were at that time. They did what they did, because they didn't know how to, or didn't want to, do things differently. The choices that they made at that time affected you – then. The choices that you make now affect your present state of mind and will create your future experiences.

As you bring your childhood memories to the surface of your mind, it is possible that you will experience emotional reactions (fear, anger, hopelessness, etc.) that were a huge component of those experiences, which may now trigger resentment toward family members. However, it is important to quickly move out of those unhealthy perceptions, because they only lead back into the Blame, Shame, and Guilt Triangle, where you will feel victimized, powerless, and more isolated.

It is normal, however, to experience sadness or remorse for what was missing at that time; what you wished you could have had; what you missed that other children your age had; or what you think that you did without. It is also normal to feel sadness, because you lost an opportunity to be close to your parents, or siblings, or peers. However, it is unproductive to lay the total amount of blame for your disconnections on the shoulders of other people. You made choices too – even as a very small child. Moving into this attitude takes you out of the VPR Cloud and puts you into a position of Personal Power.

Maintaining a willingness to understand is essential in the process of closing the distance between you and your parents. This process is so important, because the dynamic of your primary family unit was the situation in which many of your attitudes and habits were formed – both functional and dysfunctional. The good attitudes and habits need to be appreciated; however, the dysfunctional ones need to be revised and restructured. This adjustment is only possible through the position of Personal Power with guidance from your Spiritual-Body.

Being consciously aware of the attitudes and habits that you absorbed in that confusing environment is the only way to begin to alter them. Unfortunately, being aware of childhood experiences may seem impossible for some people who have blocked out their memories of painful experiences. So, let's begin by looking at some information from the history of mankind when some of our unhealthy attitudes and behaviours may have begun.

It is well known that in healthy, primitive, tribal units, new babies were seldom away from the support of a parent or family member. They were held to the mother's body by a sling, or passed around the family unit; older siblings often helped in the care and feeding of their younger brothers and sisters. Aunts and uncles were close at hand. The child was never away from human touch and support.

As the child developed, grandparents or elders taught the younger generation about their spiritual connection – a belief in a Supreme Being. Tribal elders shared stories of the myths that held the tribe together. The priest or shaman conducted ceremonies that maintained the connection with their spirit ancestors. The elders were honoured for their years of experience and the wisdom they had attained. This tradition held a strong sense of continuity and maintained a deep sense of security in their way of life.

In such a strong and protective family unit, there was a much greater probability that the children would have their physical, mental, emotional, and spiritual needs fulfilled. If by chance the parents or grandparents were unhealthy in some way, there were aunts, uncles, and close neighbours to provide support.

As the family unit became more and more decentralized by industrialization, males became absent from their families for long hours to work in factories. When they were at home, there was little energy left to nurture and teach their offspring. This change in the structure of the family unit disempowered it. It was no longer a strong force, as it had been in the days of the tribal unit. The traditional, supportive, extended family unit was wounded and in some cases totally destroyed. The tribe was fragmented and eventually broken down, until isolated family units became the "norm."

Even though civilization has created many beneficial advancements that have improved the quality of life, for the most part, by diminishing the family connection, it created an unsafe and unnatural environment in which to raise our families. This culture created a belief in lack – an illusion – a bad dream about lack of connection with other people, Mother Earth, and the God Force. This has created confusion – false beliefs that separate us from each other and prevent us from having the love and support we need to grow into healthy, mature beings.

Our present civilization creates isolated family units in which young parents are forced to be alone to tend to their offspring, with very little, if any, support from their elders. Babies are often separated from their mothers at birth and placed in plastic containers in hospital nurseries, like some alien science project. Obviously, there are times that it is necessary to place premature or very ill babies in incubators as a life-saving measure, but even then, it is critical to maintain as much physical contact with newborns as possible.

Even with healthy babies, bassinettes, baby-totes, car seats, cribs, and playpens, etc., soon replace those impersonal plastic containers. This lack of connection between the parent and child prevents healthy communication. The baby isn't able to root for the breast. The mother is too far away from the child to sense this request, so the baby learns to cry in an attempt to have its needs met. This forced isolation soon teaches children that they just have to accept the lack of human contact. They are soon convinced that they are supposed to be separated – that it is their lot in life.

The chance of this happening is increased in dysfunctional families, where parents may be too busy focusing all their attention on their addiction of choice, to have sufficient time or energy to focus the necessary attention on the needs of their children. Many children are brought up by the family television, baby-sitters, or by parents who are unable to adequately parent, because they, themselves, had little or no healthy parenting. This creates an unnatural separation between parents and children, causing children to feel ostracized from their elders and confirming their lack of connection from other people, Mother Earth, and the God Force.

As the child grows, this lack of connection often grows. The empty place, which was created by the lack of shared sustenance and comfort, opens the door to an addiction to unnatural substances, such as candy, pop, or other junk foods; or activities, such as watching TV or playing with video games, which have been introduced as different types of "pacifiers." Soon, young people are faced with more "adult" choices, such as alcohol and drugs. They feel so vulnerable that they may be willing to try anything to distract them from their pain.

Young people who were raised in confusing environments may have learned to believe that they are totally alone in the world, so they often conclude they might as well live on their own. This often motivates young adults to move away from their parents. Subsequently, when they have children, they bear all of the responsibility for rearing their offspring. This isolates the second generation from the support of their elders.

It is important to note here, that, if you are a parent, it is a waste of time to wallow in shame and guilt over the choices that you have made in the past, but it is never too late to honestly tune into your child's real needs. Even if your children are adults, you can support and nurture them in adult ways. No matter how old we are, everyone likes, and needs, to be nurtured.

When you are committed to building your true self by walking your Path to Wholeness, it is important to examine the cause of each cloud. If a cloud or lack began in your birth family, it is essential that you understand how that cloud was the product of a certain set of experiences in that family. When you take time to think about the overall dynamic of your birth family environment, you may begin to understand things differently. When you understand how the people who raised you were raised, you will usually find that they did a better job of raising you than their parents did in raising them.

You may also begin to understand why you act the way you do or why you attract certain types of people into your life. If you always look to others to fill your inner longings, it is important to examine your deeper emotions and recognize that a dysfunctional belief is probably at the core of your habit pattern. You may be unconsciously looking for your missing parent – someone to fill the wounded parts of you that were neglected or abused in your early childhood.

Often daughters of absent fathers are attracted solely to dysfunctional, "aloof" men. The same is true for sons who were not nurtured by a caring mother. If you find yourself longing for a particular type of partner and your experience has taught you that that type of relationship hasn't been satisfying to you, it is necessary to understand and release the patterns in you that continue to attract the same dysfunctional energy. It is necessary to understand that it was your unconscious recognition of this dysfunctional energy that drew you to seek out a similar type of partner as you had attracted in the past – it was familiar territory. Recognition of this habit allows you to access your Personal Power to make healthier choices in the future.

It is also essential to understand that your particular family dynamic was the arena in which you learned some of your unhealthy patterns, so healing your relationships with your parents and birth family may actually facilitate the healing of your unhealthy patterns of relating to your environment.

It may also be necessary to let go of all expectations about how you will reconnect with your birth family. If you have disconnected physically, due to their dysfunctional lifestyle, it may not be in your best interest to reconnect physically; however, you may be able to reconnect with them emotionally and mentally simply by understanding that they did the best that they knew how to, during your early years.

This book is about your healing. It gives suggestions about how you can make healthier choices. So, it is essential that you also begin to understand, and eventually forgive, others for their choices by accepting that they didn't know any better at the time. It won't serve you well to spend your energy being angry with your family for their choices.

Sometimes forgiving yourself may be necessary, before you can truly forgive others. By learning how to forgive your ignorance or lack of understanding, when you made certain choices, you can forgive others for their ignorance and their lack of understanding, when they made the choices that hurt you.

When we accept that we usually make mistakes whenever we are learning new things, we are able to see that everyone makes mistakes as they learn new things, because they don't know how to do things differently – yet. It is important to consider that making mistakes is a necessary part of the process, whenever we are learning new things.

It has been said, "To be unforgiving is like taking poison and expecting the other person to die from it." If you wish to heal your life, you must accept that you did the best thing that you knew how, and forgive yourself. By using this logic, you will be able to understand and forgive others for their past choices. Then, you will be able to focus on making your present and future choices according to your integrity, moment-by-moment.

Building Healthy Relationships

We often think of a relationship as the interaction between two romantic partners; however, you have many different types of relationships in your life. Each encounter between two people has the potential to change the dynamic of their relationship. Some relationships stay the same – year after year – and others gradually evolve into something that is very different from the original relationship; because each individual has evolved. Unfortunately, often the most seemingly "successful relationships" have never changed, because they were built on similar neuroses or addictions to the same belief systems.

It is very challenging, but not impossible, to re-create a relationship, once it has been established in a specific way. This is often the reason that people in recovery from alcoholism or drug addiction move away from their previous relationships. Running away from your past isn't always necessary; in fact, it may be hurtful to everyone concerned. It may also create a pattern of running away from challenges. However, in some cases, it may be necessary to remove yourself from certain people, if you are convinced that they are unwilling to evolve or respect your evolution. It is also possible that your absence may actually be the catalyst for the other person's growth. It is important to carefully weigh your decisions and not jump to conclusions about terminating relationships for the wrong reasons.

To build healthier relationships with yourself and others may require you to rethink your past experiences and consider the possibility that you can create relationships that are based in integrity and intimacy – even with people who have previously hurt you or whom you have hurt in some way.

Keep in mind that your integrity is the alignment of all your parts. Your spirit is a part of the God Force. Your body is a part of Mother Earth. You are part of your environment and the people in it. It is essential that you experience those connections to live within your integrity. Your level of integrity influences how you make choices. If you are living in harmony with your integrity, your choices will reflect your level of connection with yourself, other people, Mother Earth, and the God Force. You will realize that you are connected with, dependent upon, and interdependent with, all aspects of nature.

For example: When you become aware of how the rain forests in South America are part of the ecosystem that produces your daily supply of oxygen, you will make healthier choices about your consumption of non-renewable resources. You will have a greater understanding of your interconnectedness with the planet on which you live. You will thoroughly consider your choices and the impact that your choices make on your environment. It is logically impossible to isolate our lives from the other aspects of Mother Earth and pretend that we can survive without them.

When you accept that you are a part of the God Force – a divine-spark or an expression of light – you can then see each living thing in the same way. Your personal sphere of light encompasses your whole identity – your physical, mental, emotional, and spiritual aspects. Whenever you interact with others, you share energy with each other. Sometimes, you overlap another person's energy circle very briefly, such as when you are purchasing an item in a retail outlet. At other times, you choose to invest more time and energy into the interaction and develop an ongoing relationship. The illustrations below illustrate how we overlap our personal sphere of light with the people who are touching our lives.

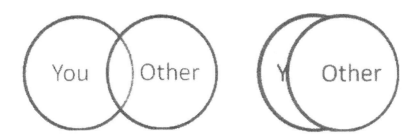

The illustration on the left shows how you share your energy with others in a healthy way – with both of you having your own separate lives and still sharing a part of yourselves. The illustration on the right shows what happens in an unhealthy relationship when another person's energy begins to overshadow you.

Your patterns of relating to the people around you are deeply affected by the patterns that you have established with yourself. If you treat others better than you, what does that say about your relationship with yourself? Observing your relationships with others can be a powerful opportunity for growth. Your observations of your relationships can, potentially, allow you to expand your awareness of any unhealthy patterns of relating or scripts that need to be healed and encourage you to explore new perceptions of your reality.

In an unhealthy relationship, each person's unique individuality is diminished; their authentic-selves are compromised or lost. Because they don't have adequate boundaries or a complete sense of themselves as divine-sparks of the God Force, they aren't able to define or delineate their own space. Because their boundaries are blurred, they may consequently be invaded.

When people are overly-dependent upon others to provide crucial aspects of their daily lives, it causes them to feel lost – they have lost parts of themselves to the relationship. Their individuality has been diminished to the point where they feel trapped in a helpless/hopeless state of mind and become unable to make healthy decisions on their own.

Resentment is the result. They may quietly suffer or lash out at the other person to "get even." They may fight for control over small things, such as where to put the toothpaste tube, simply to achieve some form of control, because they feel inadequate as individuals.

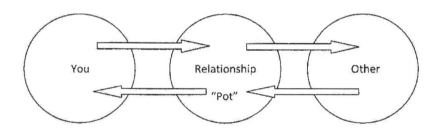

This illustration shows a balanced, functional relationship. It is helpful to see every relationship as a "pot of energy" that is separate from the individuals involved, as in the above illustration. The use of the word "pot" allows you to think of the relationship as able to hold the energy that each person contributes to the "pot." When you think of each of your relationships as a separate pot, it creates the possibility to carefully view the specific dynamic of each relationship and determine whether or not the relationship is valuable to you.

To be in a healthy relationship means that both people are contributing things to the "pot" that the other person values – things that enrich the other person's life. If one person changes what he or she puts into the "pot," the relationship automatically changes. The second person may either appreciate, or object to, the elements that the first person has altered; however, every deviation from your relationship patterns will change the relationship dynamic.

The above illustration depicts a functional relationship – one that "works well" for both people. "Work" is an action word; there is nothing stagnant about it. It means that both people are "working" on maintaining the relationship by putting valuable contributions into the "pot." Even though the relationship is always changing, the relationship remains stable, because the change is evolving the relationship; therefore, both partners are evolving.

> *Whether a relationship is sexual in nature or platonic, your relationships have the potential to be the "sandpaper" that smooths off your "rough edges," by exposing your unhealthy habits to the light of truth in your Spiritual-Body.*

To be in a healthy relationship means that the "sandpaper" of the relationship "pot" is rubbing off the rough edges of each partner on a regular basis. It is opposite to the control/compliance model in which one person decides what to do and the other person complies – where both people passively accept their "proper place" and robotically play out unhealthy patterns of relating.

A healthy relationship challenges and encourages each person into spiritual growth. It is based upon self-love and the willingness to evolve and grow together. It is based upon shared independency. This may seem to be a contradictory statement, but it is not. Independency is the maturity to function as autonomous individuals – not allowing others to control us, or unduly influence our ideas or behaviour. It means that both individuals are autonomous beings – totally accountable for their thoughts, feelings, words, and actions. It also means that we are no longer caught in the dynamic of the VPR Cloud.

Whenever we share life's experiences with a partner, the potential to expand is enhanced exponentially, especially when both parties are conscious of the value of their own unique paths and they are aware of their responsibility for their own growth. Also, if one or both partners are willing to expand themselves within the context of that relationship, the entire relationship is altered, because they will each contribute new energy into the "pot." This leads to greater awareness and evolution in both individuals.

Consequently, it is your responsibility to carefully choose the elements that you put into, and take from, the "pot" of every relationship. If you are committed to living within healthy boundaries, your integrity will determine what you are willing to give to, and accept from, others. As you develop healthier choices, you will begin to choose your thoughts, feelings, words, and actions more carefully. You will accept that you are fully responsible for everything that you think, feel, say, and do; therefore, your relationships will reflect that integrity.

When you are honest about what you are putting into the "pot" of every relationship, you will be willing to concede that your habits may have contributed to past misunderstandings with people. For example: Perhaps, you may have *thought* you wanted a person to understand you, when, in reality, you were speaking in a way that guaranteed that he or she could not relate to what you were saying. This way of speaking may have created a density or blockage of energy between the two of you. In the future, you may choose to consciously change your habits – your tone of voice, your words, your expressions – and speak in a way that the other person will clearly understand. Then, you will begin to feel understood and the density of the energy between you will lessen, because the light of truth from your Spiritual-Body will shine through.

As you become more aware of your contributions to every relationship in your environment, you will realize that every situation reflects the choices that you have made in the past. Your responses to each present situation create your future experiences. If you are committed to living in harmony with your integrity, you may also need to appreciate the value of the stress that is caused by the process of transformation. You will eventually become more committed to the new principles that you develop as you walk in your integrity. You will automatically make the choices that reflect those principles. The other people in your circle of influence will either agree or disagree with your choices. You don't have any control over their choices; but your choices must reflect your integrity, if you wish to live in harmony with yourself. Remember, wherever you go, you take yourself with you; so you must always make the decisions that you can live with in the future.

Healthy personal relationships encourage the development of Personal Power and integrity in each individual. In a healthy relationship, both individuals must have the strength and courage to risk the loss of the relationship, if necessary, to maintain their Personal Power and integrity.

> *Your soul attracts to you that which you most need to learn.*

This statement helps us understand that we have caused, or created, every interaction and situation in which we find ourselves. Therefore, you can't blame others in your circle of influence for being the only cause of any situation. You have contributed to the creation of *every* situation in which you participate. Accepting this concept of co-creation also offers you the opportunity to change your reactions to the people and situations in your life. It also allows you to be totally honest with yourself and dig deeper to define your unconscious beliefs and intentions.

Unless you accept responsibility for being a causal factor or co-creator of everything that occurs in your life, you will feel "out of the loop" – a victim of circumstances – and you will continue to repeat your lessons, until you learn from them. By acknowledging that you are responsible for having caused part of the pain and stress in every past relationship, you have an opportunity to move into a higher level of awareness, until you become more conscious of your choices. Then, you will automatically choose and create healthier relationships.

This infinity symbol shows the flow of energy in a healthy relationship between two individuals. Every time one of the partners goes out into the world to explore new information and gain new insights, the relationship is enhanced and the energy flowing between the two individuals becomes stronger.

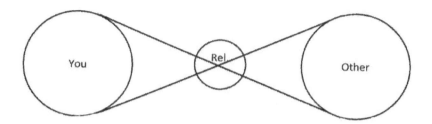

Honesty, integrity, and respect for the divinity of each other are the most valuable contributions that we can make to any relationship. These gifts offer each person the opportunity for exploration into new territories and stimulate expansion into new thought processes, personal growth, and evolution.

As you release your clouds, re-establish your connection to your intrinsic value, and live in harmony with your integrity, your ability to think independently increases and your ability to be in healthy relationships expands. As you learn to make healthier decisions about what you contribute to every relationship "pot," your self-worth grows; you increase your self-love; your connection with your divinity grows; your self-confidence and independency expand; you begin to respect the divinity of others; and, therefore, you will naturally build healthier boundaries. This leads to the healthy state of interdependency, where you share energy and material things of equal or similar value with those in your circle of influence. Relationships become filled with love and joy and opportunities for growth and you will view every relationship as a gift from the Universe.

> *Self-love always nourishes and satisfies the inner being in a "wholistic" way that isn't conditional upon the love of others. External love truly satisfies – IF it is unconditional love and IF you are able and willing to receive it.*

Learning to Love Unconditionally

To love ourselves and others unconditionally simply means to love without conditions. It means that we are open to give and receive love fully without expectations. It means that we won't stop loving ourselves or others when we, or they, make mistakes – when we, or they, say or do something that we don't like. It is being truly respectful of everyone's right to be whomever we, or they, choose to be, and the right of each person to believe, think, feel, say, and do whatever we, or they, choose.

This does not suggest, in any way, that we should allow others to disrespect or abuse us, or that we should give up a part of ourselves in order to pretend to be *loving*. The idea that we must "turn the other cheek" and allow others to treat us badly, is, in actuality, not loving. When we allow others to act disrespectfully toward us, or accept abuse from them, we are not being loving to ourselves, or them.

We are actually enabling them to continue to be unloving or abusive to others.

When we are truly committed to our spiritual growth, we appreciate the lessons that others bring to us, and we love ourselves enough to learn each lesson that is presented to us. When this is true for us, we must acknowledge that the spiritual growth of others is also vitally important to *them*. Therefore, if we don't give others the necessary feedback that would allow them to evolve and grow into their greater connection with their Total-Selves, we aren't being truly loving toward them. True, unconditional love includes the commitment to encourage and support the spiritual growth of ourselves and the people around us.

This leads to the awareness that it also would *not* be an act of unconditional love, if we were to enable others to participate in self-limiting or self-destructive behaviour. We can't stand back and let them think that we are supporting their self-limiting behaviours *and* be truly loving at the same time. There has been a media push to encourage people to prevent others from driving automobiles while intoxicated. This is an act of love. When we love and respect ourselves, we will love and respect others enough to firmly suggest that their thoughts, feelings, words, or actions seem to be inappropriate or might even lead them down the path to self-destruction.

Our ability to love others unconditionally is directly proportional to the amount of self-acceptance and unconditional love that we have for ourselves. When we truly love ourselves, we accept that we are "a work-in-progress." This leads us to understand that other people are also "a work-in-progress." When we accept that we are probably going to make mistakes, we understand that everyone else will also make mistakes. When we admit this, we will be more kind and gentle with ourselves and others. We won't expect to know everything, nor will we expect others to be perfect. We won't feel stupid when we make mistakes, nor will we try to make others feel stupid when they make mistakes.

When we love ourselves, we want to feel whole; when we love others, we want them to feel whole. When we receive unconditional love from others, we realize that we are growing and evolving into our wholeness. When we unconditionally love others, we help them expand into their wholeness.

The act of finding our wholeness includes connecting with our whole self – recognizing that we have many facets. When we accept our complexities, we can then apply that same perspective to others. They may be working on one aspect of themselves that is calling to be healed. They may need to explore that aspect, until they find their truth. Their present perspective may be very different from ours; but if we maintain our position of unconditional love, we may find that it is possible to adjust something within us that is conflicting with their perspective; and hopefully, we will learn to respect their way of finding their truth. It is also possible that they will shift to our perspective at another time; but we must also accept that it is not necessarily going to happen.

In some cases, we may find that the people in our immediate circle refuse to adjust their behaviours toward us, even after we have repeatedly stated our concerns and clearly given our opinions. In this case, our choice becomes limited to whether or not we wish to continue an association with them. Then, even if we choose to disassociate from them, this doesn't mean that we must stop loving them unconditionally. If we have the condition that we will only love someone *IF* they do as we want them to do, or *IF* they agree with our perspective, we close off our connection with them – perhaps to our detriment.

Our ability to love others unconditionally is expanded whenever we practice listening to their truth without imposing our separative thoughts or judgments upon them. If, while we are listening to others, we pay close attention to any separative thoughts or judgments that may pop up during the conversation, we can expose our limiting beliefs and control patterns to the light of truth from our Spiritual-Bodies. Loving oneself and others, unconditionally is rare in our society. So, don't wait for it to come to you from others. Be brave enough to start by loving yourself unconditionally and explore these uncharted waters.

Chapter Seven

New Beginnings

Defining Your Sacred Circle

The circle is a universal symbol of unity and the continuity of life. The circle has been used for centuries to represent community and family. It is a sacred symbol for many earth-based philosophies. In North America, Inuit people lived in circular igloos, and Native Americans lived in circular tepees. The circle represents the Wheel of Life – the cycle of birth, and death, and rebirth. In these ancient cultures, the circle is revered as a sacred space.

A circle, by nature, is constantly moving and transforming, and yet it is stationary, solid, and whole. The energy of a circle is very strong. It is very difficult to crush any object that is perfectly circular. The circle is beyond duality; it is full and yet empty; constantly filling and emptying; all and yet nothing; the beginning and the end – the Alpha and Omega. The circle represents the womb where you created your physical body within your birth mother.

The energy in a circle is also constantly changing and transforming. The only thing that is constant in the Universe is change. The movement of change creates all life. Without change, there is stagnation, atrophy, and death. The circle holds the capacity for change and can be seen as empty or full, depending upon your perspective. It represents the circle of influence in which you live; how you affect the people that you touch with your life; and how you affect Mother Earth, which is also the shape of a circle. Because there is no beginning and no end to a circle, it represents the state of openness that is often referred to as "perfect peace" in a meditative state, making it a perfect analogy for your sacred space.

As you become fully aligned with your integrity and committed to balancing your Total-Self, you become more conscious of what is in your sacred space. You pay attention to what you share with others and also what you want others to share with you. When you consider that your personal circle has boundaries, you must be fully conscious of what you invite or allow within those boundaries. Keep in mind that you have either invited or allowed everything that, and everyone who, is invading the boundaries of your personal circle. Therefore, you are totally responsible for keeping, or rejecting, every person, thought, or thing, that is inside your personal circle.

In defining your sacred circle, it is necessary to take full responsibility for your unconscious choices; you must realize that everything that is in your sacred space is there, because you have attracted it to you. If you complain about what is there, you place yourself into victim consciousness. When you accept that you are a part of the Creative Force in the Universe, you must also acknowledge that you are constantly creating or dis-creating your relationships with the people in your environments. Every decision that you make either puts life into each relationship or takes life away from that relationship.

Every relationship is different. Every relationship has a gift for you – whether it is bringing something valuable into your life or teaching you that you have the power to withdraw your energy from that person or thing.

Your soul only attracts to you that which you need – whether it is a difficult challenge or a safe haven in which to rest. This realization leads you to consider which thoughts, things, and people you choose to share space with, and consciously choose how you wish to be influenced by them. This is a crucial step in anchoring your Personal Power, because you are acknowledging your personal responsibility to make your choices according to your personal integrity. Then, you will use your time and energy wisely to achieve your personal best.

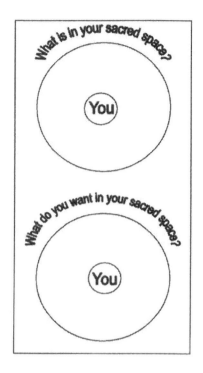

You may wish to use these illustrations as tools to explore your sacred space. Please feel free to enlarge them so they are large enough to make notes about your personal observations.

Your Total-Self is your sacred circle. Visualize your Total-Self filled with your life energy – everything you think, feel, say, and do, on a daily basis. Then, honestly assess the energy in your sacred circle. How is that energy affecting your physical body? Is your body being weakened or depleted; or is it being strengthened and balanced? Next, examine your thoughts and beliefs. Are your thoughts and beliefs creating a clear space within your sacred circle? Are your emotional responses creating a loving and harmonious environment? Is there lots of room in your sacred circle for the light of truth from your Spiritual-Body? Then, ask yourself what new energies you would like to invite into your circle on a daily basis.

It can be a valuable part of your healing process to take a few moments each day to focus on what you wish to have in your sacred circle. Begin by asking yourself what your sacred circle holds at the present time. What substances do you provide for the enrichment of your physical body? What physical environments do you choose? How do you choose to occupy your spare time? What thoughts and emotions do you dwell upon? Do you believe that you have to protect your circle from certain people or influences? If so, how do you protect your circle? Make notes in your journal and consider sharing your ideas with others who are committed to living within the boundaries of their sacred circle.

When you have a clear picture in your mind about what you would like to invite into your sacred circle, you are then in a position of Personal Power to create a new way of being in your world.

Creating A Personal Sacred Space

Down through the ages, wise spiritual leaders have taught that, when we want to make room for an intimate relationship with the God Force, it is essential to shift our normal thinking and behaviour away from the mundane. Historically, this has been done through ritual, a variety of disciplines, prayers, meditation, or contemplation. Each of these methods is a form of discontinuity, which is an interruption in our set routine. During this type of interruption, we create an empty space where we can consciously access the wisdom of the God Force.

For most people, conscious discontinuity happens because they create a discipline that breaks into their previously established habits. Consider, if you want to have a healthy relationship with your significant others, it is necessary to spend quality time with them. The same is true when you decide to build a relationship with the God Force.

Most of us have hundreds of activities that are automatic. We get up from our beds on the same side every day. We go to the bathroom and brush our teeth the same way, and so on. If we become stuck in, or addicted to, our way, we may achieve the "illusion" of security, and eventually believe that we will only be safe IF we control every aspect of our environment. Unfortunately, this belief prevents any awareness of other options or possibilities. We may even become angry with anyone who, or anything that, interrupts our routine. However, when that routine is interrupted, the sacred space of discontinuity can happen. It is in that moment of time, when no set pattern of relating is automatically operating, that creativity is possible.

It is essential to invite those moments of conscious discontinuity into our daily routine, whether it is simply the act of taking a long, slow, deep breath, during a stressful experience; exercising, if we have been too sedentary; or committing to a more intensive discipline.

If you have a busy schedule at work, it may be beneficial to take a meditation break instead of a coffee break. (Some people even meditate in the restroom on the toilet.) If you are in the habit of sleeping late in the morning, getting up early and spending time in meditation or prayer may help you become more relaxed and centered at work. If you have a chaotic lifestyle, it may be helpful to find a special place to be quiet and align with your Spiritual-Body and connect with the God Force.

Making room for meditation is an act of self-love that requires us to re-evaluate our priorities. A beautiful story about Mahatma Gandhi tells about a time when he was very much in the political spotlight. One evening, he asked his aide to awaken him an hour earlier than usual the following morning. He said that he would need two hours of meditation instead of one, because he had a very busy schedule that day. This reflected his priorities. He knew that he would be much more centered in his integrity, if he were to spend the extra time in meditation.

Setting your priorities on what is truly right for you motivates you to create a space or a time of contemplation – a sacred space. This decision releases your old patterns of relating and creates the possibility for change – the possibility for healing – the possibility of a solid connection with your Spiritual-Body.

Creating a sacred space is a very personal task: no one can do it for you or know what will work best for you. You must be willing to explore the many options available to you and choose the right method for you, at this time. You may wish to try something different from anything you have ever tried before.

If your attempts to talk to the God Force (prayer) or listen to the God Force (meditation) have been ritualistic, try a freer, more spontaneous approach. If you have been practicing a random or freeform method, it may be helpful to try a ritual. You may wish to build an altar, if your habit has been less structured, or sit in a different chair or space, if it has been your habit to meditate in only one location. The act of discontinuity may expand your conscious awareness into a new realm – one that could be more effective than those you have explored in the past.

It is through change that we are held in the balance of life and death; hope and fear; happiness and sadness. If Mother Earth were not spinning on her axis in an ever-changing spiral, she would wobble out of orbit and become a shooting star. The same is true in our personal journey. Every new moment happens, because the previous moment has died.

> *Nothing is permanent. Everything is dying and evolving simultaneously. The cycle of life creates multitudinous opportunities for growth. The only thing constant in the Universe is change.*

Because change is constant, random change happens automatically, every moment of every day. Focused and constructive change, however, requires creativity and commitment. When you want to change or transform your internal patterns of relating to your environment, you must set the stage for creativity.

Many of us have learned that it is "good" to keep busy. There are a number of old cultural adages supporting this belief – such as the suggestion that idleness is equal to slothfulness, laziness, wastefulness, uselessness, and lack of productivity. The old saying, "Idle hands are the devils' playground," suggests that, if we keep busy, the "devils" won't have the chance to influence our minds. This saying suggests that the "devils" are waiting to take over our minds. This fear tactic is the way by which we have been controlled by society's norms, keeping us from listening to our authentic-voices from our Spiritual-Bodies. This type of control is designed to create followers who are not allowed to express their creativity or live in harmony with their higher-selves.

In recent years, some Eastern concepts have become more acceptable in North America and meditation has been accepted as a form of relaxation and stress reduction. This is good; however, some forms of meditation can be perverted into an addiction to activity, if you use meditation to escape the reality in which you live. It can become a robotic-like pastime without any real contact with your Spiritual-Body. It is important to look at the intent and results of every activity to determine whether it brings you closer to, or takes you further away from, your Total-Self and the God Force.

Meditation takes many forms, and the art of meditating is thoroughly discussed in other books, including my meditation guide called, Creating a Sacred Space: A Path to Wholeness through Guided Meditation.

Creating a sacred space, whether it is only for a few minutes each day or setting aside a larger block of time, such as a retreat or vision quest, opens your Total-Self to a greater perception of the moment – the now!

Creating a sacred space allows us to acknowledge the death of the old, appreciate what we have learned from it, and welcome the new. It allows us to break from our routine, invite inspiration, gain perspective, appreciate our connection with our Spiritual-Bodies, and subsequently, the God Force.

Reconnecting with the Source of Your Being

Making time and creating space for a solid relationship with the God Force is probably the best investment in time and energy that you could possibly make. Meditation can build a gateway to your Spiritual-Body and allow you to have easy access to the wisdom of the Universe. You will then be able to access the light of truth from the God Force and draw strength and courage from the Source of your being. It allows strength and power from your Spiritual-Body to penetrate your Emotional, Mental, and Physical Bodies. This is the reason that it is so important to release any unhealthy beliefs that still cloud your connection with the God Force.

To turn your life away from separation, it is necessary to take responsibility for having chosen your previous perception of the Universe and decide whether or not it has served you well. You can stay in the fear of a chaotic Universe, created by some "giant with an absurd sense of humour," who is unwilling to love you, unless you agree with it; OR, you can see yourself as a part of a beautiful Universe that could only have been created by a loving God Force. The choice is yours.

Because you are a spark of the Creator of the Universe, you are also the creator of your universe – your personal reality. When you believe that you have the power to create, you can create a different way of perceiving your reality and you have the power to create a new way of being. This, hopefully, is a way to bring you into harmony with nature and the people around you. When you do this, a miracle happens – you will be happy, because you are fully connected with all the parts of your Total-Self;

thereby, living within the perimeters of your integrity. You will automatically attract others who are also living in harmony with their integrity and you will feel loved and supported by them. This shift in consciousness may be seen by some as a miracle.

The Course in Miracles teaches that, "A miracle is simply a shift in perception." Whenever you shift your perception, you cause a minor, or major, miracle to happen – you create a change in your Total-Self and your perception of your environment changes. You reframe (put a different framework around) your perception of reality and cause a shift to happen, because you see your environment differently. When you see your world through a narrow perception, you can't embrace all the possibilities that are available to you. If you wish to open your heart and mind to the realm of greater possibilities, it is necessary to explore a greater and wider perception of reality.

When we explore the realm of the nonphysical, it often causes us to consider that the name of God is said to be the most powerful word in all religions – a "sacred" word. When we explore that idea a bit further, we begin to consider that it is a different word in each religion and is different in each language; therefore, there are many "sacred" words. Then, if we expand that thought we may begin to consider the concept that every word that has ever been spoken in any language may be "sacred," as it has come out of the "mind" of the God Force – the Universal Mind. This leads us to consider the power of our words and encourages us to be much more accountable for our words on a moment-by-moment basis.

Perhaps, the powerful words "heaven" and "hell" are words that reflect states of mind, not locations. This theory is prevalent in Eastern philosophies. There is a Buddhist story about a young man who was studying at a temple. He approached the high priest and asked the question, "What is the difference between heaven and hell?" The priest scoffed and asked, "Aren't you the young man who came in off the street just a few days ago? And you dare to waste my time with such a profound question? Go and study and pray for at least five years, and then you can ask me that question!"

The young man was too impatient to follow this advice and said, "But I want to know, now!" Again the priest rebuffed him. The young man became more and more insistent, until the priest yelled, "Go away, you stupid man! Can't you see that I have more important things to do than to argue with you?" and he turned his back on the young man. The young man became so enraged that he pulled out his sword to strike off the priest's head. The priest calmly turned to face him and quietly said, "That, my son is hell." The young man, realizing what he had done, fell to the ground to kiss the priest's feet and ask forgiveness. The priest responded, "That, my son is heaven."

The theory that heaven and hell are states of mind opens the door to consider the possibility that each of us has a personal choice at all times and that we have the power to create our personal reality through our choices.

When we consider that an acorn always produces an oak tree, the sun shines and the rain falls on everyone – regardless of his or her faith – we then must conclude that there is an impartial order in our Universe – one that doesn't show favouritism.

We can think of the Creative Force like the power in the engine in your car. It is your choice how you will use that power. Your choice determines whether to put your foot on the gas pedal or brake. You choose which direction you will steer your vehicle. It then opens the discussion to the theory that we create our heaven or hell with our free will – our ability to choose our reality.

To move completely out of dysfunctional thinking and behaviour, it is necessary to replace the belief in a miserly god of lack with a belief in an abundant Universe that is so full that you will be able to have your needs met in a perfect, harmonious way as soon as you align yourself with that good.

When you begin to consider the idea that we live in an abundant Universe, it is much easier to believe that you are in your present circumstances for your "good." You may need to learn something that you really need to know, so you can expand and evolve to your greatest potential. Each new day becomes an "adventure in paradise" when you realize that it isn't what happens to you that determines your happiness, it is how you respond to what happens to you.

When you open new doors, you have the opportunity to explore a different reality; understand what your new life is all about; and expand your horizons. You will also have the opportunity to embrace other worldviews and respect the intrinsic value in many other belief systems.

Each time that you open your heart and mind to greater knowledge, your life becomes enriched and your connection with the bigger picture becomes more real. When you fully understand the "greatness" of the God Force and accept that there is "goodness" in the Universe, you will see yourself as a part of that "greatness" and "goodness," and you will expand into your greater potential.

Reconnecting With Your Authentic-Voice

Your authentic-voice has been called by many names – intuition, inner-voice, inner knowing, sixth sense, soul voice, and psychic awareness – to name a few. Your authentic-voice is actually the voice of your Spiritual-Body.

Most people can relate to the term "inner knowing," because they can remember a time when they "just knew" that they needed to do or say something and it turned out to be right. Or, they groan, "I knew I should have … but I did the opposite and look what happened!" Even though some people call the voice of the Spiritual-Body the "sixth sense," I think it should be called the "first sense," because it is the most important of all of our senses. Without a firm connection with the voice of our Spiritual-Bodies, we are disconnected from an essential part of ourselves, as well as other people, Mother Earth, and the God Force.

Because your Spiritual-Body is that aspect of your consciousness that connects you with all that is, it includes what some refer to as "animal instinct." It holds the ability that animals and birds use to return to the same geographical location even though they may migrate thousands of miles away for part of the year; or how flocks of hundreds of birds or fish swoop and soar in synchronicity. It seems that, in our civilization process, many humans have neglected this part of their nature and have subsequently diminished or lost a valuable tool that has the potential to steer us away from problem areas and guide us into our highest good.

Everyone has a Spiritual-Body; therefore you have access to your authentic-voice, if you listen to it and trust it when it surfaces. Reconnecting with your authentic-voice is an essential step on your Path to Wholeness. It has the potential to heal your life and allow you to fully embrace your intrinsic value, your connections with the people in your environment, Mother Earth, and the God Force.

Connecting with your authentic-voice also gradually builds a sense of safety and security – knowing that you are safe to venture forth in the world, because you have the confidence to explore new territories.

A clear connection with the truth in your Spiritual-Body dissipates all fear of death, because you know that there is no separation between you and the spiritual realm. An added bonus is that your heart opens to the wonder and beauty around you; you are gently guided to make the right decisions, moment-by-moment; and anxiety and fear are greatly reduced in your daily life.

Your life work becomes your expression of what you know to be true about you, your world, and your connection with the God Force. Your connection with your authentic-voice will also allow you to trust your own experiences and not let others tell you what to believe, think, say, or do. It will give you the self-confidence to think through a subject and come to an appropriate conclusion that is right for you.

For example: Several years ago, I had a discussion with a woman who had the opinion that my belief in reincarnation is wrong. She explained her beliefs at length to convince me that I am wrong in my beliefs. I listened patiently until she was finished, and then I quietly said, "You have a right to your opinion, but my experience is that I have lived in other times and in other bodies." That was the end of our discussion, because she turned away. She obviously didn't want to hear my point of view.

After our one-sided conversation, I remembered a saying that I had heard many years prior to that time; "A person with an opinion is no match for a person with an experience." So, my experience gave me the necessary confidence to stand true to my belief in reincarnation, and I had no need to defend it. Keep in mind that we only think that it is necessary to defend our beliefs, IF we are uncertain of them.

If you take time to listen to your authentic-voice, your Spiritual-Body opens your conscious mind to explore new ideas, where you can consider them, to see whether or not they might work for you. Pay attention to the sensation of "truth" as you play with each new idea. When you have that sense of "truth," you will know that you are on the path that is right for you. Keep in mind that your "truth" will gradually change, as you grow and change.

It is possible to use your authentic-voice to connect with each part of your being. You can gain access to the needs of your physical body by just taking a moment to connect and listen. You need a healthy body to enjoy your life to the fullest. When you focus your attention on the wisdom that is inherent within your physical body, you will get clear and strong answers. Just be quiet for a moment and let your body "speak" to you. Ask your Spiritual-Body to assist you in making the right choices of food or drink that will be the most loving to your body.

You can use the same practice when you wish to gain clarity about what is unconsciously floating around in your Mental, Emotional, or Spiritual Bodies. Just take a moment to listen carefully and you will receive insight that can guide you in your healing process. The more you access your Spiritual-Body and listen to your authentic-voice, the more you are following your Path to Wholeness. When you trust your Spiritual-Body to guide you, it will lead you to live fully, responsibly, spontaneously, and joyfully. Your Spiritual-Body holds all the information, insight, and inspiration that you need to lead a full and happy life.

The Right Use of Your Will

Throughout this book, you have read about how a child's creativity is subdued, suppressed, or diminished in confusing or unhealthy environments. However, I have then suggested that, as an adult, you must now engage in a new way of thinking and create a new plan in order to produce different outcomes. I have told you that you must be in charge of your decisions; but, how do you do that, exactly? My answer to all those questions is that you must learn the right way to use your will.

Your will is your ability to align your life with the "good" of the Universe. Your will is creating your life at all times. Either you are in alignment with good (the God Force), or you are moving away from good – creating disconnection.

If we use the analogy of the God Force as the power in the engine of your car/life, it is your choice how you will use that power. Your free will determines whether to put your foot on the gas pedal or brake. Your free will chooses which direction you will steer your vehicle.

Your will is the part of you that makes choices. You've heard the statement, "You have free will." This means that you are free to make any choice you wish to make. However, what many people forget is that you must always accept the consequences of your choices. They forget the Law of Cause and Effect. "For every action, there is an equal and opposite reaction."

What you have read throughout this book suggests that you may have learned to live in a way that is not in harmony with your Total-Self. If your connection with your will was diminished or even broken by oppression, neglect, or abuse, either from others or by your own choice, because you forfeited it in order to survive, how do you find it again? And how do you know how to use it in ways that will be right for you? So, the better question becomes, how do you use your will to get what you want out of life?

The answer comes when we carefully explore the tenet, "You have to exercise your will." That may seem to be a strange statement: but think about it! If you want to build strong biceps, you must exercise them. You can't just sit in your armchair and think about strengthening them. You have to actually practice movements that may not be easy for a beginner. You can't lift a 100 pound weight in the beginning stages, but as you grow in strength, you can do more rigorous exercises and lift a heavier burden. This is also true for the right use of your will – you have to gradually exercise it, until it becomes stronger and stronger each day.

Every choice you make, every day, even the simplest task, is an act of free will. If you have trouble making small decisions, it is because you haven't learned how to use your will. If you have given up too much of your will, you might say, "I don't know how to do it!" However, it is important to understand that you have the ability to try something different in this moment. Don't let the fear of making the wrong choice get in your way. Anything different is a step in the right direction. You can't create anything new without exercising your will in a slightly different way.

You may have to strengthen a slightly different "muscle." Perhaps you need to exercise your will to strengthen your Physical-Body, by changing what you eat or drink or adding some physical regime. Perhaps you need to exercise your will to strengthen your Mental-Body, by changing how you think and questioning what you believe to be true. Perhaps you need to exercise your will to strengthen your Emotional-Body, by delaying your emotional reactions and creating different responses. Or perhaps you need to exercise your will to strengthen your Spiritual-

Body, by spending time in meditation and developing your relationship with the God Force.

It might be helpful to think about how you have used your will to become the person you are today. When you first decided to incarnate into this reality on this physical planet, you focused your will on the direction that you wished to follow. You created a specific type of physical body in the specific type of family environment that you thought could offer the experiences that would lead you on your soul path – your purpose – your evolution.

As you moved through your early life, if you chose to relinquish parts of your will, to fit into the energy package of your family environment, there was a reason that you did that. Perhaps you did it to feel loved; or perhaps, you felt desperate and thought that it was the only way you could survive in that space – your only choice. This may or may not have actually been true, but you thought that those were the right choices at the time. However, by making that choice, you lost touch with your free will and that made you feel like a helpless victim.

It is important not to criticize yourself for that decision. It was simply the choice that you made at that time. If you accept that you were the one who made the decision to surrender your free will, keep in mind that you just didn't know any better at the time.

Other people in your environment could have advised you, or even forced you, to do something that was totally unhealthy or inappropriate; but they thought that was the right decision at the time. They didn't know any better at that time. However, if you continue to blame the people in your environment for "bullying you" into making those decisions, you continue to relinquish your connection with your free will. You continue to disempower yourself and inhibit your ability to make healthier decisions today.

Now is the time for you to exercise your will by actively making different choices. In the section of "Shoulding on Ourselves and Each Other" in Chapter 4, we discussed the power of the word "should." Now, I would like to discuss the difference between the words "should" and "want." When you internally hear the word "should," it is always an old script from an internal pattern of relating. So, if you follow the suggestions of others when they use the word "should," it is always because their suggestion matches one of your internal scripts. These scripts may or may not be in alignment with what is best for you. When you take out the word "should" and insert the word "want" into a statement, it activates your will and makes you feel responsible for your choices. If the "should" idea is not what you truly want, you must rethink the idea and make a better plan that fits in with what you actually want.

When you do this, you are setting your intention (focusing your free will) on achieving what you want, but you must be willing to follow a specific path to get it. You can't just say, "I want a new car," without doing the work that is necessary to earn the money, so you can purchase that vehicle. You must be willing to do whatever is necessary to get what you "want." Activating the will requires that a formula must be engaged. You must clearly define the steps that are necessary to achieve your desired outcome.

Many people have become involved with books and theories about manifesting what they want through contemplation or meditation, only to become disenchanted because they don't achieve their desires. When we contemplate or meditate, we may find ideas or suggestions of pathways to follow, but we must be willing to actually do the necessary work to construct the object of our desire.

It may be helpful to consider that our desire is vibrating at a specific level; however, we may be vibrating on a different frequency. To achieve our desire, we must raise or lower our frequency to vibrate on the exact same level as our desire. This is a planet of cause and effect. We must accept that we are the creator of our vibratory level and we may have to shift into a different frequency in order to achieve our desired effects.

Achieving our desired "effects" involves focusing our attention upon the goal and becoming motivated enough to do whatever is necessary to physically create it. Many people misinterpret the message of books on manifestation to mean that they just have to sit and ask for what they want and the Universe will magically provide it. This is an unrealistic expectation. Therefore, it may be necessary to carefully examine what we believe to be true about the Universe.

When you expand your thinking to contemplate the "big questions" about the workings of the Universe, you have the opportunity to explore the realm of "the great unknown" or the "mysteries of life." You also have the opportunity to explore the workings of the Universe in your life and appreciate that your will is an integral part of that Universe. When your will is in alignment with your soul's purpose, it will also be in alignment with the rest of the Universe.

Your Spiritual-Body is closely aligned with the Universe and your Physical-Body is closely aligned with the Earth Realm. To activate your will to create something specific in the Earth Realm, you must bring those two realms together through the power of your Mental and Emotional Bodies. As has been explained in other areas in this book, we must clear away any thoughts/beliefs or emotional energy that could be interfering with the natural flow between those two realms. That is why so much emphasis has been placed on clearing any clouds that may be lurking in those energy fields.

 The practice of meditation is often the link between those two realms. When you meditate, it is common that you will experience the unconditional love and support of the Universe around you, but you will also be shown what you must do to achieve your goals. Your connection with both the Universe and the Earth Realm will inspire you to rise to your greatest potential. You will fully understand that you are accountable for your actions, so you won't want to be disappointed or unhappy with your choices at a later date.

You will also give yourself permission to experience healthy remorse for making mistakes and eventually accept that your mistakes are an integral part of the greater scheme of things. You will be more inclined to genuinely ask others to forgive you, if you have hurt them, and make a commitment to them to change your unhealthy patterns of relating that caused you to act unhealthily selfish, inconsiderately, immaturely, or hurtfully. In this process, you will own the power to choose differently in the future. You may even experience more love and support, and less separation from the rest of the Universe when you accept the fact that everyone makes mistakes – that making mistakes is a natural part of the creation process.

If you do not learn from your mistakes, your constant companions will be misery, hopelessness, remorse, and self-flagellation. However, when you accept your mistakes as an integral part of your learning process, you will see that all new experiences have the potential to be educational and richly rewarding. Then, you will become more conscious of your free will to make other choices, so you won't repeatedly experience the same undesirable results in the future.

To be responsible for creating happiness means that you must actively set your goals and intentions to live on the path that leads to harmony and joy. This path isn't an easy one at first, because you have to go through the stress of change. You have to consistently and consciously engage your free will to adjust and adapt your thinking to explore each new direction – each unknown territory.

As you learn, by evaluating each situation by the effect that it has on your life and the lives of others, you will begin to forgive yourself and others for making mistakes; you could also begin to encourage others to use their free will to try something different and risk making their own mistakes.

Our minds are capable of receiving millions of perceptions and ideas every day. Each second that you are aware of your thoughts, you can observe many opportunities – directions to follow, emotional reactions and responses, inner dialogue, creative ideas, challenges – chatter of every kind. If you slow your thinking to a standstill through meditation, contemplation, or introspection, you will realize that your Spiritual-Body has a connection with the God Force, through which you can access every idea that ever was, or ever will be. While you daydream or think about your possible options, your mind has the potential to wander and "shop" for a path to follow. Your free will allows you to choose from a wide variety of possibilities.

It might be helpful to think of your decision-making process, as if there is an auctioneer calling out each of your possible options. It is up to you to decide which of the options you want to "buy into." However, it is very important to realize that there is always a "price" you must pay for "buying into" each option – and an inevitable outcome that will occur as the result of each choice.

If you want to make decisions that are healthy, each decision must be made from the place that is in harmony with all your parts – physical, mental, emotional, and spiritual – your integrity. It may be helpful to ask yourself the following questions:

1. Physical – Will this substance/relationship/activity enhance my physical body or my physical environment?

2. Mental – Will this thought/concept/belief expand my mind to greater heights of knowledge and inspire me to greatness? Within the context of this mental state, will I learn something valuable about myself or others?

3. Emotional – Will I feel good about myself, if I make this choice? Within the context of this emotional state, will I be loved and supported in such a way that I will be able to grow and evolve into a better, happier, or healthier person?

4. Spiritual – Will this choice further my connection with my Spiritual-Body and the God Force? Will this connection encourage me to be a more radiant beam of love and light to the world?

It is essential to explore each of these four aspects of your Total-Self to decide whether you are functioning within your integrity – carefully examining each aspect to decide what is best for all your "parts." It is through this inner struggle that you will grow and evolve. This process isn't easy at first; but it becomes easier with practice. After you have run through these questions a number of times, the process will become almost automatic.

As has been previously stated, all choices can be, when you are meticulously honest, divided into two categories – life wishes and death wishes – the will to live or the will to die. Some choices are counter-productive to life, and actually take you away from living in your integrity. What this actually means is that the focus of your creativity is either on change and evolution or the stagnation of the helplessness and hopelessness of victim consciousness that leads to death. If you take the time to observe where your free will is leading you, it is often much easier to change your unhealthy habits into healthy, functional ones.

If you want to be free of self-limiting habits, it is necessary to take the time to struggle with each decision. Think about what would happen, if you were to put your choice into action. Choose to stay in the state of creativity, until you create a plan that is based upon what would be totally and truly right for you. This would also include how your decision would affect others and how you would feel about the way your decision would affect them. As you learn to make decisions based upon what is truly right for you, you will quickly see that those decisions create an environment that is truly right for everyone else concerned – even if they don't agree with you, or like your choice, at the time. Your will is then in harmony with the Divine Will or the God Force.

If you carefully attune your mind to the "good of the whole," you will see that we are all connected to that good (the God Force). When you make a decision within the harmony of that good, the result will be beneficial to all concerned. Therefore, if you wish to live in harmony with your environment, you must find your personal good, based on guidance from your Spiritual-Body; because, when you are making a decision about your association with another person or group, you are actually deciding what is best for them as well.

It has been my experience that when I have an emotional connection with an individual or group, I always have something to learn from them and they have something to learn from me. If you pay attention to the potential lessons in every experience and value what you are learning from, and sharing with, the people and situations in your environment, the result of your experiences is always growth and evolution.

It is, however, very important to be totally honest with yourself about your capacity to resist temptation at any given moment. If you feel vulnerable or weak, it would be foolish to associate with people who usually try to tempt you to do something that is not in your best interest. Until you are strong enough to resist those temptations, it is probably best to avoid those associations. If you conclude that you aren't strong enough to resist the choices that certain people are making and you decide to disassociate yourself from them, your next choices are much more difficult. You will be faced with deciding whether or not you will disassociate from them temporarily or permanently. Then, you will have to decide how you are going to create the separation.

Some people believe that it is wrong to disassociate from others – that we should be able to get along with everyone. However, when you have committed to follow a specific path, it is essential to respect the fact that others may need to follow a very different path. If those paths are parallel, you may be able to connect occasionally; however if those paths are divergent, then that has to be respected as well. Sometimes, we simply must take divergent paths.

Every living organism is constantly in a state of change. Unless there is change, it stagnates, atrophies, and dies. The cells in your body either continually reproduce themselves in healthy ways or physical disease develops and your body atrophies and dies. Either your mind continues to expand and explore the Universe or tunnel vision and rigidity occur. If you fail to express your emotions in healthy ways, emotional stagnation and apathy occur. Either you explore your connection with the God Force or it becomes stifled and eventually forgotten.

When you include your perception of the God Force in the idea that everything in the Universe is constantly changing and you realize that the God Force is a dynamic, changing force – not a fixed one – you may begin to wonder whether the God Force ever made any mistakes. (I'm sure you can think of a few examples. I, personally, would include mosquitoes, black flies, and poison ivy on my list. However, I also understand how each of these pests has a purpose on this planet.)

If you are able to entertain the idea of a dynamic, evolving God Force, you will be more likely to forgive yourself when you make mistakes and realize that every mistake is just one possible outcome in the process of trying something new. You might even consider the possibility that you are on this planet to create new experiences with the specific intention that you will expand or evolve. You might also consider the possibility that as you expand, you are actually expanding the rest of the Universe.

As you consciously use your free will to change the way you interact with your personal environment, your small universe changes; but the greater Universe also changes. The underlying intent behind your thoughts, feelings, words, or actions is the causal factor or the creator of those changes. This leads us to consider that we are a part of the Creative Force of the Universe – a God Spark.

If you objectively observe the results of your thoughts, feelings, words, or actions, they reveal your underlying intention, (or how you have focused your free will) to your conscious awareness. If you honestly observe the effects (results) that you have created, you will have the opportunity to take responsibility for your choices, making it possible for you to choose differently the next time a similar opportunity presents itself.

You are then able to align your will with your higher purpose, change the direction of your free will, and create something that will make your life better in some way. It may be helpful to consider the following steps when you want to create a new choice:

1. Clearly determine what you actually want by connecting your thoughts/beliefs and feelings with your Spiritual Body through contemplation or meditation.

2. Realize that it is your responsibility to remove any obstacles that may be preventing you from achieving your goal.

3. Define the steps that you will need to take to achieve your desired goal.

4. Activate your will by believing that it is possible to achieve your goal.

5. Accept that you will probably make mistakes along your path and treat them as learning experiences.

6. Alter your direction, whenever necessary, if you find that you have made choices that are not working for you.

7. Try something different, until you succeed.

8. Enjoy the results of your effort!

This illustration shows how the Total-Self becomes balanced and whole. As we penetrate our clouds with the light of truth from our Spiritual Body, we begin to live in harmony within our balanced Total-Selves and attract more positive energy that automatically changes our lives.

Expressing Your Balanced Total-Self

There comes a time when you have let go of your separative belief systems; you've made a strong connection with the authentic-voice of your Spiritual-Body; you understand that you are the creator of your reality; and now, you are ready to take responsibility for what you express into your personal circle. So, the next step will be to find ways of outwardly expressing your balanced Total-Self.

If you are truly honest with yourself, you will acknowledge that you enjoy doing certain things more than others. For example: You may find pleasure in playing a musical instrument, singing, writing, preparing food, gardening, or woodworking. It is important to pay attention to what gives *you* pleasure, because the act of doing that special thing will give expression to a beautiful aspect of yourself, which you are then able to share with others.

Each one of us has our own unique way of expressing our balanced Total-Self. Your way isn't the same as any other person; so you must follow your own *Path to Wholeness* to find your unique expression – your passions, your purpose.

When you find your special interests, talents, and abilities, you must next find a practical way of sharing them. For example: If you have a love of music, it is very nurturing and self-loving to sit and absorb it; however, it isn't enough to just listen to it, if you want it to be an *expression* of your unique talents. You have to be able to share it as your special way of expressing your balanced Total-Self. There are many ways to do this. You could learn to play an instrument; but if that isn't an option, find another way – even if it is just volunteering to be an usher at a community concert. The gift of your time, when it is given from a place of love and joy, is always an expression of your Total-Self.

A few years ago, I met a beautiful woman who cooks food in a huge community kitchen to feed street people. She told me about how she had begun to feel "empty inside," when her children went away to college. By being very honest with herself, she finally realized that the thing she missed most was the time that she had spent cooking for them. So, she began volunteering her time at a community kitchen. She said, "It has become a great joy for me." Can you imagine the love and caring that goes into the food that she prepares? What a perfect gift she is giving! And, she is receiving so much from it!

My own personal sharing of my Total-Self takes many forms. One of my special gifts is the ability to play the piano. This talent was obvious when I was a very young child. However, I allowed the cruel treatment of a piano teacher to stifle my talent. Some years ago, I healed those old clouds and allowed my talent to be more fully expressed. Now, I play for myself with great joy and have stretched into a space where I feel comfortable enough to play for others. There are times when I am *at one* with the music and have a sense of pureness that reminds me of the Source of all music and I know I am connected with that Source. There are other times when I am *at one* with the other musicians. I am fully experiencing the joy of contributing to the sound that we are creating together. My gift to the sound becomes a joyful experience for myself and others. I am expressing my Total-Self by bringing joy to others.

Another joy, and expression of my Total-Self, is my writing. Often, when I write, I sit back afterward and joyfully exclaim, "Wow! I wrote that!" My Mental-Self recognizes that "I" alone, could not have written such profound truths and I'm shocked that those words came through me. I recognize my connection with a much greater Source of wisdom. My surprise is because the integration of my Mental-Self with my Spiritual-Body isn't complete, yet. It is my desire and intent, however, to continue my healing process to let go of any belief that I still carry, which makes me think that I am separated from the God Force, until I am fully living in my balanced Total-Self every moment of every day – living in Unity Consciousness.

What do you want in your life? Think of each of your dreams, aspirations, and goals. Allow yourself to become completely honest about what would happen if a particular goal were to manifest in your life. Is that goal truly what you want? If it is, be grateful. If you discover that it isn't, also be grateful, because it will reveal one option that you didn't truly want. It could have unconsciously created a future that would not be in harmony with whom you truly are. Then, you will have the opportunity to change what you have been unconsciously "putting out" to the

Universe. You are then able to consciously create something different in your future, if you so choose.

This present time can be the most wonderful time of your life – if you honour your ability to contribute something of value to your environment. You can become focused on the expression of your Total-Self and your purpose in life! Each time you express your unique gifts to your world as a gesture of love and joy, you are expanding your sacred circle to embrace your world. As you share your gifts, you focus your will on turning up the volume on your connection with your Spiritual-Body, and express it outwardly. Soon, you will be so full of wonderful things to do, there won't be any time or space in your life for unhealthy thoughts and habits! The following list of suggestions may help you become more conscious of your choices:

1. Be on guard for any separative beliefs that may still creep into your thinking, which you would have previously tried to fill with addictions.

2. Observe your thoughts, feelings, words, and actions as you become more and more responsible for what you attract, invite, and allow into your sacred space.

3. Make time to understand, process, and heal any remaining unhealthy beliefs or habits.

4. Be courageous enough to share your fears and pain with others and ask for their assistance.

5. Stretch your boundaries by fully experiencing your fears, facing them, and doing whatever you need to do to explore your greater potential.

6. Take time for self-nurturing activities and meditation.

7. Find unique ways to express your Total-Self by exploring what you love to do and are truly passionate about.

8. Step out in faith and trust your Spiritual guidance to lead you.

Be gentle with yourself. Remind yourself that, whenever you wish to experiment with new ideas and projects, you must give yourself permission to make mistakes. There are so many options to play with and you have so many opportunities to explore, you will always find some that work and some that don't. The Universe is a place of abundance, containing a multitude of possibilities, because a loving God Force created it and it is constantly expanding every moment of every day.

Let your imagination take you to the space where anything is possible. Imagine yourself without your past excuses, without any self-limiting thoughts or beliefs. Imagine yourself as capable, competent, and talented in a variety of ways. Imagine yourself as a child – dancing freely in the field of possibilities. Let your hopes and dreams come to the surface of your conscious mind. Let your spirit soar!

Listen to your authentic-voice and let it guide you to the perfect expression of your Total-Self.

After you get in the habit of being conscious of every aspect of your life, you will automatically make healthier choices. Once you have become fully responsible for what you invite in, and express from, your circle of influence, it is time to relax and enjoy your life. Your ultimate goal is to be happy! When you are happy, you make the world a better place!

As you expand your expression of your unique balanced Total-Self, you become a bright and shining star. You automatically brighten up the area where you are! Each time you choose to let your inner light shine, you are opening your life to unlimited possibilities. You will find that you become increasingly balanced, so you begin to experience more true happiness every day. You become excited about sharing your happiness with others.

As you begin your journey into sharing with others in new ways, you will find that you attract people to you who are also willing and able to be loving and supportive toward you. As you lovingly connect with other people, you create a bond of light and joy. You will find that your circle of friends will change, as soon as you create opportunities to share your light with others who appreciate your vibration.

There may be people who will try to put you back in the old boxes, but living in those old ways will no longer be appealing to you. Once you begin to follow the light of truth from your Spiritual-Body, that light will guide you to be in the appropriate place at all times. So, your choices will become easier and it will be more natural for you to be in a constant state of happiness and clarity. You will find that your excitement will grow into a passion for life that allows you to share your light in ever-widening circles.

As you interact with others by expressing the light of truth from your Spiritual-Body, observe how that light trails behind you – like the tail on a shooting star – wherever you go, and behind others, wherever they go. Consider the idea that every time you think about another person, you are connecting with them. What do you want to give to them and receive back? Each time you shine brightly, you expand your circle of light. As your light touches the people in your circle, their circles touch the circles of others, and soon that series of circles covers the whole planet and flows out into the rest of the Universe.

My love and light is expressed to you in every word of this book. Thank you for allowing me to enter your sacred space. Each time you think of this book, my love will be present for you, if you choose to feel it. My hope and prayer is that you will have the courage to let your unique, personal light shine throughout the world – with passion and joy!

THE BEGINNING!

Testimonials

"Tashene, I have just finished *A Path to Wholeness* and I must say that it is one of the best books on addictions that I have ever read." Jeff Wilbee, Discovering Recovery, www.jeffwilbeespeaks.com

"Tashene, I love your book, *A Path to Wholeness*. I took copious notes and took them to my husband's and my counsellor. After discussing them for weeks ... specifically the VPR Triangle and how it plays out in both our relationship and our families, my counsellor asked how to get a copy of your book. He was especially interested in how you tie it all into personal growth. Thank you for all you do!" Jan Sterling

"An empowering, eye-opening, great 'AHA' experience! I now know how to consciously create healthy patterns in my life." Bobbie Kalman, author, www.crabtreebooks.com

"This book offers the reader an opportunity for self-empowerment and personal maturity." Paul Prozeller

"In a world that undervalues common sense and values quantity over quality, Tashene offers us practical and sensible lessons in self-awareness leading to self-improvement. If we implement these lessons, it will enable us to improve the quality of our lives and the lives of those close to us. Tashene is a natural born healer!" Amanda J. Smith, DIHom, DHM. www.amandajsmith.net

"When school curriculums include books like this, we will be giving our children the tools to discover the treasure within themselves." Wendy Everett

"*A Path to Wholeness* is more than an aid to personal development. It will also help you grow spiritually. After studying and learning the lessons provided throughout these pages, you will be able to look in the mirror and be happy with the person you see and who you have become." James A Watt

"I have read *A Path to Wholeness* and have attended the *Hooked on Wholeness Workshop* that is based on this book. Both experiences were most empowering and have changed my life. This book has set me free from physical and emotional ailments and given me keys to healing my relationships. Tashene shows you how to be responsible for your thoughts, words and actions." Sharon Kaesler

"In these economic times, *A Path to Wholeness* is just what is needed to get a person through each day; feeling not as taxed by the stresses, expectations, and rigmarole of society. Its simplistic principles will last a lifetime; and have you realize that sometimes that term 'selfish' is 'focus' in disguise. It's when you realize you are not complete and something is missing, and you want to know 'why?' you'll need this unique book. Salvador SeBasco, www.theinsideviewshow.com

"I love this book. Honest, to the point, beautifully written! Tashene, your book gives me the understanding to move forward in my soul's journey, with enthusiasm." Debbie Wallace

"I would highly recommend *A Path to Wholeness* to anyone who wants to understand the dynamics in relationships and how to defuse unhealthy patterns. When I think of Tashene, I think of Light, Love, Laughter, and Healing. Everything she does is full of integrity and insight. Tashene is gifted and very talented and it shows in every aspect of her work and teaching." Heather Hudson, Holistic Practitioner http://www.samurais.ca

"I have been on a spiritual journey and have read many spiritual books. All the books helped me find my path, but I wasn't finding a way to pull all that I have leaned together-to begin to live my spiritual self and walk that path – until I was given the book *A Path to Wholeness*. It was the thread I needed that pulled all that I have learned and all of my experiences together. This book has brought my spirit back home ... to me. Thank You!" Susan J. S. RN

"Meeting Tashene and reading her book, *A Path to Wholeness* has offered me a new perspective and perception in thinking about my life. *A Path to Wholeness* offered me many insights into my past, gave me permission to let go of the things that had held me back, and opened up a willingness to look and move forward. I have given *A Path to Wholeness* to family and friends as presents. It's a gift that will always keep giving, and a book that I will read over and over as I continue to grow! Thank-you Tashene! My life has never been the same." Carmelina Cannella SSW, RSSW.

"Hello Tashene, I just read your revised Chapter One. I think it is just amazing! I can't wait to read the entire book. I learned more about myself by reading it and took note of what emotions I felt as I read it through. I know I have a lot to work on, which, at times can seem very overwhelming. But having your books and you there supporting me gives me hope that there is true light at the end of the tunnel. Also, that reaching that light is a possible achievement. I am grateful everyday that you have come into my life. Thank you for being you." Ann Howe

"I am truly impressed by, and grateful for, the words of wisdom contained in *A Path to Wholeness*. The content is relevant for everyone. *Path to Wholeness* is written with such clarity and practicality that I found the absorption of information simply effortless. I love that the explanations provide the reader with an understanding of how our reactions, though harmful to our development, are 'normal' when viewed in the context of our modern human conditioning.

A Path to Wholeness opens up pathways to knowing ourselves without blaming ourselves or feeling ashamed of the many coping mechanisms that we all use in our daily lives. Many books offer solutions to problems without first uncovering the root causes or issues at play and therefore the foundation for healing is not properly established. Without uncovering root issues, our power to be extraordinary, rather than simply sleepwalking and reacting to life, cannot be sustained.

A Path to Wholeness is a pivotal key to transformation for the reader. It is a gift and contains the inspiration and understanding to heal; and thus become a whole and conscious being. Many, many blessings to you, Tashene." Amy Whitney Inspirational Transformational TV Show, youtube.com/user/ittvshow

Made in the USA
Charleston, SC
22 March 2015